The Winner's Circle® V
Wealth Management Insights from America's Best Financial Advisory Teams

Foreword by Charles D. Johnston
President, Citi Global Wealth Management

Introduction by Jerry Miller
President and Chief Executive Officer
Van Kampen Investments

R.J. Shook

HORIZON
Publishers Group

Library of Congress Cataloguing-in-Publication Data
Shook, R.J. (Robert James)
  The Winner's Circle V: Wealth Management Insights from America's Best
Financial Advisors / R.J. Shook
  p. cm.
  ISBN 0-9721622-3-2
1. Financial Advisors—United States. 2. Investing.
I. Shook, Robert J.,   II. Title
338.7—dc21   2009

This publication is designed to provide accurate and authoritative information to the subject matter covered. It is sold with the understanding that neither the publisher nor the author is engaged in rendering legal, accounting, or other professional services. If legal advice or other expert assistance is required, the services of a competent professional person should be sought. The views expressed by these advisors may not represent the views expressed by their companies.

—From a Declaration of Principles Jointly Adopted by a Committee of the American Bar Association and a Committee of Publishers and Associations

The Winner's Circle® is a registered trademark of The Winner's Circle, LLC.

ISBN 0-9721622-3-2

Published by

HORIZON
Horizon Publishers Group
Printed in the United States

10 9 8 7 6 5 4 3 2 1

To Elisabeth, Jacob, Jamie-Brooke and Jeremy ...
I love you ... forever and ever and ever

CONTENTS

Acknowledgments vii

Foreword: Charles D. Johnston ix

Introduction: Jerry Miller xi

Preface: R.J. Shook xv

CHAPTER 1: DWYER & ASSOCIATES 1
   Merrill Lynch & Co., Inc.

CHAPTER 2: BRIAN PFEIFLER AND TEAM 27
   Morgan Stanley

CHAPTER 3: THE HANSBERGER GROUP 43
   Smith Barney

CHAPTER 4: NCA FINANCIAL PLANNERS 73
   NCA Financial Planners (Royal Alliance)

CHAPTER 5: THE CURTIS GROUP 99
   Smith Barney

CHAPTER 6: THE HALBFINGER GROUP 115
   UBS Financial Services

CHAPTER 7: BOGGS WEALTH MANAGEMENT GROUP 139
   Wachovia Securities

CHAPTER 8: THE OBERLANDER GROUP 159
   Merrill Lynch & Co., Inc.

CHAPTER 9: 545 GROUP 183

Morgan Stanley

CHAPTER 10: HUDOCK MOYER WEALTH MANAGEMENT 207

Hudock Moyer Wealth Management (Wachovia)

CHAPTER 11: CHRIS BALDWIN AND TEAM 227

Credit Suisse Securities (USA) LLC

CHAPTER 12: THE LOCNISKAR GROUP 249

Merrill Lynch & Co., Inc.

CHAPTER 13: NADIA CAVNER GROUP 267

BancorpSouth Investment Services (National Financial)

ACKNOWLEDGMENTS

Similar to every project we pursue at The Winner's Circle, it's a team effort. Hundreds of individuals contribute to make projects like The Winner's Circle V possible. These individuals—and the entire industry for that matter—contribute to the efforts of The Winner's Circle Organization because they care about this industry. These individuals include our world-class advisory board of industry leaders, individuals in the areas of compliance, media relations, marketing, financial advisors, and all layers of management. On behalf of The Winner's Circle, I appreciate all of their hard work, dedication, and passion—without which The Winner's Circle simply wouldn't exist.

Special gratitude is due to The Winner's Circle financial advisors and their teams who took the time to contribute to this book. These financial advisors need not seek publicity. Their dedication to clients keeps them busy enough. However, they are dedicated to giving back to the industry to help raise professional standards.

Other industry professionals have contributed countless hours toward The Winner's Circle, to whom I am very appreciative: Jim Wiggins, Michael O'Looney, Karina Byrne, Allison Chin-Leong, Christina Pollak, Susan Zurbin, Alexandra Reilly, Heather Rynasiewicz, Katrina Clay, Darin Oduyoye, Lisa Palmer, Kandis Bates, Joanne Caruso, David Linton, and Jim Ryan. Like the advisors in this book, I rely on a world-class team to help with the editing, writing, and administration. This includes my incredibly talented writer Jordan Gruber; editor Claire Zuckermann; Debbie Watts; Brian Boucher for cover design; Fred Dahl who managed production; my world-class agent Al Zuckerman, and other professionals at Horizon Publishers Group.

FOREWORD

By Charles D. Johnston
President, Citi Global Wealth Management

It's become a commonplace to say that being a successful financial advisor requires a holistic approach to wealth management. But as I read the profiles that R.J. Shook has compiled here, it strikes me that talking about that approach and actually delivering the breadth and depth of services it implies are two entirely different things. The fact is, walking the walk of holistic wealth management demands extraordinary range. You have to demonstrate excellence—and not just proficiency—as an investment manager, chief financial advisor, strategic advisor, analyst, confidant, and even therapist at times. And you have to move seamlessly and spontaneouslyamong these roles. The FAs you'll read about in this book do all this as well as anyone in the business.

Each member of the Winner's Circle has a different story, but I find some clear (and very instructive) similarities among all of them. For starters, there's the technical mastery required to do this work at the highest level. Picking individual investments, the bread-and-butter of the old-fashioned financial pro, is only the start these days—one facet of a financial planning process that incorporates wealth preservation, trust and estate, tax, business strategy and succession, and philanthropic issues. What's more, as the financial world has grown more complex, the advice of financial advisors has had to grow more sophisticated and keep pace with change in each of these areas. Asset allocation, to take just one example, was once a simple matter of dividing a client's money among a few basic asset classes; today, maximizing efficiency requires vastly more complex models that can figure hedge funds, real estate, private-equity investments, and other "alternative" assets into the mix.

Another characteristic that these all-star FAs share is an intense focus on always, always doing the right thing for their clients, even if that means (gently) disagreeing with the client's initial wishes or settling on a personally less profitable solution. You'll read about one FA, for example, who turned away the opportunity to manage a $50 million investment because he felt the client would have been taking on unnecessary risk. Over the long run, such decisions are likely to cement a client's loyalty.

Another theme running through these stories has to do with problem solving. The FAs in the Winner's Circle are not fundamentally interested in offering products to their clients; they are interested in finding solutions to financial challenges—and any products they end up selling are merely a means to that end. In my experience, all really successful FAs get most of their satisfaction from making a difference in someone's life—enabling them to, say, put their kids through grad school or retire early.

In a similar vein, they also tend to be extraordinary listeners—so much so that they often see their clients' dreams (and worries) more clearly than the clients do themselves. As such, they can anticipate needs, ask questions their clients have a hard time asking themselves, and eliminate financial worries, often before they even surface.

There is no job on the planet that asks so much of one person and demands so much of those who want to reach the top ranks. The FAs in this book are truly a rare bunch. Learn from their stories. I find them inspiring. I hope you will too.

Charles D. Johnston
President
Citi Global Wealth Management

Charles D. Johnston is president of Citi Global Wealth Management for the United States and Canada. He oversees the firm's Smith Barney and Private Bank client-facing organizations, responsible for one of the nation's leading private banking and wealth management businesses, with approximately 700 branch offices, 13,000 financial advisors and bankers, and approximately 6 million client accounts representing over $1.3 trillion in client assets. He is on the Citi Senior Leadership Committee.

Citi is a leading global financial services company and has a presence in more than 100 countries. The Citi brand is the most recognized in the financial services industry. Citi is known around the world for market leadership, global product excellence, outstanding talent, strong regional and product franchises, and commitment to providing the highest-quality service to its clients.

INTRODUCTION

By Jerry Miller
President and Chief Executive Officer
Van Kampen Investments

F irst and foremost, this is a book about interpreters—talented individuals who are highly skilled in the art of translation. They take what is confusing, opaque, inexplicable, and turn it into something clear, understandable, even logical. It's not alchemy, but it is a rare combination of science and art. We see exactly how rare it is when we encounter a period of severe market volatility.

One way of thinking about the global financial tumult that began unfolding in the summer of 2007 is to contemplate one of the classic postulates of chaos theory, which goes like this: The flap of a butterfly's wings in Brazil sets off a chain reaction that ultimately results in a tornado in Texas.

If there is a corollary in the financial world, perhaps it goes something like this: The collapse of a hedge fund invested heavily in exotic subprime mortgage securities leads inexorably to a half-trillion dollars in asset write-downs by the world's banks, with resulting collateral damage to stock and bond markets worldwide.

Yes, the physical universe and the financial universe are chaotic places. There are causes, and there are effects. But frequently, the connections between the two are either indiscernible or apparent only after the fact, when it is too late to take corrective action that could prevent an undesirable outcome.

In finance, we derive comfort from concrete things that we can measure and label with familiar acronyms: ROE, P/E, EBITDA, AAA. Surely, these accountings give us certainty of what a company, a bond, a share of stock, or even a derivatives contract is actually worth. Of course they do, at least until they are rendered utterly meaningless by the madness of crowds, the panicked run on the bank. Yes, the financial universe is a chaotic place.

Enter the financial advisor, or, more specifically, the financial advisors profiled in this book. They understand the real nature of the world in which they operate. They are masters of the technical knowledge required to manage an investment portfolio. They are relentlessly focused on outcomes, because they know there's great clarity in the way you keep score in wealth management. You only win if the client can (a) send three children to college debt-free, (b) establish a long-planned family foundation, or (c) buy that vintage, red Mustang convertible, if that's what they want to do. Wealth, after all, is nothing more than a means to make the world a better place—for oneself and for others.

As knowledgeable as these financial advisors are about the mechanics of managing and growing wealth, they demonstrate an equal mastery of the intangibles and the "unknown unknowns," to paraphrase a recent defense secretary, that are as important, or maybe even more important, to the people they serve. They ask questions like, "How well can my client sleep at night, knowing what we have in the portfolio?" Or, "If a '100-year flood' hits twice in ten years, what's the most we can lose?" They not only know that the unpredictable might happen—they know it will happen. Chaos theory? They get it. They get it completely.

In my career, I have been fortunate to be a financial advisor, to manage financial advisors, and to manage people who manage money for financial advisors and their clients. I have had the privilege of working with many extraordinary professionals, and I have found that the best ones share two characteristics in particular. The first is humility. They understand that good fortune and a bit of chance have played a role in their success.

The second is generosity. Someone gave them a helping hand along the way, and they are more than willing to do a similar good turn for the next person. Such generosity is evident in this book; some of our finest practitioners have been willing to take the time to share the secrets of their success, so that standards can be raised across the entire industry.

This combination of humility and generosity leads them naturally to act in the best interests of their clients. They don't get hung up over narrow, legalistic definitions of what's "fiduciary" and what isn't. They put their clients' interests first. It's as simple as that.

At Van Kampen, we are proud sponsors of The Winner's Circle. We work hard to deliver solid, long-term investment performance, tailored to each individual client through our invaluable partnership with the financial advisor. We are inspired by the stories that follow, and we think you will be, too.

Jerry W. Miller
President and CEO
Van Kampen Investments

Jerry W. Miller is president and chief executive officer of Van Kampen Investments, Inc. He joined Van Kampen after serving as central division director for the Global Wealth Management Group of Morgan Stanley. Prior to that, Mr. Miller enjoyed a 22-year tenure at Merrill Lynch, where he held a succession of management positions in both the wealth management and asset management businesses. He began his career in Institutional Equity Sales at Brown Brothers Harriman & Co. Mr. Miller holds a BA from Swarthmore College and is a graduate of Harvard Business School's Advanced Management Program.

PREFACE

By R.J. Shook

The Winner's Circle V, like previous books in this series, profiles some of the country's most outstanding financial advisors and their teams, and does so with two primary audiences in mind.

The first audience is financial advisors and other industry professionals who are interested in learning how these elite advisors, in concert with their partners, team members, and firms, are providing superior client service and advice. To that end, this book focuses in detail on the kinds of best practices, actionable ideas, and implementable strategies that truly set these advisors apart, especially in the context of providing comprehensive wealth management services, a topic I'll return to shortly. I've also aimed to convey a sense of the extraordinary integrity and professionalism that characterizes every one of these advisors, criteria that are essential to their being selected to be part of The Winner's Circle in the first place.

Before going further, let me take a quick step back and describe the origins of The Winners Circle Organization. I started as a retail advisor in a small branch office of a major wirehouse in the late 1980s. The training I was given wasn't quite what I had hoped for, and I soon realized that I was going to have to figure out a great deal on my own. At that point I heard my father's voice ringing in my ears: "If you want to be the best," he said, "then you have to learn from the best." But who were the best advisors, and how could I learn from them?

ORIGINS AND MISSION

I knew I had to start somewhere, so I began calling the top advisors at my firm to ask them how they built their businesses and how they developed relationships with their clients. A few of them gave me a small amount of their time, but I quickly realized that if I was going to learn from the best, I would need to have in-depth conversations, and not just with the top producers in my firm, but with the best brokers throughout the industry. Coming from a family of book writers, it soon dawned on me that many other beginning financial advisors probably also wanted to learn from the best, and that I should write a book about industry best practices.

I called senior leadership at the major securities firms and asked them who they would want to represent their firm in my book. I put forward a set of quantitative and qualitative criteria that would one day become the basis of all The Winner's Circle lists, criteria that you can read about at The Winner's Circle Organization Web site at http://www.WCorg.com. These industry leaders were very cooperative and provided me with nominations, and based on my criteria, I developed my first so-called top advisors' list—advisors whose lives and practices formed the first of The Winner's Circle books that were published.

Since that time, and with the further encouragement and support of many industry leaders, The Winner's Circle has become a formal organization that embraces outstanding advisors from all firms. As such, The Winner's Circle Organization promotes a dual mission, the first part of which focuses on promoting the best practices of advisors—and the highest code of ethics, integrity, and industry professionalism.

The second part of our mission concerns the clients of financial advisors, without whom there would be no investment industry, and these clients are the second audience for whom this book is written. Along these lines, The Winner's Circle aims to raise investor confidence by promoting the value of receiving sound advice from financial advisors and also helps investors find a trusted advisor in the first place.

If, then, you are not a financial advisor but seek to work with one (or to work with a better one), the profiles in this book will give you a clear idea of what—and whom—to shoot for. And while it's true that many (but not all) of the financial advisors in this book work mainly with high-net-worth clients, it's also true that investors at all wealth levels will benefit from understanding how the very best advisors operate and what they do for their clients.

THE EVOLUTION OF RELATIONSHIP MANAGEMENT AND WEALTH MANAGEMENT

More so than the other books in this series, The Winners Circle V focuses on the simultaneous evolution of wealth management and relationship management. Now, ever since I've been involved in the industry, the best financial advisors have always focused on deepening their relationships with their clients. This makes sense, because for advisors to truly serve their clients and put their interests first, they must know their clients' minds and hearts. That is, to truly serve the client's best interests and make sure that they are moving their clients towards their life goals and dreams, they must know what those life goals and dreams are, and that can only happen in the context of an in-depth personal relationship.

Similarly, a client's portfolio cannot be properly invested and asset allocated unless an advisor knows the client's risk tolerance, that is, how much volatility the client can stand and how much money the client is comfortable with the possibility of losing. And risk tolerance simply isn't the kind of thing that can be understood with just a few minutes' conversation or the quick review of a questionnaire and a few balance statements. As you will see, the best advisors make both an art and a science out of getting to know their clients extremely well. In many cases this includes the development of close personal relationships, but in all cases it requires the advisor and his or her team to really get inside the client's thoughts and feelings, to figure out what really matters to the client so the client can both be properly invested and properly attended to when things get rough.

Because, as you'll see, many of the advisors profiled in this book say the same thing about why they are being hired by a client. In part, it's for good returns, but in a sense that's just "table stakes." A client expects his or her advisor to be competent at investing money—whether the investing is done in-house or by outside money managers or other experts—or why else would the advisor be in the business? But even more important than investing competently, is knowing how to work with a client so that he or she doesn't make bad mistakes when the markets go down. Studies consistently show that the key to investor success is "time in the market, not timing the market." A great deal of the value from having a top-notch advisor, therefore, comes from the advisor's willingness and ability to make regular contact, hand-hold, and offer steady encouragement when the markets are sharply down or even up (like during the "irrational exuberance" witnessed during the tech bubble).

Again, then, we return to the importance of building in-depth relationships. And while this is something that everybody talks about doing, the advisors in this book have truly understood both the necessity of building such relationships and the ways in which such relationships can be built.

Such in-depth relationships are even more important for the advisor seeking to work with high-net-worth clients—as well as high-net-worth clients seeking to find the right advisor—as we move further into the era of comprehensive wealth management. A wealth manager is a financial advisor who not only assists with investments, but who provides high-net-worth clients with a full spectrum of financial and wealth-related services including those addressing private banking needs, estate planning, insurance needs, and other elements from the right side of the balance sheet.

Interestingly, not only do clients who receive such services have their complex lives made simpler and therefore better, but advisors with a true wealth management focus also end up faring better. For example, although clients in the $2.5- to $5-million range of net worth typically have most of their assets in a liquid form, once they reach the $25 million level or above, a good two-thirds of those assets tend to be illiquid. But working with these illiquid assets—with insurance needs, with real estate, with the making of personal and business loans—tends to be a highly profitable endeavor. Similarly, compared to advisors who only offer one product (that is, investments), advisors who offer multiple products including loans, trusts, insurance products, and so on tend to have much higher revenue per client (and they tend to keep their clients much longer).

So for those advisors who want to focus on building their businesses by building scale and moving up market, it makes all the sense in the world for them to offer comprehensive wealth management services and to develop the kinds of relationships that attract high-net-worth and ultra-high-net-worth clients in the first place. But not only must they know how to competently serve their clients and develop ever-deepening relationships, they must also know how to build a team that will support the deepening of relationships and the delivery of comprehensive wealth management services.

Every advisor profiled in this book will tell you that without their team, they could not possibly do what they do, and you'll note that many of these elite advisors have team members who have been with them for many years. Once again, it's about the relationship. Team members who are treated well are happier, are more productive, and do a better job for clients. And similarly, by teaching and encouraging team members to appropriately develop their own relationships with clients, advisors are freed up to further leverage themselves and to pay attention in the moment where it is most needed.

THE GOLDEN RULE

In a certain sense, none of this is a secret: By developing in-depth relationships and paying careful attention to people (including clients, partners, team members, and even outside fund managers and money managers), the best advisors find out what these other people need and want, what they can offer, and how they can best be served. In fact, this is at the core of their belief to treat others the way you would want to be treated, but also the way that they want to be treated.

So while none of this is a secret, there's still a whole lot to admire—and a whole lot to learn—from those who have figured out how to effectively put this knowledge to use. As you read the stories of the fourteen advisors and advisor teams in the coming chapters, you'll see that while the advisors come from remarkably different backgrounds, they all aim at the same place: a level of excellence, integrity, and service that raises their work from a simple job to something like a "calling," a calling that often also involves giving back prodigiously to their firms, and to community and charitable concerns, while still making their own family the highest of priorities.

So whether you are an advisor yourself or the client or potential client of an advisor, you can rest assured in the knowledge that the evolution of the financial services industry is moving forward hand in hand with the evolution of ever-deeper advisor-client relationships, to the mutual advantage and betterment of everyone involved. Truly, this is a great time to be involved with our industry, whether as client or advisor, and I feel honored to be able to present you with the stories of some of the advisors who have truly taken their practices, and their commitment to others, to the next level.

R.J. Shook
Founder
The Winner's Circle Organization

CHAPTER 1: DWYER & ASSOCIATES

MERRILL LYNCH & CO., INC.
MIAMI, FLORIDA

(Back Row from Left to Right) Marcel Laniado, Rafael Fernandez, Richard Grodin, Mike Romanchuk, Patrick Dwyer

(Front Row from Left to Right) Maria Kattan, Jessica Collante

Patrick Dwyer's success can be defined partly by the roughly $2 billion that he and his team of six manage for Merrill Lynch. More importantly, Patrick has created exactly the kind of practice he most desired. Over time he has found a way to work with considerably fewer but increasingly wealthier families. Thus he can serve these ultra-high-net-worth clients with the in-depth personal attention and private banking services necessary to truly satisfy them. Moreover, Patrick has devised a process-driven investment methodology that consistently delivers the investment performance results needed to attract and retain his wealthy clients.

In addition to his genuine likability and great native intelligence, there are two fundamental keys to Patrick's success. The first is his long-term perspective on what it takes to be happy and successful as a financial advisor. "I'm a long-termer," he says. "This is a marathon, not a sprint. *My philosophy is that you've really got to figure out what you'd like to do, whom you'd like to serve, and how you'd like to do it.* If this is of value to somebody, and you go and do it, you'll be happy. But if you're serving the wrong constituency, or if you're not doing the business the way you really think it should be done, then you're not going to be very happy."

The second key is Patrick's pragmatic, real-world approach to satisfying his clients. "I'm very goal-oriented as a person," he says, "and very process-oriented in how I approach things. You need to have a process that gets you to your goals, and this translates into what we do for our clients. I want to get my clients on the path to success, and what most of them are really looking for is for us to simplify something that's very complicated—the management of their personal lives and personal finances. That's what we try to do, and so far we seem to be pretty good at it."

LIKE FATHER, LIKE SON

Patrick's introduction to the financial services industry came early. "My father was a manager in the industry," he says, "and always loved the business. He was a partner for a large firm and a regional manager of private client businesses, and enjoyed it so thoroughly that he never wanted to retire (although he did retire the same year I got into the business). His one regret—something that influenced me later on—was going into management, because he enjoyed being a financial advisor more."

"Like most kids," Patrick continues, "I always looked up to my father and wanted to be just like him. So I've followed stocks since I was a kid, because that's what my dad was interested in—he loved the markets—and that's what we talked about at the kitchen table in the Dwyer household. I was reading the *Wall Street Journal* when I was twelve, and have pretty much always enjoyed following and watching the capital markets. Over time I became a voracious reader of business information, and I learned a lot about the markets that way."

Having grown up mainly in New Jersey, Patrick went to Providence College in Rhode Island, where he was a history major with a business minor. "History has been much more useful in the investment business than business," Patrick notes, "because history repeats itself over and over again. The more you are aware of history, the more you are aware that there's nothing new under the sun." After graduating in 1991, Patrick went to the University of Miami for his MBA, which he received in 1993.

A PIVOTAL CHOICE

Patrick started working for Merrill Lynch in July of 1993. "The only place I've ever worked full-time has been Merrill Lynch," he says. "I started in the Private Client Development Program. This was an elite management training program out of the Princeton office that took two to three MBAs and about ten college graduates and trained them to be in senior management."

Patrick continues, "At twenty-five, I decided that what I really wanted to do at Merrill Lynch was to become a financial advisor. In the management-training program, it became clear to me that although I might ultimately be in a branch management or leadership position, I wanted to be a financial advisor. So, in December of 1994 I became a financial advisor in the firm's Miami office. I chose Miami because I had gone to graduate school there, and I thought it was an interesting and up-and-coming town, a place with a lot of opportunity."

Patrick's decision turned out to be the right one. "I quickly found that I took great pleasure in my client relationships, and these made my job very fulfilling. This was the component that was missing while working at corporate headquarters in Princeton. I had enjoyed the capital markets part of the job, but I was missing something. As a financial advisor, I got the whole package. In addition to an ongoing focus on the capital markets, I got the enjoyment of working with clients, and to this day I look forward to client meetings more than anything else in the business."

TALKING TO THE WALL

"When I started out as a financial advisor in Miami," Patrick says, "I had no clients. And I knew absolutely no one in Miami except for three people: Marisa, my girlfriend, who is now my wife, a college buddy, and one fellow I went to graduate school with. So I went from this elite management program—where I was treated extremely well and pampered, and where I worked for some very senior people and got to sit in on lots of important meetings—to starting from scratch."

"By my third day in the branch office," Patrick recalls, "I had reorganized my desk twice. I was starting to get really worried as I realized that I had to go out and find clients. Well, there I was reorganizing my desk when the manager came up to me and said, 'Pat, there are no clients on your desk,' and he handed me the telephone book and told me to start calling. I think I turned three shades of red. I was terrified, because I knew this was where the rubber met the road. I knew what a financial advisor did because my father had been in the business, and I had even made cold calls for brokers before as an intern. But I'd never had to do it for myself, and going from my pampered position in the Princeton office to having to actually pick up the phone and build a client base from nothing was very, very scary. But it was also really exciting. So I just did it. I picked up the phone and started making calls."

"Eventually," Patrick recounts, "I figured out something that I was truly comfortable with. I found that I was a really big believer in financial planning, and I began building my business by doing financial planning seminars for people, something not too many people were involved with back in 1995. This was something I truly believed in, and I wanted to get better at my delivery, so I would come in at 6:45 a.m. or so and practice my presentation on financial planning in the conference room. I had never done any public speaking before I became a financial advisor, so I had to learn how to communicate my knowledge."

"I would talk to the wall for about forty-five minutes every morning," Patrick says with a smile. "Since the conference room and break room were separated only by a divider, as people came in to work and went into the break room, they could hear me ... and they would laugh. They actually laughed at me. But I persevered and continued to practice my presentation every day for months, until I eventually began doing my first seminars with CPAs and attorneys, who would invite their clients just as I would invite my prospective clients."

"I quickly realized that I *was* a good speaker and that this was much better than cold calling as a format for me to talk to people. Here, they could properly evaluate whether they wanted to work with me or not, and if they didn't want to work with me, they wouldn't waste their time. And if they did want to work with me, they would approach me. Well, it worked out pretty well—I had a few successful presentations where I developed some good client relationships—but overall it was hard. Sometimes fifty people would show up, but sometimes I'd spend two weeks preparing for a seminar that no one would come to. I kept at it, though, knowing that I had to build my business one client at a time. I had other motivating factors too: I wanted to be financially successful so that I could get married, and I liked the job and really wanted to succeed as an advisor."

"My first big clients," Patrick continues, "came in about my third month, and I still have these relationships to this day. It was a competitive situation involving two guys selling a beer distributorship, and I was very motivated to win the relationship. I met with them and presented what we did, and brought some of Merrill Lynch's asset management expertise to help me out. Well, even though I was just twenty-five, we won the business of these two individuals, who were in their early fifties. This was a $16 million relationship, which was a really big deal for any advisor in 1995. And for a guy whose length of service was just three months, this was an unusual thing to have happened. I learned a tremendous amount working with these two very nice entrepreneurs, and they appreciated my hustle and how hard I worked for the relationship. Most of my relationships after that were much smaller for quite a while—you take a lot of rejection in the job early on—so this first big relationship really kept me going."

REFOCUSING THE "WHAT"

Consider, again, Patrick's core philosophy: "You've really got to figure out what you'd like to do, whom you'd like to serve, and how you'd like to do it." By determining that he really wanted to be a financial advisor rather than a manager, Patrick had gone a long way in determining the "what" of his career. "When I first started out," Patrick notes, "I was a traditional Merrill Lynch financial advisor. I had a planning-based business, and my accounts ranged anywhere from $1 to $25 million. I had myself and an assistant, and then eventually a second assistant." Clearly, as a traditional financial advisor,

Patrick was rapidly becoming more successful: five years after he started, he was already one of the top advisors at Merrill Lynch.

"Two thousand was a big year," Patrick says. "My business was up 100 percent. I had achieved tremendous growth, but I didn't like the business I had. We had done a good job with our clients between 1995 and 2000, but we had a reactive service model because we were willing to take all types of clients and provide them with a broad product mix. I felt we needed to think about things differently. My team, I thought, was overworked, and because of the broad set of things we did I needed team members with a huge skill set. It was hard to find people like that and then integrate them into the team."

"I asked myself what I really wanted to accomplish, and I realized that I wanted to be a trusted advisor to a small number of families. I didn't want to have a lot of clients. I wanted to give the clients that I had a tremendous amount of time so that I could be a great investment advisor as well as a good overall financial advisor."

As fate would have it, in 1999 Merrill Lynch introduced a new training program that was ideal for Patrick. "In 1999, the firm created its Private Banking and Investment Group, which focused on ultra-high-net-worth clients. The new program focused on the consulting process, something that I was very interested in and felt I was good at. I also felt that I understood the needs of ultra-high-net-worth clients and was able to connect with them. I had already been attracting a lot of larger clients, especially considering my age. These clients just seemed to like me."

"The program involved an accreditation process," Patrick continues, "and if you passed you received a special title, 'Private Wealth Advisor.' When the opportunity to be part of this program presented itself in 1999, I said, 'This is for me.' About forty of us went through the program, which basically consisted of an all-day series of interviews and presentations that you had to give, in addition to postmeeting tests. I was one of the four or five who passed that day. Once I completed the written criteria, which included getting my CFM® [Certified Financial Manager®] and meeting some other requirements, I became the first person in the firm to actually get the title 'Private Wealth Advisor.'"

ZEROING IN ON THE "WHO"

"Once I became a Private Wealth Advisor, I had to change my business model in every respect. I had to begin to focus my business on serving only one client segment, not three or four. Up until that point I ran a very traditional Merrill Lynch business, which meant that if somebody came to me with an opportunity, I would take a serious look at it, no matter what it was or whether it was something I knew a lot or a little about. But as I said, I wasn't enjoying that, and wanted to have a different kind of business. I wanted to be a trusted advisor to a very small number of very-high-net-worth individuals. That's what I wanted to do."

"I figured that, ideally, the greatest number of clients I would like to handle would be fifty to sixty ultra-high-net-worth families. I really wanted to work on a fee-basis-only and not be involved with commissions, and I wanted to spend meaningful face-to-face time with all my clients. To really get to know the families, to understand their issues, and to be able to explain things to them, I've always felt that there's no substitute for face-to-face time. So I wanted to be able to spend at least a half a day a year with each client in a one-on-one meeting followed by a meal."

"The reason this face-to-face time is so important," Patrick continues, "is that I can't successfully serve clients unless they truly understand what we're trying to accomplish with their portfolios. And unless they have this understanding, I won't be able to keep them on track with their investments through difficult market periods. A failed relationship is one where the client unwinds his long-term investment plan because he is not comfortable enough with what he owns to ride through periodic stresses caused by the market. And the only way you get clients comfortable with their investment strategy, and ultimately be successful in helping them achieve their long-term goals, is by spending a lot of one-on-one face time with them. Fortunately, what I like to do most is be with my clients."

"I wanted to build a business model I could feel good about," Patrick states, "and that I could make work. I wanted to spend a lot less time marketing, and devote my time and effort to face-to-face meetings with clients. I also wanted to improve our service level and investment process, which meant that I needed to build a quality investment and service team. I also thought about the types of accounts I wanted to bring in, namely, two to three meaningful new relationships per year, amounting to $100 to $150 million in net new fee-based assets per year. It could be one client or three clients, but something in that range was what I felt I could do and would be a manageable pace of growth."

"I also wanted to stop working on weekends," Patrick notes. "I had worked every weekend for my first six years in the business— that's how you go from zero business in 1994 to being a top advisor in 2000—but I was working six days and at least eighty hours a week. And by this time, my wife and I had two kids and were on our way to four. I needed to get some balance in my life, and couldn't possibly achieve my ultimate revenue goal by 2010 unless I worked with fewer clients and built a sustainable process."

"The good news was that big clients liked me. For some reason, the group that most identifies with me has been very wealthy people, particularly entrepreneurs and CEOs. And I liked them. I somehow work well with, relate to, and enjoy being with men and women who are successful entrepreneurs and CEOs, and the feeling seems to be mutual. Clients pick you and you pick them, and I always want to work with people who like me and whom I like. For example, I don't enjoy working with institutions or foundations, partly because I don't enjoy group settings. I will work with a client's foundation, but will not have a separate foundation as a client."

"I also don't enjoy working with inherited wealth as much as I enjoy working with entrepreneurs," Patrick notes. "Inherited wealth is a different animal. From my perspective, people who have worked for a living have a certain appreciation and respect for other people who are working for a living. For whatever reason, I just don't appeal as well to those with inherited wealth as I do to wealth creators. There are, simply, different dynamics with different types of clients, and you cannot appeal to everyone. It's not important to understand why you don't appeal to everyone; what's important is to understand whom you appeal to. I realized that the types of client I wanted to serve were these entrepreneurs and their families. I wanted to get to know them, and as I did get to know them and their kids, and as I saw what I could do for them as their investment advisor and financial consultant, I just loved it."

"What I say today," Patrick adds, "is that I serve wealth creators whether they are company founders or corporate executives. Those who have run their own businesses or who have run public companies are the types of clients we serve best and with whom we work best, because they understand what we can and can't do. They have realistic expectations, and they understand our value proposition. They are a pleasure to work with, and are also, in our opinion, the most fun clients."

RIGHT-SIZING REQUIREMENTS

To implement his new business model and right-size his business, Patrick had to change certain things and put certain requirements in place. "One thing I had to have was a minimum account size," he says. "In 2000 I decided my minimum was going to be $10 million, which would enable me to focus on $10- to $100-million-dollar relationships. Today, my minimum is $25 million plus. Having only clients of a significant size enables us to have a tighter investment model. Similarly, in terms of our service model, we just manage private wealth for individuals or families, not corporations or retirement plans or anything like that. We used to service whatever came along. If the client wanted us to open an account and do a business loan, we'd do that, but not today. If a client wanted us to run the pension plan for his business, we would do it, but not today. Today, if a private foundation came to us and said, 'Would you bid on our $50 million foundation?' we would say 'Thanks, but no.' We don't do that. We only work with high-net-worth individuals and families. That's it."

"It's also important to understand," Patrick adds, "that today we are concentrating on one segment of the market, which is not just clients of a significant size, but clients who want our advice and guidance and are ready and willing to turn over the management of their money to us. We are not looking for clients who want to manage their money themselves and just use us to do it. We are looking for clients who want to turn all of that over to us, in part because I'm not going to watch somebody commit financial suicide. Fortunately, the first-generation wealth creators whom we work with have a certain mindset that we like and feel comfortable with. These people are good delegators, and we want to be delegated to. We want individuals and families who will turn over all their work to us and let us do our thing. If they're not going to listen to us, why hire us and pay us?"

When a client won't listen, Patrick simply won't take them on to begin with. "Over time, we've come around to realize that if someone is not your client up front, they are never going to be your client, so why take them on and have both sides be disappointed? We simply don't want to preside over financial disasters, and whether they are of the client's making or not doesn't really matter. Some people just seem to have a knack for blowing themselves up, and we'll get tainted by being near the explosion."

Another requirement is that clients fully understand and accept Patrick's basic consultative terms. "Our clients have to agree to work the way we want to work or we won't take them on. This means working on a fee-based model and using a consultative process to arrive at a long-term investment strategy. We also want to be the only investment advisor to the family. Generally speaking, if a client has under $50 million and says, 'Look, I want to split it twenty-five with you and twenty-five with another advisor,' we will say, 'We appreciate it, but no thank you. We want to be the only advisor on the account because we feel that we can add the most value if we are looking at everything and are working side-by-side with the client, not in constant conflict or competition with somebody else. That just doesn't seem to add as much value.' However, we don't insist on this when families get over $50 million, because they're just going to do what they want to do. But the vast majority of our clients do have all their money with us."

With these various requirements in place, how far has Patrick come toward achieving the goals set out in the business model that he revised after he became a Private Wealth Advisor? By 2006 Patrick was down to 100 total households yet his revenue was up 40 percent, and by 2007 Patrick was down to just 68 households with revenues up another 27 percent, and, together with his high qualitative rankings, earned a spot on The Winner's Circle top-100 advisors list in Barron's. Understandably pleased with his progress, Patrick says, "With the number of clients going down and the dollar amount we are managing going up, we aren't downsizing our business, we are right-sizing it. We are actually continuing to shrink the business; we now have fewer than 50 total clients. Basically, we have given away everything under $10 million—that is, we have found other advisors at Merrill Lynch to service those relationships."

Have there been any downsides to right-sizing his business in this way? "It took a lot of willpower," Patrick says. "I had to forego a lot of short-term compensation. That's what it's really all about: Can you defer immediate gratification and say 'No' to tons of referrals that are just too small? It wasn't easy to do that, especially as the market was going down. But what happens is you finally come to the cold reality of what you can and can't deliver. Do I really want to go out and tell a guy I'll do this and that for him and then not deliver? If I get a $3 million client, I can make him feel very good and do a nice asset allocation for him, but ultimately he will not get the same experience as a $50 million client, and he will leave. He'll be disappointed that he just doesn't have the connectivity he wants with me, and he'll walk out."

"In this business," Patrick emphasizes, "the hardest thing is to admit that you can't be everything to everybody, and then refer potential business to others who are better suited for it. It takes some business maturity, and you can't be greedy. But ultimately, you'll make more money this way, if you have the skill set to bring in the big clients. You can wish a business any way you want it, but you've got to be able to attract the right clients as you downsize your book. Knock on wood, so far we've been able to do that."

There is one more potential downside, but Patrick is not too concerned about it. "When you have fewer but bigger clients, each one has more control over your personal financial destiny, and you are taking on some different risk characteristics. Fortunately, even though we have lots of big clients, none of them does more than about 4 percent of our business. It would scare me to have a single client who dominated our book. I have some friends who have one client who does 25 or 30 percent of their business. That would make me really nervous and I wouldn't be able to sleep at night. I'd just be too uncomfortable with that. I want a more consistent type of business."

DELIVERING WHAT'S PROMISED

"Having become a Private Wealth Advisor," Patrick continues, "I was determined to promise my clients a value and service proposition and then deliver as promised. I never want to overpromise; lots of people promise things and don't deliver. I therefore had to think about doing fewer things but doing them extremely well, and doing them in a way that would be tailored to and meaningful to families with significant wealth. As a result, I became very clear on what I will and won't do with the families I work with, and one thing that I did want to promise and deliver on as part of my being compensated on a fee basis was family office services."

"Think of it this way," Patrick suggests. "Most of our clients have run a business where they are the CEO or founder of a company, and then they sell that business for an amount that becomes their wealth. We, essentially, become that business, which is really the residual liquidity from those events. I wanted, therefore, to standardize our service process so we could deliver the same kind of service experience that a client would expect from the Ritz Carlton. If you go to the Ritz Carlton, no matter whom you touch in the organization, if you have a problem, that person will resolve it. I've instituted that same standard in my team to make sure that we deliver a very, very high level of service to the clients we are fortunate enough to do business with."

"When a significant client hands over his wealth to me—when he chooses me—it's an incredible feeling, because it's a huge leap of faith. Our clients give me their trust and confidence, and I take it very seriously. I have to deliver for them, and I want to make their financial life better, easier, and more pleasant. We start with the day-to-day things, the mundane things that people don't like to talk about but that are really important to them. For example, most of our clients have staff, and on a typical day we interact with their staff so that the clients don't have to deal with day-to-day matters."

"Basically, we provide full family office services, including, of course, investment management services and a full financial plan every three years to keep the family on track, as well as many other things—assistance with checking, credit cards, bill payments, automatic bill payments, wire transfers, finding and paying domestic staff and boat crews, travel planning, boat and plane financing, providing all necessary year-end tax documentation, making sure lines of credit and similar financial vehicles are set up to take advantage of whatever opportunity the client might see, providing consolidated performance reporting and making sure it's electronically delivered the same day every month, and scheduling three in-person meetings a year. This is the universe we work in, and I make sure we take care of all these things and do them well."

"We wanted to be and have become very good at a small set of things. We know what we know, and we know what we don't know, and if a client wants to do something outside of our sphere, then we'll refer them to someone who can help. For example, if a client wants to trade silver futures, that's not something we do. We don't have expertise there, and we aren't going to pretend that we do. So we'll find a partner in the firm, somebody who is an expert on this, and then deliver the client to that person. Another example: We have a significant family as a client that's involved in real estate and they wanted introductions to somebody who would lend against their real estate and investment banking holdings. We took them to a financial advisor who specializes in this. We made the introduction and said he would handle this for them. We always want to make very sure that we do not misrepresent what our areas of expertise are. Clients really appreciate it when you are up front with them about what you do know and don't know."

"We are, however, always looking to extend our competencies and go one step above and beyond for all the families we work with.

For example, we've been working on getting everybody completely paperless with regard to performance and tax statement organization. To make this happen, we have to talk to each CPA firm so our clients can electronically download the tax information they need daily. This is a huge project, because we have to go through it forty-five times, and each CPA firm works a little bit differently. But it's a huge value add to our clients, because it means the time spent by their CPA collecting their Merrill Lynch statements is going to get cut from twenty hours a year to zero hours."

"That's our initiative for this year," Patrick adds. "We always like to have a new initiative, something we can do better for our clients. We want to be one step ahead of everybody else, and we want to be indispensable. I can't make the market go up, but I can make sure that we deliver on what we promise."

OUTSOURCING HIS MONEY MANAGEMENT

In addition to delivering a Ritz Carlton level of service, Patrick delivers excellent investment performance through his process-oriented approach, beginning with setting realistic expectations. "I want to generate solid and consistent investment results for my clients in the context of a diversified portfolio, which means I only take on clients who want a diversified portfolio. It could be an aggressive diversified portfolio or a conservative diversified portfolio, but it has to be diversified. And I've always thought the best way to go was to use an endowment-like approach with all my clients, meaning a combination of active and passive management, traditional investment, and alternative investments."

Importantly, Patrick learned early in his career that he was far better off outsourcing the actual management of money than attempting to be his own part-time portfolio manager. "The bottom line is whether or not you are adding value for your clients," he says. "My conclusion is that it's extraordinarily difficult for an advisor who is focused on managing relationships and helping clients with their complex personal financial needs to also be a world-class stock picker. In fact, I think it's impossible. It's difficult enough for a full-time investment professional with lots and lots of experience to outperform [the market], and even more so for a financial advisor. Many financial advisors who are picking stocks are charging the same fees as if they were professional money managers. I just don't see the value that their clients are getting for their money."

"Admittedly, managing the money by yourself may be a more profitable business model," Patrick adds. "But even though my business model may be inherently less profitable in that sense, I think it allows me to be much more objective, and to sit as close to my clients on the same side of the table as I realistically can. There are always going to be conflicts of interest in the world, but if you're managing the money on your own, you're not going to fire yourself, no matter how poorly you're doing, especially if you're earning 100 basis points on it."

"My ultimate reason for not managing the money," Patrick goes on, "is that I truly feel it's not in the best interests of my clients. Keep in mind that the way you create wealth for your clients isn't just by doing a great asset allocation, adding a tactical overlay, and picking great managers. The real key is the mental and emotional commitment you make to help the client through periods of great stress in the markets, which, of course, requires face time with the client. Often, the best thing you will ever do for a wealthy family is to keep that family on track with their investment objectives through a difficult period. When everybody wants to get out of the market, that's usually the exact wrong time to do so. This kind of communication with clients is, in my mind, much more valuable than having a financial advisor who, with zero information advantage, tries to personally beat the S&P 500."

Still, given Patrick's love of the capital markets, does he miss the actual management of his clients' money? "I find it quite interesting and challenging," he says, "to focus on the top-down investment process that we use, starting with our long-term asset allocation and then the tactical allocation over that, along with manager selection. In many ways, picking managers is like picking stocks, and I enjoy understanding what the managers are doing and what they are buying, and whether they are doing what they are supposed to be doing or not. Essentially, I'm still in the process of managing money, just at a higher level."

THE INVESTMENT PROCESS AND
TAX-EFFICIENT INDEXING

"Our investment process uses a consulting-driven model," Patrick states. "We use long-term asset allocation models based on the firm's private bank's research along with tactical overlays also based on the firm's research and provided to us by our chief investment strategist. Basically, our building block models are our five-year forecasts of index return expectations. So we essentially have models that say we can guess what a client's return and likely standard deviation or volatility will be. On top of these building blocks we have tactical bets that we overlay across these longer-term models, and, of course, we believe in focusing on a blend of alpha and beta." [*Alpha* refers to added returns above a benchmark index, and *beta* refers to the volatility, or systematic risk, of a portfolio compared to the market as a whole.]

"Basically, we create models based on our long-term view," Patrick says, "and then we plug in a combination of indexes and active managers. In fact, we think that a client should have at least 45 percent of his or her portfolio indexed, but we use *tax-efficient indexing* to increase the odds of hitting our projected returns and then hopefully outperforming them by about 200 basis points. Using these tax-efficient indices as the core of our equity model allows us, in our choice of non-index managers, to hire those who really don't look anything like the benchmark. They have a much higher standard deviation than managers you'd typically hire, which means that they really have an opportunity to outperform. The managers we hire are unique, and can really hit the ball out of the park. Because we have the comfort of knowing that we have the indexes, we can also have these sluggers in our clients' portfolios. Last year, for instance, our active managers really outperformed their benchmarks, but this year it's the benchmarks that are carrying the portfolio."

How does tax-efficient indexing work? "Essentially," Patrick says, "we hire a manager to construct an index for the client, such as an S&P 500 index, an S&P 600 index, or the EAFA index, which is a large cap international index. There are basically three companies out there that will create a separate account for each index, and we've been using them since about 2000 to do this. The manager buys the individual stocks in the index, and then does tax loss harvesting on a monthly basis while still replicating the benchmark as closely as possible. The client has the benefit of the short-term tax losses, which are worth 35 cents on the dollar against short-term capital gains across the client's entire portfolio. With this approach we've found that on an after-tax basis we are able to beat the indexes we've chosen by about 100 basis points a year. This has worked extremely well. In fact, the more volatile the markets, the better this kind of tax-efficient indexing works."

"What happens," Patrick continues, "is that you have this 'tax alpha' and for the first six to seven years the manager is able to harvest a lot of losses. For example, during this volatile year, a million dollars in a tax-efficient S&P index would enable a client to harvest on average about $200,000 of short-term losses even though the S&P 500 is only down 5 percent. So the portfolio is down $50,000, just like any index, but the client has been able to harvest $200,000 worth of short-term tax losses, assuming a maximum if they earn 35 percent capital gains rate. This is extremely valuable to the client who has short-term capital gains—typically he or she will end up having short-term capital gains somewhere else in their portfolio— or if they carry the losses forward to future years."

"Over time," Patrick continues, "this allows the client to spend less money on taxes the first six years or so, which means the portfolio will compound at a higher rate because there is more capital invested. So, just like a 'J' curve in private equity, it goes negative in the beginning and then goes positive. In our case, it never really goes negative, but it becomes more meaningful as time goes on. We feel that this kind of tax-efficient indexing is a very powerful tool, and that any high-net-worth individual who has any belief at all in the notion of reversion to the mean should use it."

"Basically, you have to index, because it's unrealistic to think you are going to pick managers who are in the top quartile consistently over a ten-year period. You can pick some good managers, but you will also pick some who don't achieve their objectives. By indexing, you hedge your bets, and if you hold the view, as we do, that we're in for a decade of lower returns and higher risks, then indexing absolutely has to be a key part of your strategy. Smaller clients are going to use ETFs, and bigger clients will use tax-efficient indexing. You need to make sure that if the market is going to deliver 9 percent, you get that 9 percent. This is something that's often lost on people. They always assume they are going to get more than what the market delivers, but 50 percent of the people out there always get less than the average."

"So, first and foremost," Patrick continues, "indexing makes sense generally, and second, tax-efficient indexing makes even more sense to high-net-worth individuals, because it enables them to replicate the return of the benchmark and then get a tax-related improvement over that return. You really have to be focused on delivering consistent after-tax results over the long haul. I don't dislike ETFs, which also rely on indexing; it's just that they don't have any tax efficiency benefits. Overall, then, tax-efficient indexes work really well for us, and that's why they are a minimum of 40 to 45 percent of the equity side of our clients' portfolios."

"Probably, over time, even more of the equity portions of our portfolios will be indexed and actively managed. Right now we are about 45 percent indexed, and our typical portfolio has 25 to 35 different investment components in it, including a very well diversified municipal bond portfolio. We also use a lot of taxable fixed-income vehicles, and we have a significant weighting into alternative instruments including both hedge funds and private equity. For clients with significant assets, we believe that private equity is one of the best places to build long-term wealth, giving them a great opportunity to experience 10-plus percent returns. So, we use multiple managers in municipal bonds and multiple managers in equities, and we use all active management."

If tax-efficient indexing makes so much sense, why don't more advisors use it? "First," Patrick says, "many people, including clients, don't understand it. They don't see the tax efficiency. It doesn't show up on a typical performance statement, and most clients focus on pretax numbers, which they shouldn't do. As they become more sophisticated and better educated, clients focus more on after-tax results. Second, the minimums are higher here. The minimum for a small cap or international tax efficient index is about a million dollars, so it won't work for smaller clients. My sense, however, is that the minimum for tax-efficient indexing will be going down to as low as a quarter of a million dollars within a year or two. Lastly, management fees are only 35 basis points on tax-efficient indexing, so it's not very profitable. And since it's not very profitable, it's not normally worth marketing. In our business, though, given what we are doing for our clients, tax-efficient indexing makes infinite sense. We don't get paid money management fees; so we are more than happy to find a cheap, tax-efficient solution for our clients, just as we are more than willing to pay a high fee to a money manager who is worth it."

ASSET ALLOCATION AND CLIENT CUSTOMIZATION

"A balance between different strategies—between efficient indexing, active managers, private equity, and the fixed income component of a portfolio—is the right way to manage our clients' money," Patrick says. "Everybody talks about the Harvard and Yale endowments, and certain other foundations that have had such great success, and this kind of balance between indexing and active management is exactly what they do. But really, when you look at these endowments, their performance has first and foremost been dependent on their asset allocation strategy. They put their money in the right buckets to begin with, and that's also what we try to do."

"That's why we take a long-term view and look at major turns in the cycle," Patrick notes. "So, for example, we look at reversion to the mean, and we want to overweight the parts of the market that have done poorly. And since our portfolios have such a high percentage in tax-efficient indexes, it's really important for us to get our top-down asset allocation mix correct and pick the right indexes in the first place. And we also keep an eye on dividends and cash flow, because even in an aggressive portfolio a good cash flow acts as an inflation hedge."

Given the macro views that Patrick and his team have of the markets, how do they customize each client's portfolio? "The way we invest is very similar for all our clients—both the equity model we use and the alternative investment and fixed-income models. It's just that the dollar amount in each of those three buckets is very different depending on the client's risk profile."

"It's not as if we'll have a very different equity investment strategy for a really conservative client. We have one equity investment strategy, one fixed-income strategy, and one alternative investments strategy, and we mix those differently depending on the client. The biggest difference comes in the private equity area, where there is more customization. Private equity is a really important asset class for ultra-high-net-worth individuals, because that's where the best returns have come from in the last eight years. But some clients, typically those in their fifties and sixties, tend to be more comfortable with private equity than others. And clients in their seventies and beyond often aren't as interested in private equity because of the long time horizons it requires. Also, because private equity isn't an asset class you can just buy off the shelf, there tends to be a lot of customization within our portfolios. Good funds do come out and open, but then they close, and there might not be another for two years. So private equity is really quite different."

To ensure that he and his team get the right asset allocation mix in place for each of their clients, Patrick pays special attention to the way he communicates with each client. "Client communication must always be clear and consistent," he says. "What's very important about having a successful client is having a client understand our strategy and our thought process. If the client doesn't understand our strategy, he or she won't stay with it when things get tough. Clearly, the reason most investors aren't successful in mutual funds is because they never stay in them, and in adverse market conditions they get out. Our job is to make sure that our clients understand what the long-term strategy is, why they are in what they're in, and, as best they can, the risks that are inherent in their portfolio."

Patrick continues, "We spend a long time with each client explaining how we select the building blocks that constitute their portfolios. And we focus on what our return expectations are for the different asset classes. The biggest thing is for us to have them understand the building blocks. If we are only expecting an 8 percent return on the S&P with an 18-point standard deviation, having clients understand that is really important. If they walk away thinking they are going to make 25 percent a year on their equities, they are dead wrong. So when a client sees the market drop 10 points and is upset, we can say, 'Listen, we are still within a one standard deviation move in the S&P. That's pretty normal.' That's the kind of thing they have to be able to understand."

Ongoing feedback from clients is also important in adjusting and rebalancing portfolios over time. "As part of our investment process we use our building blocks to build appropriate models for our clients and then tweak them either at our introductory review or at subsequent reviews. Most of the changes we make during the review process are minor, but we are always tilting the portfolio in one direction or another depending on whether our thesis is working out overall. But we keep the focus at the asset class level, which helps clients step back and not get overfocused on details that may not really be relevant to generating the returns they want."

THE RIGHT STAFF

To make sure he delivers on his promises—both with respect to family office services and investment services—the size of Patrick's staff has been increasing, even though the total number of households the team serves has been going down. "We actually just added another person," Patrick notes. "Keep in mind that one $100-million client is not only worth far more to us than several under-$10-million accounts, but the reality is that there is more that we can do, and need to do, for a larger client like this."

Patrick relies on a competent and well trained team, starting with Maria Kattan, Senior Client Service Associate, who has been with Merrill Lynch since 1985. "Maria, who is also known as 'Ricki,' acts as my head private banker," Patrick says. "She is key in delivering high-level client services to our ultra-high-net-worth families. She's really been an integral part of my success in building the business."

Rafael Fernandez, Investment Analyst, has been with Patrick since 2003. "Rafael came to me right out of the University of Florida, where he was a business major. He has specific expertise in concentrated stock positions," Patrick adds. "He understands virtually everything there is to understand about concentrated stock risks, rules, and regulatory paperwork, which is especially important because we are a self-clearing team—that is, we can clear a trade without going through the normal apparatus at Merrill Lynch. Rafael also focuses on derivative work and alternative investments, and because he's quite knowledgeable in lending, he's often involved in complicated deals. Right now we're arranging financing for a private jet, and Rafael is the person who takes care of that. And, like Ricki, Rafael is fluent in Spanish as well as English—Miami's Spanish-speaking population outnumbers English speakers."

Richard Grodin, who's been with Merrill Lynch since 2006, is another of the team's Investment Analysts. "Richard was a financial advisor in our office when we hired him to be on our team," Patrick says. "He really wanted to learn the business, and felt that being on our team represented a better learning opportunity. He's been with us for three years now, and in addition to being a very smart guy, he's a Level II Chartered Financial Analyst® [CFA®]. Richard works with our investment research group and our investment management consulting group on asset allocation, tactical asset allocation, and manager selection. And then, secondarily, he's involved with portfolio reviews."

"Another former financial advisor at Merrill Lynch who's joined our team is Marcel Laniado," Patrick says. "With a BS from Syracuse University and fluency in Spanish, he's now an Investment Analyst and reports to Richard Grodin. Marcel works primarily on the marketing side, does investment presentations for prospective clients, and assists with client reviews."

Also fluent in Spanish is Jessica Collante. Patrick says, "Her mother and father both work in our office as well. Jessica reports to Ricki, and works in customer service and private banking for the 45 families we now serve."

The newest team member is Michael Romanchuk. "Michael received his BA in finance from Michigan State University and was hired by Merrill Lynch in March 2006," Patrick says. "He was a financial advisor in another office but wanted to get more experience and really learn the business from the ground up. He's a financial analyst and involved with basic portfolio construction."

To make sure that the overall team and each team member shines as brightly as possible, Patrick constantly focuses on training and upgrading skills. "We try to have everybody cross-trained in everything," Patrick says. "So, for example, while Rafael has great expertise in concentrated stocks, he's teaching somebody else about this as well. We make sure that we have an ongoing cross-pollination of skills so that everybody has a really strong foundation in the different things that our team does."

Educational opportunities with resepct to investment products are also a regular feature of the team's environment. "Money managers constantly roll through our office, coming to meet with us and show us their products," Patrick notes. "Everybody on the team is welcome to sit in on those meetings. Whether or not a team member is in an investment role doesn't matter, because we feel those meetings are a great learning opportunity and we want everyone on our team to have as high an awareness level as possible of the investment options that are out there, because we are always looking for where the next opportunity is going to be."

To ensure the free flow of ideas and the best possible communication, the team members sit in an open office environment. "We all sit in an open area," Patrick notes, "and in the next phase they're going to open it up into one giant room. We will be even closer together, and that's important for communication purposes. I don't have a separate office. I sit out there with everybody else, so everybody can hear what's going on. In fact, most of the private banking teams at Merrill Lynch are set up this way, which I like. I would never want to be in an office by myself. I would feel too disconnected. I prefer to be able to hear every phone call that comes in. It works out better this way. Of course, we also have a big conference room for meeting with clients."

Although Patrick is clearly the team leader, he makes sure to listen to the input of his staff, especially when they don't agree with him. "I've been overruled a few times," he says. "I definitely listen to my staff. And when they shout loud enough, I know I'm probably wrong."

LEARNING FROM MISTAKES

When looking at Patrick's rapid rise to the top ranks of financial advisors, one might be tempted to think that he has made few mistakes and has had few setbacks along the way, but Patrick readily admits that this is not the case. "Mistakes? Sure. Absolutely. I've had all kinds of setbacks. Where would you like to start?" The important thing, of course, is that Patrick learns from his mistakes and makes necessary and appropriate course corrections.

"For example," he says, "in 2000 and 2001, as I was building my new business as a Private Wealth Advisor, I thought I would bring in a junior partner and have that person take over some of my relationships. I brought in a very smart and talented guy who was a CFA and experienced money manager. I thought I could hand some of my client relationships over to him and that he could take care of them. But what I quickly realized was that my clients did not hire him; they hired me. So if I was committing to a client, and they in turn were saying, 'Yes, I'm going to give you my money,' then I had to be the person servicing them, at least from an investment perspective although not necessarily on the day-to-day kind of things."

"This was a real learning experience," Patrick notes. "I found out, first, that my clients simply were not going to accept somebody else in the investment role. I also found out that even if someone is smart and has a money management background, if he has never really serviced clients, he may not have sufficient skills and empathy to do it, particularly for working with clients when the markets are going down. Clients understand risk in a different way than we do. It's their money, and they worked for it their entire career; if they become irrational, you need to talk them through those periods and keep them focused on their longer-term goals. So, this fellow I hired, as talented a professional as he was, was not able to take over my relationship role, because the clients really expected me to be there."

"This was a painful experience, as well as a valuable lesson. Whatever deliverables I had offered my clients, I was the one who had to deliver them personally. Nothing more, nothing less. From that day forward I became very clear with every existing and prospective team member that as long as I was around, I would be doing the client reviews. Clients like mine expect you to spend meaningful time with them. Not phone time, but unhurried time in front of them, sitting down, spending as long as they want to spend in a meeting. To really understand what's going on in a client's life, you must sit down with them frequently, one on one, for a meaningful and unhurried amount of time. This is absolutely the key to building successful relationships."

"At minimum," Patrick continues, "we meet with each client three times a year. This week, I'm only doing one meeting, on Thursday, and it will start at 10:00 a.m. and finish around 4:30. I'm meeting first with the husband and wife, spending about two hours going through their portfolio. Then we are going to have lunch and afterward we'll meet with their family office staff for a couple of hours. On average, I probably talk to only three clients a day on the phone. I simply don't have that many clients, and I aspire to having fewer so I can do more for the ones I do have."

"We want to build very strong relationships," Patrick adds, "because a client's financial success is fundamentally a by-product of a strong relationship. I'm very confident that we can deliver good financial performance, but only if we have a strong relationship and can keep a client on track. In a year like this, for example, it's hard to keep clients from liquidating everything and putting their money into municipal bonds. We have to keep them focused on their long-term objectives and not let them get caught up in the news flows. You have to be confident and comfortable with your clients, and that only happens if you spend time with them. Also, you build credibility by consistently delivering over time and by being balanced in your views. You don't want to be too excited when things go well, nor too pessimistic when things go poorly. We strive to take a middle view of things."

Patrick learned a different kind of lesson when he brought someone onto his team to manage money. "I hired a fellow who was a CFA and portfolio manager with professional experience to run an equity portfolio for us. We thought he would do customized portfolios for our clients, but it was a mistake. In a world where you can go out and buy expertise cheaply from different money managers around the world, it's just not necessary to try to create alpha on your own team. In fact, I think there's very little value added that you can deliver like this."

"We were doing this as an accommodation to clients who wanted an in-house stock picker. But I quickly began to realize that there was no value in it, whether the clients wanted it or not, or, put differently, we couldn't deliver enough value to make it worthwhile. Conflicts of interest inevitably arise in this situation, and I want to be as objective as possible when dealing with clients' money. So I really think it's important to outsource and separate yourself from the asset management function. It's hard enough to beat the market even if you have a team of full-time investment professionals dedicated to it."

Another lesson involved an attempt to do *too much* for clients. "At one point we got in the situation of trying to overcustomize certain things. Consider, for example, performance reporting. If you get into lots of hand work in customizing reports, you end up making mistakes. So now, in everything we do, we really try to have as many things as possible be process-driven. We use the same process for everybody because it really minimizes human error and increases the quality of the product at the end of the day for all our clients."

One final lesson concerned the need to diversify during over-heated markets, like the dot-com bust. "We begged our clients to diversify," Patrick says, "but some held on too long and their stocks never came back. That's just what happens after you've had a twenty-year bull market like we had in the eighties and nineties and you got bailed out of every mistake you made. The lesson everybody learned during those twenty years was that if you just hang on, it will all eventually come back, because everything *had* come back. Unfortunately, in the last eight years this hasn't been the case, and a lot of folks who didn't diversify simply are no longer as wealthy as they were. It was a brutal lesson for all, me included. You wish you could go back and be more forceful with your clients, but at the end of the day, people make their own decisions on these things. Since then, we haven't taken on a concentrated stock client who won't agree up front to diversify. We just don't want to go through that kind of drama again."

Having made some mistakes and learned from them, Patrick is generous with his time when it comes to advising newcomers to the business. "I really enjoy helping the new guys in the business because that was the most fun part of my career. About four times a year I run meetings where I give the younger financial advisors half a day and walk them through my entire process, soup to nuts. We cover everything from how we market and how we manage money to how we talk to clients and what we do to help them. It's very rewarding for me, and we're happy to mentor people if they ask."

A GOOD LIFE

"I think it's really important to play to your strengths," Patrick repeats. "I'm not good at everything. I'm very aware of what I'm not good at, and I try to focus on doing the things I do well. Where I have gaps in my skill set, I try to fill them with other people who are extremely talented in those areas, and give those people, especially my team members, the autonomy needed to be successful. My philosophy, I suppose, is to give people opportunities and let them run with them. I really enjoy working with people who are positive, who really want to do a good job every day, and who come to work looking for new opportunities, challenges, and rewards."

"That's how I operate as well," Patrick continues. "I work hard, and I play hard. I get up at 4:45 or 5:00 in the morning and go for a ten- or eleven-mile bike ride or go to the gym. Then I come home, have breakfast with the kids, and go to work. I love working fifty or sixty hours a week. I consider it a privilege to have a good job and clients that I like. I don't take it for granted. Humility is around every corner and since life will inevitably humble you, you just have to enjoy it. If you've built a great situation, you've got to enjoy it while you can, because you never know what's coming."

"Ultimately," Patrick adds, "I'm a positive family guy, not a complicated guy. And I'm loyal. Same wife. Same job. Same assistants. Same firm. So part of my philosophy is to not overcommit. My weekends are 100 percent for my family, my wife and four children, and that means Friday night, Saturday, and Sunday. I'm not there with my kids every night, but I'm there a lot, and I control what I can. It took me a long time to become mature enough to say 'no' to various offers. I'm an enthusiastic person and I want to say 'yes' to everything, but you just can't. No one knows who I am at my golf club; I haven't picked up my clubs since my second child arrived. But I will play golf again one day. And while I can't be the main coach for my kids' teams, I'm often an assistant coach. I work hard at finding a good balance. And I make sure to take my vacations. I take off about five weeks a year, and spend them with my wife and the kids, because it's important time that I'll never get back."

"I have to repeat that having a job like mine is a great privilege," Patrick says. "I'm grateful to each and every one of my clients for the opportunity they have given me. That's why I have to deliver on what I've promised. That's my responsibility. If I didn't want the responsibility, I didn't have to take it, which is what I remind myself of when I might be getting annoyed one day about this or that. 'Hey,' I tell myself, 'I said yes to this person, and they are paying me, and I've got to deliver for them.'"

Patrick also delivers in his community. "I've gotten really involved with my kids' schools," he says. "They are taking care of my most precious resource, my children, and I like to give back where I can. I'm on the Pacesetters Committee, which is focusing on a major new reconstruction development for the school. And recently, the town elders of Key Biscayne, where we live, asked me to be on the board of the Key Biscayne Community Foundation. My wife and I are the chairpersons of the annual fund drive this year at St. Stephen's Episcopal Church. I'm also on the Advisory Council to Management for Merrill Lynch. There's so much to do that it can get overwhelming, so I have to decide which activities I can manage."

One more thing Patrick has to juggle is his personal relationships with his clients. "Since we spend a lot of time with our clients, I'm pretty good friends with the vast majority of them. I'm not sure I will ever retire because I would just end up calling the same people a lot of the time. I don't have too many clients my age, though, since most of them are in their fifties and sixties, and a few of them are in their seventies. But I do have a couple of clients my age, and I like them a lot."

"The bottom line," Patrick continues, "is that you inevitably become friends with your clients. On the weekends I spend all my time with my family, but during the week I thoroughly enjoy the time I spend with my clients. Because we spend so much time together, many of them become as close to me as my close personal friends. In part, it's because we like each other that they are still working with me ten years later. To me, this is part of the pleasure of life and of work. You can have meaningful, long-term relationships with your clients, and that makes work much more satisfying. For example, when I have a really good relationship with a client family and go visit them at their summer home to do their review, they invite me to stay with them. This lets me know that they really trust me and care about me the way I care about them."

Is Patrick ever jealous of the great wealth of many of his clients? "No, not at all," he says. "I don't have aspirations to five homes and lots of complexity. Really, I feel that I've always had what I wanted, perhaps because my wants are not as complicated as some people's. I do get a kick out of knowing people who are as interesting, fun, and successful as the folks I work with. But I'm not a 'grass-is-greener someplace else' kind of guy. I do my exercise in the morning, I love my kids and my wife—we met when she was nineteen and I was twenty-three—and I greatly enjoy working hard for my clients. I love traveling around the world, and I'm a gourmet chef. Cooking is one of my passions, and I actually love to read cookbooks, cook for the family, and make things like homemade pasta. Ultimately, I have the life that I want, and I wouldn't want a different one." No doubt Patrick's clients feel the same way about having him as their financial advisor.

CHAPTER 2: BRIAN PFEIFLER AND TEAM

MORGAN STANLEY PRIVATE WEALTH MANAGEMENT
NEW YORK, NEW YORK

Brian Pfeifler

B rian Pfeifler, consistently ranked by The Winner's Circle in the top echelon of the nation's very best financial advisors, is a study in contrasts.

On the one hand, Brian's focus on investing his ultra-high-net-worth clients' assets to deliver the best possible returns has brought him to and beyond the leading edge of implementing customized asset allocation and opportunistic investing. Following extensive research and contemplation, Brian incorporates a heavy dose of alternative and international investments and is not afraid to move away from what have traditionally been major components of a typical portfolio's asset allocation (e.g., for the last several years, he has recommended a substantial underweighting of fixed-income investments). With a work ethic that flows directly from his investment banking and institutional bond trading background, Brian has managed to deliver favorable returns on the roughly $4 billion he manages for some twenty-five client relationships.

On the other hand, Brian has eschewed certain conventional notions, such as working as part of a team of advisors who collectively make investment decisions or offering clients a wide range of family office services. The core reason that clients come to an advisor like Brian is to have their money well managed, and that is what Brian is all about. He delegates the day-to-day operations of his business and gains new clients only through referrals. His partner, Laura Norman, handles the former, and the latter takes care of itself based on Brian's reputation and ongoing success. Thus, with a team that—including Brian—totals just five individuals, he exemplifies what an intelligent, dedicated, and focused investment representative can achieve on behalf of a few dozen extremely wealthy clients both in the United States and abroad.

INTO THE FRAY

Brian was born in 1967 in Milwaukee, Wisconsin. At the age of four, he moved with his parents to Gulf Stream, Florida, and attended St. Andrews School in Boca Raton. After high school, Brian received his BA from Amherst College in Massachusetts, spending one of his four college years in London at the prestigious London School of Economics. After finishing college in 1990, Brian went straight to work for Morgan Stanley in New York City as an investment banking analyst.

Brian's father was a commercial banker. "Finance and stocks were always discussed," he says. "While in college, I realized that I wanted to live in a big city. So I spent a year in London and realized I wanted to start my career in New York City. I thought the most logical place to derive a positive experience was from an investment bank's analyst training program where you would work ninety hours a week and gain five years' worth of knowledge in two years. I received offers for a number of jobs and concluded that Morgan Stanley was the best place for me."

Brian started as an analyst in the M&A (mergers and acquisitions) department, where he remained for two years. "At the time, Morgan Stanley hired about a hundred people worldwide in investment banking on the analyst side. About sixty of those were in New York, and about fifteen of us were in M&A. We were part of a pool, and, as deals came in, they assigned us to teams. We modeled the deals in the 'computer room,' where we basically lived for two years. I worked with many good people back then. Of the original hundred, eight to ten individuals remain in senior roles throughout the firm."

Brian moved to high-yield trading from 1992 to 1996, with the last two years spent in London. "When I was in M&A," Brian says, "I knew that investment banking was great training, but it wasn't something I wanted to spend the rest of my life doing. Having focused a fair amount on going to companies and pitching Morgan Stanley's high-yield bond capabilities, I wanted to explore the trading side, and I was able to get a position doing that after two years."

Eventually, Brian came back to New York and joined the PCS (private client services) division, where he has remained ever since. "After four years of trading—two in New York and two in London—I read the handwriting on the wall and realized the Internet could take away some of the advantages of corporate bond traders and salespersons. In addition, I wanted to manage money. I had worked quite closely with a number of the high-net-worth salespeople while in London and thought, 'Well, this is a very interesting job. You get to interact with self-made people who are extremely successful and usually quite interesting. Moreover, these clients invest in all asset classes.' I was in London in 1994 when the bond market got crushed and a large number of employees of the fixed-income division were let go. I realized that the careers of the research salespeople and traders depended upon the performance of the underlying market."

"In contrast," Brian continues, "on the private wealth management side, the business is much more resilient. If bonds were underperforming, one could reallocate to equities or another asset class. One has the ability to adjust an allocation to whichever asset class provides the most opportunity. I view this to be a resilient business model. The idea of assuming investment responsibility was, and remains, very interesting to me. A typical trader at the time attempted to make a few basis points per trade, but you never really owned anything. I thought that, on a long-term basis, it was going to be most fulfilling to manage money and that actually turned out to be the case. I really enjoy the money management side."

THE EVOLUTION OF A TEAM AND ITS FOCUS

The PCS team that Brian joined was already up and running, and it consisted of three professionals, including Brian. In 1998, after two years, the team's composition started changing. "What happened," Brian says, "is that one person on the team took a job in management and ultimately left the firm. When he left our team, we added another person, so it was three professionals again. Then, in about 2001, another partner left to start a hedge fund, and there were just two of us. Then in 2002, my partner left to run the family office of one of our largest clients—they remain good clients of ours today. I have been on my own for the past six years. In the meantime, my colleague Laura Norman was promoted and is now my partner. We also have three other members of our team, but they are not equity partners."

Brian's duties changed as the team changed. "Initially I was going to run high-yield portfolios for our clients, with the possibility of branching out and running high-yield components for other teams as well. I did that for some time, and it worked out very well. Later, I began to manage the equities for our team as well and migrated to running more and more of the money on the investment side of the business. Over time, I went from being a pure money manager within the team to basically running the team. As the business has changed and as new products have become available, we've continued to shift the focus of what I do."

With respect to raising money, Brian says, "When I initially joined the team, my two partners were entirely focused on raising assets. My first break occurred when a successful car dealer I knew from Florida sold his business, and the timing worked out really well. He received a large amount of stock, and we did one of the first prepaid forwards for him, an interesting tax structure around a collar. From there, it just grew."

"I frequently tell people entering the business," Brian continues, "that there are situations where you know someone for five, six, or seven years before you finally see the relationship come to fruition. It takes a long time to develop the right clients and the right contacts who can get you introductions to the right clients, which is equally as important as prospecting directly. It's all about having people who are in contact with wealth creation situations who know you, who know what you can do, and who can refer people to you. It takes time for people to understand that you're in the business and to start thinking, 'Oh yes, Brian's the guy to go to if this kind of situation arises.' That's true both within the firm and externally as well."

"So eventually," Brian says, "I became responsible not just for managing money, but for bringing in assets as well. But we got to a point where I didn't really have a desire to focus on bringing in more assets. Of course, you always want to have more assets, but I didn't want to spend any time on the marketing side at the expense of performance. Over the years, we added other people, including a dedicated trader and additional assistants, all whom have improved the client experience. I see some advisors where the raising of money is the primary focus and the actual managing of the assets is secondary. My model is different. I spend my time determining asset allocation, managing money, and evaluating third-party managers. The few clients we add per year are exclusively through referrals."

THE RIGHT TEAM AND THE RIGHT SIZE BUSINESS

Of course, Brian would not be able to spend so much time on the investment side if the rest of his team weren't extremely capable. He says, "The team is set up so that I make all the investment decisions, and Laura runs all other aspects of the business. Very honestly, the day-to-day mechanics don't hold much interest for me, and there are people who can do it much better than I who can focus on it 100 percent of the time. Our processes for investing and disseminating information are very well established and followed consistently among our client base. It's lucky for me that I've got a great team behind me and that things run very smoothly. This allows me to travel in search of the best managers and investment ideas."

As for optimal team size, Brian says, "Each situation is different and each team is different as to what the right dynamic is. Especially for newcomers, there's a kind of catch-22 here. In order to be successful in the long-term, one needs to be a savvy investor. However, when building a new business, you can't spend all your time on investing. You can have the greatest ideas in the world, but if you don't have clients, what does it matter? So, you have to spend a lot of your time on the noninvestment side, which is a very tough thing.

Then, even for advisors who are successful at raising money, the challenge is to take it to the next level and deliver strong results."

"Also," Brian continues, "when you have people who enter our business from other industries, a lot of times they are good at raising assets from investors, but they are not experienced in investing. Some don't really have the desire to invest. My model is entirely inappropriate for them. Other people come laterally from the institutional side. They are senior people who have been successful on the institutional side of the business but they are inexperienced in recruiting clients. Often such hires become quite frustrated because prior experience is of little help to them. They are obliged to spend the vast majority of their time on operations and recruiting clients, and that can be quite frustrating. It's a tough thing this business asks you to do in general, and it's interesting that what enables you to be initially successful is not necessarily what enables you to be a really good investor or build a great business."

Brian is quite satisfied with the overall size of his business. "There are a number of funds whose goal is really to get to be the biggest. That is the kind of business they want to be in—they really want to grow to a multifaceted investment firm. There are hedge funds whose sole focus is maximizing returns on a single fund. I could easily go out and start hiring a ton of junior partners to raise money and make it more institutionalized. That doesn't interest me. The prospect of expanding the business at the expense of returns is not something I am willing to do. What we are trying to do is grow our assets through performance, and then very selectively add one or two new clients a year. We turn away a lot more business than we accept."

Indeed, Brian is quite satisfied with his current client base—roughly 25 relationships—and the quality of those clients. "I'm not looking to have the most clients," he says. "What I really want to have is the smartest clients, really big clients, clients to whom I can give ideas and who share ideas with me. We have a lot of clients who are very well-known people and also very good investors."

Brian limits the number of clients because he wants to ensure that each one gets the best possible service. "I'm not going to add clients knowing we would not be able to service them properly. I truly believe that all you have in this business is your reputation. When you lose it, you can never get it back. Ideally, we would like to double the business in five years through performance. If we outperform markets, the business will grow on its own merit."

"At the end of the day," Brian adds, "if we have really bad performance for an extended period of time, we could lose all of our assets. So if I were to spend a lot of time raising money, and I had bad performance, then I could easily lose a large portion of our overall assets. I've always thought the best way to raise assets was to grow the current assets through performance and referrals, and for me that's been the right decision."

THE BUCK STOPS (AND GROWS) HERE

One of the places where Brian's thinking stands out most clearly is his dedication to going it alone as the single individual who makes investment decisions for his clients. In a day and age when the trend toward horizontal teams with distributed investment decision-making power is gaining in popularity (as seen by the prominence of some of the other teams in this book), Brian says, "It's just not right for me."

"Most successful organizations have one person who is the real decision maker. Yet, in our industry, there is a belief that you should have multiple people sharing that responsibility. People will come up to me and say, 'Gosh, you don't have a partner?' But really, it's our industry that's the anomaly."

"Second," Brian continues, "I'm very comfortable taking full responsibility. I don't ever want to be in a situation where decisions were made that I didn't agree with but that, when they didn't work out, I had to go to the client and represent that I was a part of the decision-making process. In other words, a situation where I didn't make the decision or agree with it, but I had to defend it."

"Third," Brian continues, "many advisors don't manage money. Often they just raise money for third-party managers. I would estimate that 75 percent of financial advisors are asset gatherers. It's a different business model than mine. I can appreciate that if the focus is asset gathering, then the multiple partner model could make sense."

But what about the frequently asserted notion that there is a big advantage to having equal partners to mull things over with and share new ideas? Brian points out that he has no lack of talented and informed individuals to dialogue with. "I'm bouncing ideas off people all the time," he says, "but it just doesn't happen to be partners of mine sitting next to me doing the same thing that I'm doing. I don't think that's a necessary requirement. What is required is talking to hedge fund managers, to outside managers, to our internal resources, and, most importantly, to our clients."

But still, what if something happens to a sole investment decision maker such as Brian? "While there's always a risk that something might happen to me," he says, "that's a risk that you have in any fund or business."

TIME WELL SPENT

"I see a number of people in our industry," Brian says, "who go through a fire drill whenever they have an idea—struggling as to whom they should call with the idea, how they actually do the trade, and so on. If there's a trade break, the advisor is working with the back office trying to resolve or understand it, or you see advisors themselves handling wire transfers or putting books together, formatting things in Excel or PowerPoint, and going to the print room."

"In my view," Brian adds, "that would be a terrible waste of my time. I should really be thinking only about investments. So where a lot of people spend, in many instances, 50 percent or more of their time on internal operational-type issues, and let's say another 20 or 30 percent prospecting, then all they really have left for investment ideas is 20 percent of their time. Admittedly, you can't divorce yourself 100 percent from operational issues because problems do arise that require your involvement. But I've tried to arrange it so that 95 percent of my time is spent purely on the investment process or on meeting with clients."

"Luckily," he adds, "with Laura running the day-to-day business operations, including the management of team members, I'm freed up to concentrate on the investment side." More specifically, Brian estimates that he spends about 50 percent or more of his time meeting with money managers and industry professionals (long managers, alternative managers, private equity interests, proprietary traders, and other people in the business), 35 percent reading and thinking, and the other 15 percent meeting with clients. "Obviously," Brian says, "those numbers are not precise, and there's a lot of overlap, because sometimes when I'm sitting down with clients we're also sharing ideas and thinking of new opportunities."

The amount of time that he spends with each client varies according to how long-standing the relationship is, how volatile the markets have been, and a number of other factors. "We have few enough relationships," Brian says, "that we have the time for frequent discussions with our clients. Typically, it's not so much that we have a schedule—'I'm going to call you every month at this time.' Instead, it's more like a relationship with a colleague. When clients are available, we will meet with them or speak to them about their investments and the markets. Typically, I prefer to sit down on a semiannual basis and have a thorough review of performance and asset allocation. Ideally such meetings are in person. I find that at the outset of a relationship, we meet more frequently, perhaps even monthly. Certainly, some people are more high touch and others are very hands off. It all depends on the client."

"Also," Brian concedes, "a lot of this has to do with performance. We had more client contact in 2001 and 2002 than we have had from 2005 through the middle of 2007. When markets are rising and performance is good, clients are typically comfortable with fewer meetings. When you see big dislocations in the market, believe me, you have a lot more contact. Eventually the markets will not be as good as they've been the last few years and we'll have more dislocations, and, when that occurs, we'll seek more contact. We're ready for that."

One way Brian leverages his time is by sending his clients a weekly email. "It takes me two to three hours every Monday to write it," he says, "and it's a very useful exercise to crystallize my thoughts. It is also very useful for clients because they know that wherever they are in the world, they are going to receive an update from me every Monday that tells them exactly what I'm thinking."

But it's the thinking, reading, and research with a nearly pure investment focus that really sets Brian apart. "We're not making changes every day to the portfolios I manage, but I'm always considering new ways to improve our positioning. I know all the stocks we own, and I'm always thinking about them whether I'm in the office or on the road. What is really key is sitting back and reading, and most people probably do far too little of that. The one consistent trait of the most successful investors we deal with is that they devote significant amounts of time to reading and research."

"I have one client," Brian notes, "who is one of the better investors I know, and who has had impressive returns for an extended period of time. He is a bit of a mentor to me and is always challenging me: 'How many hours did you read today? How many hours did you get off the desk and just do research and reading? You should take a minimum of five hours a day to be off the desk doing reading and research.' I probably spend two hours every morning and an hour every evening doing reading and research, and if I can get the time, I do more during the day. I hate to say it, but you're just not adding that much value when you're talking about last night's baseball game."

Ultimately, Brian's numbers speak for themselves. "Our clients have been happy with our performance, and our assets have grown."

UNCONVENTIONAL MONEY MAKING

Being the one person at the helm for all investment decisions gives Brian the flexibility to consider unconventional ideas. "Following conventional beliefs in the stock market is typically not how you make your money," Brian says. "To make money, you have to move out of consensus beliefs and ways of managing money and running teams. If you are just doing the same things as everyone else, then you are the market, and you are never going to have outsized returns."

"The classic way of running a team," Brian continues, "is that one person manages equities, one person manages fixed income, and others have money-raising responsibilities. I have been very bearish toward fixed income and credit for the past three years, and, for the most part, we've been underweight in fixed income. We have reallocated such funds toward alternatives and other investments. Now, if we had a team, with one person whose sole focus was managing fixed income, would such a decision have been possible? I doubt it, because if we are partners, and one person is managing fixed income, would such a person ever say to the other partners, 'I think fixed income stinks right now. Let's take all the money away from my area of focus and reallocate to more attractive opportunities and I will just sit around all day and wait until fixed income comes back again.'"

"In this way," Brian continues, "intrateam dynamics have the potential to compromise the asset allocation process. The fixed income manager in this situation would likely say, 'No way, I'm not going to agree to that, because my job would basically be going away.' They might compromise and underweight the position and take the allocation to 35 percent instead of 40 percent, but that would be it. Human nature and personalities get involved, and that is just the nature of the way these things work. In my opinion, it's not an efficient way of maximizing returns."

WORKING WITH CLIENTS AND CUSTOMIZING ASSET ALLOCATION

Of Brian's roughly 25 relationships or households, roughly 25 percent are domiciled outside of the United States, thanks in part to the relationships Brian developed during his time in London. As for the average total net worth of these families, Brian says, "We certainly do not know precisely, but the smallest is probably $30 to $50 million, and the largest is in the billions. Our focus is on individuals or families with a minimum of $20 million to invest. That is where I feel we can add the most value. In some of these twenty-five relationships, we work directly with one individual. In other situations, we work with a family office or a board of a foundation."

To stay prioritized on investing his clients' money, Brian and his team do not offer their clients a wide array of noninvestment-related services. "To be very honest, there are a lot of people in this business who view themselves as private bankers and who get involved in everything," Brian says. "I was just on a call with somebody who has an account elsewhere. She commented that her advisor pays her bills and arranges her trips to New York, and she wanted to know if we do anything like that. Well, we don't. There are other people who focus on selling insurance, home loans, and a variety of other services for their clients. I don't do any of that. My view is that if they require such services, we have many resources here at the firm that I can put them in touch with. I know what my strength is and I don't deviate from it."

"I am here," Brian emphasizes, "to manage money. I'm not purporting to be a private banker or a family office. People should hire me if they want to seek superior investment returns. If I don't deliver that, they should fire me. But don't hire me and pay me to do anything else because that would not be my strength. My clients hire me to manage their money, and then they hold me accountable for providing favorable returns."

How, then, does Brian actually work with each client? "Typically, we get involved when someone has had a capital-raising situation, such as selling stock in a company they own or selling the entire company. It usually begins with a face-to-face meeting, often with one or more family members. We begin by looking at their entire balance sheet, including what they have at other firms. If private businesses are involved, we look at the characteristics and dynamics of those underlying businesses to see how the markets affect them. We get as much information as we can about their financial history and background, level of sophistication, and financial goals. We consider everything, including their personal real estate holdings, any estate planning needs, dependents, and philanthropic efforts. We have dedicated professionals at Morgan Stanley who can advise on estate planning, and they are an integral part of our process. While we do not provide any drafting of legal documents, we do incorporate clients' estate planning needs from the very beginning. Really, the goal is to get to know the client."

"It's not a science," Brian notes. "There isn't a questionnaire that can provide complete answers on these topics. It's really about spending hours and hours with a client to understand all of these dynamics and get a better sense of their risk tolerance. It's understanding how prepared a client is for market volatility. That's why this is an art and not a science. It takes many conversations to really flush these things out."

"From this point, in conjunction with the client, we derive what we believe is an appropriate asset allocation. I present my view on the markets," Brian says, "and what my one-, three-, and five-year views are toward various asset classes. In this way, clients understand my perspective and thought process. It's important that they understand my investment philosophy, because some people are comfortable with it and others are not."

"After multiple discussions, I provide a preliminary asset allocation including recommended managers. Typically we go back and forth and refine the asset allocation. Very rarely do we end up precisely where we started in terms of a recommendation. Next comes the implementation stage, and that can take up to a year depending on market conditions."

ACTUAL INVESTMENT CHOICES: RISK AND REWARD

Where does Brian actually end up putting his clients' assets? "We manage close to a billion dollars right now just in alternatives," he says, "and that includes hedge funds, private equity, and real estate investments. We essentially run our own fund of funds, which means I put money with outside hedge funds that I choose. We also probably have approximately $1 billion in long-only equities, a portion of which I manage and a portion of which is managed by third-party managers. The remainder of our assets are in fixed income, cash, and concentrated stock positions."

"Ultimately," Brian believes, "it's all about risk and reward. The investment process revolves around risk and reward. I am very comfortable taking risk if the reward is commensurate, and I'm very uncomfortable taking risk if the reward is not appropriate. That's my investment philosophy, and it extends to every asset class."

As for whether he has made any mistakes, Brian says, "Yes, we make mistakes. Everyone makes mistakes all the time, especially in terms of stock selection and manager selection. But we hope to make fewer mistakes over time, and we try to make sure that when we do make mistakes, they have a minimal effect on performance. Specifically, we've learned how to better handle and manage our mistakes, and we've also learned how to better scale positions to improve pricing and transaction execution for clients."

As for Brian's current views on overall asset allocation, he says, "My starting framework is probably a third in equities, a third in alternatives, and a third in fixed income, and then at any given point in time, I overweight and underweight. Right now, I am underweight in fixed income and overweight in equities and alternatives. So, instead of roughly 30 percent in fixed income, I am between 5 and 10 percent, and in the range of 30 to 50 percent alternatives and 30 to 50 percent equities. Then, of course, there are choices within alternatives and within equities. So for example, within alternatives I am very underweight in venture capital and overweight in Asian and emerging market private equity. These are my general views, with specific allocations depending on the individual client."

FIELD TRIP!

One way Brian has broken new ground with respect to expanding his network is by taking his clients with him on so-called field trips to investigate potential international investment opportunities. "Morgan Stanley holds conferences for select clients globally. I thought going was a great idea," Brian says, "because I am always looking to increase my knowledge as well. I often invite clients to join me. In many instances, my clients have good contacts in these local markets, and we can mutually benefit from the trip."

"It started a long time ago," Brian continues. "Our first trips were to London. Then a few years ago, we wanted to learn more about what was going on in China and Asia. So I attended our hedge fund conference in Shanghai with several of our clients. After the conference in Shanghai, we went to Vietnam to meet with several local managers. Our trip resulted in our making multiple investments, many of which we exited with substantial profits. Subsequently, we have made trips to Russia, Hong Kong, Singapore, India, and the Middle East."

"I really like getting our clients to meet interesting people in areas where we think there are going to be attractive investment opportunities. I believe it is essential to see things firsthand and meet managers in person. At a lunch the other day, there was a gentleman visiting from Hong Kong who was one of the owners of a company that we visited in Vietnam. We were talking about Asian economies and the particulars of what he was seeing on a local basis. You get to know each other a little better, and get a better feel for what you think is really going on if you have a face-to-face relationship with someone. If you're talking over the phone, sometimes you may just be an anonymous voice and you don't really have a relationship. If you get to know them personally, it's much more likely you'll learn more from them, and information is a necessary ingredient in successful investing."

"You don't quite know what you are going to come away with on these trips," Brian adds, "but you usually come away with something that's investable in some way. In part, it's just increasing your sphere of contacts so that you are in a better position overall, and sometimes you'll just suddenly see an opportunity. The firm is very generous in allowing me to do these trips. It's something I will continue doing, and I think I should probably be doing even more of it."

A DIFFERENT VIEW

Brian has always worked hard, and still works long hours. "I get in at 7:30 a.m. and we stay until 7:30 p.m. or later. When we were building the business, we would stay until midnight every night. Now I think my time is better spent with clients or hedge fund managers or traveling to meet potential new managers. I'm always trying to improve performance and make our business unlike what anybody else is doing on the Street."

"In essence we are trying to approach the management of each of our client's assets the way a great investment banker would approach covering a company like IBM. You rarely see this approach on the private client side of the business."

Still, on top of his hard work and dedication, Brian also has a well-rounded personal life. He and his wife have a very young son, and, when he has free time, Brian likes to play golf. He is also on the board of the Concert Artists Guild in New York City. "It's been around for fifty years," Brian says, "and runs a competition every year for up-and-coming young artists and people who are going to become professional musicians. It manages their careers in the early stages and provides them with professional support."

Brian also manages to take off some time every August. "Outside of that," he says, "we are very focused on the business." While he agrees that he might take off more time as his son gets older, he wryly adds, "Yes, maybe. That's one of the reasons why I waited this long to have children." That's Brian for you: always keeping things in professional focus and always taking a different view to generate the kind of returns and build the kind of business that have made him one of the very best financial advisors in the world.

CHAPTER 3: THE HANSBERGER GROUP

SMITH BARNEY
ATLANTA, GEORGIA

(Back Row Left to Right) Morty Levey, Jim Hansberger, Jr., Ross Caphton

(Front Row Left to Right) Marsha Smith; Jim Hansberger, Sr.

T he number of people who describe Jim Hansberger as "an incredibly deep thinker" might surprise you—that is, until you get to know him. Then you'll find that Jim's reputation is well deserved and, if anything, understated. Not only does he look deeply into everything from the fundamentals of the companies he invests in to the best in business management and self-development literature, he achieves success on multiple fronts with a rare combination of excellence, integrity, and humility.

For example, The Hansberger Group, a wealth management team at Smith Barney, which Jim founded and oversees as Managing Director, advises on roughly $2 billion of assets for some 300 total households. Unlike most other groups or even boutiques entrusted with this level of assets, however, Jim and his team directly invest the majority of their clients' money, making their own investment decisions rather than assigning them to outside money managers. The result, according to Winner's Circle estimates, is risk-adjusted returns well above industry benchmarks over the past couple of decades. Another example: Jim takes health and fitness seriously enough to have been featured, along with his wife, Lyn, on a CNN primetime show on the search for the fountain of youth!

What's the secret of Jim's success? He thinks hard, works hard, and consistently applies principles and formulas for success, always recognizing that "the devil is in the details, the devil is in the execution." This is true whether he's talking about modern portfolio theory and asset allocation, evaluating the worth and purchase value of a company, or holding a client's hand through a difficult transition period.

Of course, an important part of Jim's success is found in the strong relationships he naturally cultivates with others: his clients; the talented professionals that make up The Hansberger Group, including his son, Jim Hansberger, Jr.; other financial advisors around the country in "virtual partnerships" with The Hansberger Group; and of course, Jim's friends and family. It's this combination of open-minded deep thinking, superlative execution in multiple areas, and relationship-focused depth of soul, that truly sets Jim Hansberger apart.

As Jim Jr. says of his father, "He's the same person on Saturday night that he is on Sunday morning. That's one of the reasons he's such a good role model. And he really cares for the client. When he's sitting in front of a client, talking about his own life and how he feels, it's 100 percent genuine. Clients trust him so much because he has such obvious integrity."

Jim's work with a European client starting in the early 1980s exemplifies this kind of trust building. "Over time," Jim says, "this client went through all sorts of machinations and peaks and valleys with his manufacturing business, and just recently sold it for tens of millions of dollars. When we started working with him, he didn't know a lot about investing, was completely focused on his business, and was not particularly adept in American ways of doing things. My experience is that many Europeans distrust much of what we take for granted because of their much longer experience with recession, depression, war, illegitimate or corrupt regimes, taxation, and government intervention. I've found that it takes longer to build a European client's trust, and you sure as heck better deliver, because they will be ten times more skeptical if things don't work out. Over a long period of time I helped him to understand something other than just pure fixed income markets, including the whole world of hedging strategies, private equity, and money management generally. In many cases this involved holding his feet to the fire while holding his hands. There were so many times he wanted to exit completely, as in 1987."

"I was privy to some of those meetings," says Jim Jr., who is Jim's partner in money management and who now does all of the trading for The Hansberger Group. "This man became emotional when there were market sell-offs. In particular, terrorist attacks upset him, because he grew up in Germany during World War II. With any kind of market sell-off or terrorist attack he truly needed to be comforted, to have his hand held and be educated so he didn't think the U.S. economy was returning to 1929. I honestly think that if he hadn't had my father by his side, he would have changed portfolio managers fifty times, selling at the bottoms and buying at the tops, and been a lot worse off. This is the kind of thing my dad is very good at. He's a genuine guy, he's absolutely trustworthy, and even with people from totally different backgrounds, he forges great friendships and partnerships."

A LIFE-CHANGING CROSSROAD

Jim Hansberger was born in Atlanta, "at a very young age." (Who says that incredible focus and intensity can't go hand-in-hand with humor?) He and his older brother had a very happy childhood, as Jim puts it, "straight out of *Ozzie and Harriet*, with a little white picket fence around a small house in a terrific neighborhood. We went to church every Sunday, and I rode my bike backward and no-hands for years. Atlanta, of course, was a totally different place back then. Considering what life is like today in much of the world, certainly in American cities, I'm on my knees every day in gratitude to have had that kind of background and upbringing."

Jim's love of physical fitness started early. "I threw myself into sports as a kid. I went to a public high school, played on every sports team, and was a star, as a kid, especially in baseball. Sports did a great deal for my self-image. I mention this because I think there are many excellent metaphors and analogies to sports in our business."

Jim's father was a non-practicing lawyer who worked in the insurance business for Aetna on the casualty side. "He retired right on target at age sixty-five, kicking and screaming, having to be pulled out of the office," Jim relates. "My dad was convinced he was going to live for only another ten years and that he'd just live off the Aetna pension. He ended up being retired longer than he worked, and died a while back at ninety-three. I've repeated this story to clients for decades, because they always think they're not going to outlive their income. My dad's story shows the importance of injecting growth into any kind of income investment, because obviously, 5 percent growth is not going to buy you the same goods and services that it does today in five, ten, or twenty years."

Jim enrolled in the University of Georgia. Having heard his father say that he wished he'd actually practiced law, his goal—besides having fun and meeting people—was to go to law school and then practice. Jim joined Sigma Alpha Epsilon fraternity, entered the pre-law program, and did well academically in his first three years of college. He then met his wife, to whom he's now been married for over 40 years. Overall, Jim found college to be "an enhancing and well-rounding experience." In his senior year, however, he became impatient to start a career.

Jim started an investment club during his senior year. "I can't say I had some kind of eureka moment or any burning passion about the industry that I ended up choosing," Jim says, "but I don't think I had ever heard of anybody starting an investment club while still in college."

Jim joined the National Guard army unit and reserves, along with about 100 of his peers and fraternity members. "I was the only one called up, so I had to leave school. Fortunately, I wasn't sent to Vietnam, but my plans did change pretty dramatically. After about six months in the service, I just wanted to get married and get on with my life. I had studied the investment business while in the service, was very interested in it, and had no interest in spending another three years in law school. We got married in the summer of

1968. We both finished school, then I started in the investment business in 1969."

THE CALLS OF EARLY SUCCESS

By chance, Jim's next-door neighbor was the brother of a highly placed official in one of the nation's largest investment firms. This led to an interview with the firm's Atlanta branch manager. "I was twenty-two years old, wearing a white suit, and had slicked-back black hair," Jim says. "I'm embarrassed when I think about it now. The branch manager looked at me and proceeded to tell me that I was way too young. And I'm not sure where it came from, but I said, 'Somebody's got to be the youngest person you've ever hired.' He said he'd call me that afternoon. My wife was still in Athens, because we had not moved from University yet, so I went to my parents' house and just sat on the bed praying. Then the phone rang. The manager said that they'd love to have me come to work. I bought a bottle of champagne and a dozen roses to take home to my wife, and the rest is history."

Jim started in the summer of 1969, went through training, and began as an advisor in 1970. "My wife and I didn't come from any kind of money, and we didn't have any particular connections. Even my fraternity brothers who came from money were young at the time and didn't have any personal money. So I did what other people did, just called people out of the newspaper or phone book. There were certainly no telemarketing rules back then, and people appreciated you calling them as long as you didn't interrupt their dinner at night, which I never did."

"One seemingly ridiculous thing I did," Jim says, "was to start at Z and go back to A, and in that first year I had something like fourteen clients whose last names started with Z. And then one morning my wife said, 'Here's what we're going to do. I'll look up the names for you. I'll give you fifty names every day, you call them, and we'll be in this together.' Sure enough, we came up with a pattern. We found that if you made fifty calls and talked to twenty people, ten would be interested and one would open an account."

With his wife's help, Jim opened up at least one account a day, every day, for the next three years or so. At the age of 23, as a rookie at his firm, he was a star. "I did the most business anyone had ever done in his first year. This is something we're very proud of." Asked if he'd recommend this approach to younger advisors coming up now, Jim says, "The numbers would be slightly different, and the types of people you'd call would be slightly different, but I'd tell them the same thing. The fifty, twenty, ten, one rule really does work. I believe our business is all art and all science. If you have one without the other, you have an incomplete experience. This call method was the scientific part of how we approached things."

SEISMIC SHIFTS IN CAREER TRAJECTORY

After about three years Jim had built up a good business, but he soon recognized that the largest producers in his firm had an institutional focus, not an ordinary retail one. "If your clients were investment departments at banks, large mutual funds, insurance companies, or state-owned pension funds, they would naturally be much larger clients. Having the opportunity to write five-thousand-share tickets was very different from writing hundred-share tickets. So I went to one of these producers and literally offered to carry his briefcase for a year or so for no compensation, while I was still doing my own business. That's how I learned the institutional business."

"I was willing to take a step backward in order to take a quantum leap forward," Jim says. "To this day, I don't believe there's any substitute for experience. No matter how gifted a salesman or how knowledgeable a young advisor might be, he would be well served to marry up with experience for at least a few years. His clients will be much better served, and he will create a longer and more prosperous career for himself."

As luck would have it, a friend from another firm called Jim and asked him if he'd be interested in opening an institution-focused branch office in Atlanta. Although Jim was successful and happy at his first firm, he says that "I wanted to get into the institutional business, and back then I was cocky enough not to want some kind of ceiling or to have to wait my turn. I wanted to do a kind of business that other people weren't doing, one that would let me 'look around corners'—see where the world was going and be where the opportunities really were, rather than just marching along."

Jim joined the new firm, and shortly thereafter yet another firm acquired it, and before long the CEO of the acquiring firm called him on the phone and said he was looking forward to meeting Jim. For most of the 1970s all the way through 1981, Jim was running the acquiring firm's institutional effort for a large part of the country.

An even bigger shift occurred in 1981. After speaking with some of his mentors, including former CEO and chairman Sandy Weill and legendary investor Sir John Templeton, Jim says, "One day in

1981—absolutely cold turkey—I sold the institutional business to the partners I had hired and started over. I began what's now called The Hansberger Group to focus very specifically on the high-net-worth marketplace. I did this because over the course of the 1970s the environment for traditional investing had been extremely negative. You had Vietnam and Watergate and the oil embargo, and interest rates got up to 20 percent. There was very little demand for traditional stocks and bonds other than in the institutional marketplace, and there were no alternative investments. Wall Street started marketing tax shelters, annuities, and other products simply because of the lack of demand for traditional investments. By the early 1980s many companies in America were selling below working capital."

"With record inflation and interest rates," Jim continues, "there was now a wonderful opportunity. Around here we frequently use the phrase 'look around corners.' Someone with a little bit of vision and some sense of financial history could have seen that every imaginable negative was front and center; in other words, all the negativity you could imagine, and then some, was already factored into the markets. So I spent some time with two of my mentors, and we all agreed that here was an opportunity to build wealth on traditional means, unlike what had happened in the 1970s. We felt that the high-net-worth marketplace was really underserved, and that at some point investors were going to return big time to traditional investments. After ten or twelve years of working with some of the very best institutional investors in and out of the country, we felt we knew what we were doing, that we had gone through a maturation process and learned about portfolio management and research. Here was our chance to focus."

"For all practical purposes," Jim adds, "that was the beginning of The Hansberger Group, although we didn't call it that at the time. I remember how passionate I was when I started with my first firm, and I remember the same kind of adrenaline and enthusiasm when I started again, and over the next year we began to put things into place."

At this point Jim had only a few retail clients left. He did not go back to the phone book to use the fifty, twenty, ten, one process, but he did do something that was similar "on a mathematical conceptual basis. There were an awful lot of people to whom I had said for many years, 'No I'm not in that business.' So I quickly let them know that I was now out of the institutional business and wanted to represent them. It was warm calling, not cold calling, and the business ramped up pretty fast. Our existing client base helped a lot. It wasn't that large, but it included the governor of the state, a senator, and a handful of wealthy people. So our success resulted from a combination of our effort, our experience, and help from our existing clients."

At the core of Jim's efforts, however, was a principle that The Hansberger Group still relies on: "The money management stops with us, and we are fully accountable for it. I fully recognized that it made sense to have the money management in-house. I wanted to make sure that we were the axe, that *we needed to be the axe*, so we could grind it ourselves."

"What John Templeton taught me," Jim offers, "is what makes a great portfolio manager. We certainly didn't consider ourselves the very best portfolio managers, but we felt we knew how to manage money. And it wasn't just because we were taking some idea from a firm. It was all research based. We had studied portfolio managers for at least ten years—bad ones, good ones—in every way possible, and I decided that this was going to be the crux of our business as we went back to serving private clients. So we started a discretionary investment management business, meaning that we make all investment decisions in a fiduciary capacity, within the umbrella of a brokerage model. With our institutional background, the various learning techniques we were using, and the advent of charging on a fee basis, it worked. It was 1988, and we were among the first people in a Wall Street firm to be in the portfolio management business. I wanted us to be new and different, innovative and unconventional, and to provide overachieving results."

A VERTICAL HUB-AND-SPOKES MODEL

No financial advisor is an island, and Jim Hansberger readily acknowledges the contributions of his team members. Jim uses different terms, including "vertical team" and "hub-and-spokes," to describe how The Hansberger Group functions. To understand what these terms mean, it's helpful first to know the players.

When Jim talks about the early years of his business and uses the term "we," he is quick to point out that, in addition to his wife, "we" includes one of his long-time assistants and senior administrator, Marsha Smith. Marsha's domain is everything from expenses, travel, and scheduling to opening accounts, handling wire transfers, and making sure people get paid on time. She is particularly well-known for not taking no for an answer until somebody gives her a good enough reason why something can't be done. She is at her very best when the team is the busiest.

"Marsha has been with me some thirty years," Jim says, "and she teaches everybody how to do everything from scratch. In reality, she talks to many more clients more frequently than any of us. Ultimately, she's the problem solver. You can do a lot of things right, but when something goes wrong, years of work can be ruined, and Marsha is wonderful at handling problems. At one point Marsha was away for a couple of years, and when she returned, I can't tell you how many people said, 'Thank God Marsha is back.' She has her head on straight, her value system is terrific, and she's very valuable and loyal to the group. And she knew Jim when he was a baby."

In this case, "Jim" is Jim Hansberger, Jr., who has now been in the business for ten years. He is one of the group's portfolio managers and handles a good deal of client contact and new business development. "Jim does an extraordinary job, well-versed beyond his years," says his father. "He worked here summers, and then I started him off in a research capacity to learn the way we manage money. Portfolio management is his strength, and he's very good at it. He's learned quickly. It's kind of in his DNA anyway, since he's my son. And he has excelled despite that fact, not because of it. I am as proud as I can be. He has an outstanding work ethic and a true nose for ideas, particularly in emerging, breakthrough products and solutions. This, in turn, assists us in attracting new clients and referrals from existing investors. In addition, he has added an important new dimension to our trading approach."

"The father/son thing has really been an advantage for me, as my dad has pretty much molded and taught me from day one," Jim Jr. says. When asked if he enjoys the business, Jim Jr. responds, "Absolutely. I love it. It's one of those things that I always wanted to do, in part because I knew he really would teach me. We've hit a tempo now where we can finish each other's sentences, and we play off each other well. Obviously, he's leaps and bounds more competent than I am. But I feel he's really brought me up so that I'm able to contribute and pay him back."

Another key team member is Morty Levey, a CPA for 25 years, who once ran the estate planning effort for the largest accounting firm in Atlanta. Morty joined The Hansberger Group in 2000, and "has made a big difference as far as what we can do with estate planning, financial planning, cash flow advice, and other wealth advisory services," says the senior Jim. "Frankly, I have worked with lots of attorneys, accountants and planners for years, and nobody has more insight, asks better questions, or has as good a service element as Morty."

According to Morty, "Jim and I shared a lot of mutual clients. I contacted him and said I wanted to round out my experience; he, coincidentally, was considering how to round out his team to become a leader in private wealth management. I resigned from the accounting firm, sold back my stock, and got out of the accounting business. I've been doing this since 2001, and now I get to do everything I enjoy doing. Before we even meet a client, we do as much up-front work as we do when we plan to invest in a company. It's the same. We want to know everything about the client. We want to make sure it's a good fit. If the client meets all of our criteria, only then do we actually sit down with him and make a presentation."

A good example of how Morty's considerable talents strengthen The Hansberger Group concerns a leading M&A attorney who was about to retire. Jim had met with this prospect a couple of times and knew that he had a lot to consider in contemplation of his retirement from his firm. "Jim had a meeting scheduled with him the Tuesday before Thanksgiving," says Morty, "and the fellow suddenly realized he'd be retiring at the end of December. I think he stayed up the Monday night before Thanksgiving and finally emailed Jim all of the information about his retirement, including his personal life, concerns, and assets. All the pertinent information was there, but it was five pages of rambling. Jim received the email while he was out of town for the holiday, called me on the Friday after Thanksgiving, and asked if I could come to New York and make a presentation based on the five-page email. I said, 'Sure, why not?' So I studied the email and created a twenty-five-year cash flow projection of exactly where he was and what kind of demands he was going to be making on his portfolio, and made recommendations on whether he should take a single or joint life annuity from the firm. I prepared all of this and we showed up on Tuesday."

"I want to make sure Morty gets credit for this," Jim says. "He generated an enormous amount of data in a short period of time. This came from his many years of being a CPA, the productivity that flows from his competence, and his commitment to providing service. And it also came from years of getting two or three shoe boxes full of stuff from a client and sorting through it. We sat down with the prospect and his wife, and about thirty minutes into our meeting he asked how we had done it, because he thought he had sent us a bunch of garbage and that for sure we were going to cancel or reschedule because we wouldn't have enough time to deal with it. But at this session, it all came together in one picture for him, and we saw the lightbulb go on in his head and in his wife's head."

"I couldn't have done it by myself," Jim adds, "because I didn't have the time, nor did I have the background or competency for some of it. This was classic professional teamwork, and we were able to provide solutions for the client's retirement. We showed what their life would look like after retirement and reassured them that even without the income they were used to having, they would be able to live well and do things for their kids without tapping out their assets."

The core of The Hansberger Group is rounded out by Ross Caphton, a full-time research analyst and portfolio management associate, who focuses on both quantitative and qualitative research. "Ross is one of the most ambitious young men I've known," Jim says. "He has his CFA and all the credentials of a much older analyst. He has reached every goal that he has set for himself or that I have set for him."

Additionally, for a few years The Hansberger Group itself has been in a kind of "virtual partnership" with advisory teams around the United States. While The Hansberger Group is focused on hands-on investment management and asset allocation, other teams may be geared towards private equity, deal making, preplanning before liquidity events, and various other capital strategies for entrepreneurs and business owners. One such team they partner with is the Maverick Group, headed by Allan Yarkin in Florida. When acting together, these two groups provide each other with greater leverage by taking advantage of each other's strengths.

In describing how all these relationships hold together and function, Jim uses both vertical team and hub-and-spokes metaphors. Regarding the vertical team, Jim says, "obviously the mental image that comes from 'vertical' is something at the top that then flows down. But what I'm trying to do is to *not* have that kind of relationship with all of my partners and team members. I want to be in the middle, instead of above, so that while I do have a pure vertical relationship with each of the team members, the team as a whole is something in the middle that splinters out."

"The intent," Jim continues, "is for me to be the hub, but I don't mean that I'm the crowning glory or anything like that. I believe that I have a real partnership with my son as a portfolio manager, a real partnership with Morty and his focus on planning and estate matters, and a real partnership with other financial advisors. I have a real partnership with Marsha and Ross and all the research and administrative people. They have a relationship with one another as well, but it is nothing like their relationship with me. Hub and spoke together make the wheel, and so far ours is rolling along pretty well, though still a work in progress."

As for the team's vertical nature, Jim says, "Ours continues to be a vertical team. That's not to say that it's my fiefdom. But a vertical team is very different from a horizontal team in the sense that in horizontal structures, priorities are split, and vision and direction are split. Now, in order to create the most viable model for legacy and pride and life, a more horizontal model is desirable, and we are slowly moving toward that. I have many friends in the business who marry up with other advisors and none of them own more than half. That's not what I want to do. It isn't the ownership part; it's the control part, and the ability to carry things up to where they really need to be. So I know that I want it to remain a vertical model for a while longer."

As to how the team actually functions, Jim is not always the lead advisor in every client relationship. "There have been many times when I originated an opportunity, and Morty or Jim took it from there. I do try to make sure that I meet and know every client, but we are constantly looking for the best chemistry. Any one of us could be the lead." Morty echoes this: "Jim's done a really good job of getting other team members involved in the more important things on a day-to-day basis. There are some clients he's had a long relationship with, and when certain things happen during their lifetimes they are going to call him for advice. But Jim has done a good job of getting the rest of the team involved in meeting with clients and learning about them so that we can handle a lot of what's needed, thereby freeing up Jim to do other things."

With his vertical, hub-and-spokes team in place, Jim is able to set his weekly timetable in a way that maximizes his efforts. "Mondays are set aside for internal meetings. I have a Monday lunch with Jim Jr. that is strictly about portfolio management and research. We get away from everything else and do our review in two to four hours. And Mondays at four o'clock there is a meeting on client matters. I've taken off every Friday for the last twenty-odd years to be alone with a legal pad, a pen, and my thoughts. When I walk in the door on Monday, knowing I have four days ahead instead of five, I reflect on everything I've thought about during the previous Friday and the weekend. It's one of the most valuable things I've ever done. So everything else that we are trying to implement—meeting clients, new business, whatever it might be—has to happen on Tuesday, Wednesday, and Thursday. Our team organization has allowed me to function this way and not be pulled in crazy directions."

THE SIX PILLARS

In addition to the quality of its people, the core foundation of The Hansberger Group's success is what Jim calls the Six Pillars. These are:

- Performance.
- Client management.
- New business development.
- Business management.
- Teamwork.
- Self-management.

The Six Pillars derive from Jim's determination to create a long-lasting, successful organization. "One thing I've tried to do is make sure we've created a real foundation, a real sticking point, upon which we can build a legacy of professionalism that goes way past me. These are principles people can go back to, and as long as we are adhering to them, our model should be able to run forever."

The Six Pillars can be best understood in the context of the group's overarching annual goal, which can be summed up as 10+10+10. Jim explains that, "If every year you could grow clients' assets a minimum of 10 percent, and if you could raise 10 percent new assets from your existing clients, and if you could create 10 percent new business, then you would double your business every 2.5 years. These are lofty goals, but we do go through periods where we achieve them. There are periods when we achieve only one, and periods when we don't achieve any. But every single year, starting on day one, it's our goal."

The first pillar, performance, "kind of speaks for itself," says Jim. "It includes asset management and how we actually manage investments, whether we manage them ourselves or allocate them to others. This includes public and private equities, fixed income, all of the different asset classes, commodities, tangible assets including energy and metals, and currencies."

The second pillar, client management, involves segmenting clients into different classes so that an appropriate amount of time and effort can be spent on each one. "This segmentation is based upon fees or assets," Jim says. "Everybody has some form of it, but most people talk about it and don't do it. So we consider the potential of each client, along with minimum fee and service levels. It's awfully easy to find yourself spending too much time concentrating on your weakest accounts. At a minimum, client management allows each group member to focus on his best relationships and on bringing clients to a higher level. It also covers our need to stay in touch with our clients. Many advisors know that they should be in touch with their clients, but they don't have an absolute model on paper that says, 'On Friday I've got to call Mr. Jones because I haven't seen him in such a long time.' We have an automatic system that prompts one of our sales assistants to call clients to establish meetings."

Related to client management is the question of minimums. "We've played with the concept of minimums for years," says Jim. "For all practical purposes, at our lowest level clients pay at least $10,000 in yearly fees in order to keep our attention. That's basically where we want to draw the line, because that's where we can do the best job for people. But there are always reasons we might take someone else, for example, friends and family or entrepreneurs with bright futures. In general, our clients range from $1 million to well over $100 million in investable assets, and their net worths go far above these figures."

The third pillar is new business development, previously mentioned as part of the 10+10+10 performance goal. To some degree, every member of The Hansberger Group is focused on new business development—especially the younger advisors—starting with the art of how they dress and present themselves. As for particular types of potential new clients, the group targets private business owners, corporate executives, particularly "the number one or two guy in a public company, or board members, private business owners. We can do a lot for the head of a company or a private business owner relative to retirement planning and estate planning as the dominos fall following his stock options."

Jim adds that in the last few years, in concert with their virtual partnership with Allan Yarkin, a Smith Barney advisor in Hallendale, Florida, his group has had a strong focus on private equity partners and firms as clients. "A few years ago," says Jim, "we were 'looking around the corner' and realized that private equity was going to play a much larger role. There is now something on the order of $1.5 trillion dollars just sitting in private equity funds. If we can source deals for those private equity firms, understanding that it's going to take years to develop the necessary relationships, then at some time in the future they'll open their portfolios to us and let us help sell the companies. Typically, they've never had any money, and suddenly they're getting ready to make

$50 to $100 million, yet have done nothing to plan for it. If we can play a role and have built good will, all sorts of dominos can begin to fall: estate planning, reinvestment, investment banking possibilities, retirement plans, stock options, stock purchase plans ... a whole host of things. The company can be sold or it can go public, and although there's definitely a long lead time, it's a very significant opportunity."

The fourth pillar is business management, or how the group runs its own business. Jim somewhat ruefully states that "the vast majority of people in this business certainly don't spend any time on running their business as a business. In our own way we know what our return on equity is, we know what our expenses are, and we think we know how to run a business." He adds, "We've created a couple of COOs, a chief administrative officer, and a chief operating officer inside the group to make sure our business is indeed being run as a business, as if it were completely separate from Citigroup and Smith Barney."

The fifth pillar, teamwork, is "a very, very big deal" for Jim, and is "something that we are constantly working on. If somebody doesn't get along with somebody else, we have a problem." Significantly, this pillar dovetails with the sixth pillar, self-management, which could also be called self-development, a field that Jim has personally explored in great depth, and that he consistently invites other group members, both directly and through example, to investigate.

"Self-management has always been a big deal to me," says Jim. "Many years ago I heard this expression: 'Five years from now you'll be the same person you are today, except for the books you read and the people you meet.' I have found that to be absolutely, categorically true. All the great knowledge in the world is out there in some book, or on some tape or CD, and all you have to do is go out and find it and act on it. You are not going to reinvent the wheel. I have a very strong conviction about this, and I require that the members of this team read. The two non-negotiables are that they work hard and long hours, and that they read."

"Self-management," Jim continues, "is a requirement because people constantly need to improve themselves in a world that's as commoditized as our business is now. What are you doing to differentiate yourself? There is an art and science to differentiation. You can differentiate yourself artfully, on how you look, how you dress, the pen you carry, and the car you drive. It's sales, skills, and communication. And on the science side, frankly, there are too many people winging it in our business. Your science really has to be based on something. That's why I'm glad to have been in the institutional business, because it demands that I flat out know my stuff."

WEALTH MANAGEMENT AND THE DISCOVERY PROCESS

The term "wealth management" has perhaps been overused in recent years. For Jim, "True wealth management is, of course, asset management, but it's also risk management, liability management, lifestyle management, and a holistic approach to the client's situation all the way around. That means you need to have outstanding planning and advisory services in-house relevant to issues that don't have anything to do directly with investing. We do a lot of work in estate planning, trusts, family partnerships, philanthropy, and so on."

"On the asset management side," Jim continues, "things can't be as narrow as they used to be. There's no question that our business will probably always be top-heavy in portfolio management because I still believe that the equity markets are the single best way to build significant net worth over time and remain liquid, especially with 15 percent taxes on gains and dividends. But it doesn't mean that the people who have already made their wealth need to be riding up and down all the time. There are other strategies that we use."

To determine which opportunities to focus on, Jim and his team implement an in-depth discovery process when first meeting with a client. "Anybody who claims to be in the wealth management business these days would say that they are really proud of their profiling and asset gathering approach, as do we. Our guidelines are quite detailed and go into a lot more depth than just assets. If a client is ever sitting in one of those chairs and I hear the words 'This is how I feel' about risk or about a company, or about anything else, that's when we listen and don't talk. We are constantly trying to ask the 'feel' questions. Some people want to do everything in their power to make life for their children easier than it was for them; for others, it's the opposite, and they worry about making it too easy for their children. We are constantly trying to determine how people feel about philanthropy, generational wealth, risk tolerance, and so on. We are trying to provide advice in areas that most people never really think about."

"I can't tell you," Jim continues, "how many times somebody has sold a business and been referred to us and we quickly learn about their situation and the only thing we can say is 'Good grief, I wish you had talked to us before you sold that business.' There are so many opportunities in the preplanning work to freeze an estate and save estate taxes, and Morty does a magnificent job of that. That's what we are trying to pinpoint in the discovery process."

A perfect example of this was a client who had entered into a prepaid forward sale. "He had hedged a transaction in his stock," says Morty, "and the stock had run up. It was short-term stock, so if he got out of it—if the transaction went away—he would have had to pay short-term taxes on it. I immediately knew how we could save him money. We actually contacted him along with the Citigroup Private Bank and created a lending vehicle, an almost $20 million line of credit, to buy the stock back out of the contract so he could hold it for the remainder of the holding period and then liquidate the stock and pay 15 instead of 40 percent capital gains. You've got to know the client, you've got to know what's out there, and you've got to know the capabilities of the firm."

Another example of proactive forward thinking was when the father of a friend of Jim Jr. came to The Hansberger Group near the end of the roaring nineties. "He had just sold his company, had about $40 million worth of company stock, and basically didn't know what to do next," says Jim Jr. "He had built this company from the ground up, so he was truly at a crossroad. We put together a strategy—a forward variable sale, which is basically like the fifth generation of a collar—that was able to give him almost 90 percent of his assets up front without selling the stock. At the time this was one of the largest forward variable sales that had been done at Citigroup, one of the pioneers of this strategy."

"We were able to save him massive amounts of taxes and spread them over many years in the future," Jim Jr. continues, "and give him the liquidity to make other investments and bump up his lifestyle. Well, we all know what happened to the market over the next year or so, and his stock was down literally 70 or 80 percent not eight months after we did the transaction. This is one of those cases where we feel we really did right by the client and changed his family's life. Because of our knowledge and understanding, we were able to offer him something that other groups didn't even know about."

The discovery process also gives Jim and his team the opportunity to provide new clients critical "housekeeping" advice. "For example," says Jim, "we regularly tell clients to take out umbrella insurance policies. If they suddenly make $50 or $100 million, and then their sixteen-year-old daughter hits somebody with a car, all that money can disappear. They can pay $4,000 and get $20 million worth of coverage immediately. It's the seemingly little things that arise within the questionnaire and in the discovery process that are important, in addition to all of the information as to trusts, partnerships, entities, other advisors, and assets. There are six or seven things about which we usually say, 'This is something you are going to agree to do before you walk out of this office.' They stop, take an oath, and we make sure they do it. These things can really make a difference, and that's why our discovery process has to go much deeper than that of the client's accountant or attorney."

"You certainly have to know your client," Jim concludes. "You must know his level of risk tolerance, experience, and goals. If you don't know his goals, you have to help identify them, and it really, truly runs the gamut. Is this a person who cares a great deal about leaving assets to charity or to his heirs? Is this someone who is a big spender? Is this person a true consumer who is going to run through all his money? Does he want to make a lot more money? Who is he going to be responsible for in the future? If something were to happen to him, how would he want his assets disbursed? Where does he see himself ten years from now? The list goes on and on, and so we have an extraordinarily detailed profiling session, face-to-face. We certainly don't rely on a pat questionnaire. There are scientific approaches to this, but it's also definitely an art."

CLIENT EDUCATION AND THE ASSET ALLOCATION PROCESS

In their initial meetings with clients, Jim says that he and his team members "talk in detail about asset allocation, explaining the concept of various asset classes and probable levels of risk and return." Jim adds, "If there is any one thing that comes across to the client it is the importance of education. Once somebody has made his money—serious money—it's absolutely necessary for him to be educated and to have a comfort level where he can preserve his capital, first and foremost, but still grow it. You do that through consistency of performance, and you don't get consistency of performance by having only one or two asset classes. Also, it's important to remember that money does not equal sophistication as an investor. A lot of people are just now getting familiar with how they can invest in private equity or hedge funds. Of course, everything depends on the client."

Importantly, Jim's view of asset allocation differs from the standard one. "When we sit down with a prospective client," Jim says, "we say that we believe it is the allocation of assets that creates and maintains wealth. Certainly in the equity management portion, we think that stock selection is most important, whereas at the asset class level, it's the allocation of assets that creates and maintains wealth. That does not automatically mean that a very broad diversification of assets makes sense and is the best way to create consistent performance. Once again, the devil is in the details, the devil is in the execution. A lot of people simply interpret asset allocation to mean broadly spraying across untold numbers of different asset classes and subasset classes, automatically accomplishing your goals. I don't necessarily think that's true. By no means do I automatically buy into modern portfolio theory, where you measure risk by volatility. And let's not forget that modern portfolio theory in its finest form is best applied at the institutional level with tax-free, extremely long-term, accounts."

"Let me take this a step further," Jim continues. "Basically, despite all the hullabaloo, there are only four asset classes: equities, fixed income, commodities, and currencies. That's it. Everything else is a subsector. In the identification of the traditional risk/reward ratios for those four classes, one thing I've noticed an awful lot of people not paying enough attention to is liquidity. Is a private equity or real estate investment that has capital calls for five years in a row, and that is completely unsalable, comparable to a common stock that pays a dividend and that's salable every day? Are the two equal? I don't think so. It's a big deal, and I put a huge premium on liquidity. And what about taxes? Is it ordinary income or capital gains tax? Projected returns broken down by asset class or by risk level is not enough. It's got to be tax efficient. We must consider liquidity whether we are talking about a foundation, a trust, a taxable account, or a tax-free account, and whether someone is investing for himself or his heirs."

To make sure that the client's education continues outside the office, Jim says, "Very importantly, we ask our clients to read a lot. One of the first books we purchased and sent to every client was David Swensen's *Pioneering Portfolio Management: An Unconventional Approach to Institutional Investment* (Free Press, 2000). Swensen is very critical of traditional investing." But the reading list for clients doesn't stop there. Jim himself has written *A Guide to Excellence—The 100 Most Important Principles*, which he sends out to his clients every

year or two. The pamphlet contains one hundred investing principles, each about a paragraph long. "On the back we give credit to
Warren Buffett, Peter Lynch, and Sir John Templeton as coining or
phrasing a lot of the principles. There is so much noise and so much
clutter, and there are twenty hours of TV programming a day about
the stock market. We reprint this once a year to get people back to
basics, to remind them they own a business, not a stock. I've said for
years that a diet of BLTs—Buffett, Lynch, and Templeton—would
make an investor very healthy!"

Jim has also written a book called *Nice Guys Finish Rich*. An
audio version, available through Nightingale-Conant, is used by
Smith Barney to train new investment professionals. "In the late
eighties I had been making a number of speeches and the more I
talked, the more I realized that, no matter how great you look, and
no matter what image you present, there are an awful lot of people
out there who are hurting, with things not so great behind the
scenes in terms of money, marriage, health, and so on. If we can
realize that about our clients and each other, we will be a different
kind of advisor. We will be a different kind of friend. And so, some
of the chapters in *Nice Guys Finish Rich* measure wealth in ways
other than just monetary."

Additionally, The Hansberger Group presents an investor conference every November, where new books, ideas, and possibilities
are discussed. The group also maintains an online bibliography
that's updated regularly. The bibliography includes books like
Steven Covey's venerable *The 7 Habits of Highly Effective People* (Free
Press, 1990), Michael Lewis's thought-provoking *Moneyball: The Art
of Winning an Unfair Game* (W. W. Norton, 2003), and William Taylor
and Polly LaBarre's *Mavericks at Work: Why the Most Original Minds
in Business Win* (William Morrow, 2006).

To make sure that they've adequately captured the relevant
information for each client, from risk profile to goals and dreams,
the group gives each one a short summary of his or her profile. "We
give them the profile itself," says Jim. "We want to make sure that
we are in agreement, so we ask them if we've gotten anything
wrong, or if there is anything they would like to elaborate on. It's
essentially spitting back to them the answers they gave us. Keep in
mind, they never saw the questions—they just heard them. But
when they see the profile in the form of a subject-by-subject account,
they realize that there's a lot more involved than signing a signature
card to open a checking account."

After the client's profile is finalized, Jim and his team "promise that we will have a proposal to them in a short period of time. It includes a breakdown by asset class and projected targeted returns per asset class." After any additional client feedback and any necessary changes, the team implements the proposal. Following that, there are quarterly meetings and an annual review. "We talk in terms of quarterly meetings," says Jim, "but the reality is that quarters come around a lot faster than people realize. And no matter how many times we talk to a client, we certainly want to make sure that we have a very serious, lengthy annual meeting, and it's then that we talk about rebalancing. Obviously, if there's been some extraordinary change in asset classes over the course of the year, or if something dramatic has changed with the client, we won't wait until the end of the year to rebalance. In general, we use the annual meeting as the most serious opportunity to focus on where we've been, where we're going, and what the proper percentages are. And there's nothing that says you have to do any rebalancing at the annual meeting. Since you are only dealing with those four asset classes, I think that a lot of people may overplay rebalancing and make too many small moves."

PORTFOLIO MANAGEMENT AND INVESTMENT CHOICES

The Hansberger Group directly manages the great majority of its clients' money. They do make use of some international managers, some private equity and hedge funds, and one or two outside managers whom they have known well for years. "Our investment business is equities management and some fixed income," Jim says. "The vast majority of our clients are probably in a higher percentage of equities than most—depending, of course, on the needs of the client."

How does The Hansberger Group make its investment choices? Jim says that it all starts with "the reasons I wanted to be on the investment management side of things in the first place, as opposed to continuing in the institutional business or playing the role of salesman or consultant. I believe strongly in certain precepts of people like Templeton and Buffett, although we don't copy what they do. Importantly, I never believed that the ownership of a stock was the same thing as the ownership of a great business. Everything we talk about relative to equity and investment management is based on the fact that behind every stock lies a tangible operating business."

"When we talk with clients, when we write our quarterly pieces, we are always talking in terms of businesses rather than common stocks," Jim says. "Our average holding period is three to five years, and we've owned many of our largest holdings for much more than a decade. If a company can continue to achieve what we are looking for, why would we want to sell it?"

"We are really looking for businesses whose market value will one day equal the value of the business—what some people might call 'intrinsic value,'" Jim adds. "We therefore strongly believe that a stock can only do as well as the underlying company itself. That means we have to identify which companies are great companies. We have identified some characteristics that are essential: a 15 percent return on equity, 15 percent earnings growth, a balance sheet with less than 40 percent debt, a management team that still has the majority of its net worth tied to the business, and significant cash flow. Think about it for a moment. If a company is not constantly capital intensive and opening factories and so on, they can use their cash flow to buy other companies, pay down debt, pay dividends, or buy back their own stock. So cash flow is obviously crucial."

"Pricing flexibility is also a very big deal to us," Jim continues. "We've owned a particular retail chain for almost ten years, and to this day we are astounded that when the company continues to raise its prices, it is openly and fully accepted. That pricing flexibility is critical if you expect to increase your profit margins when commodity costs, labor costs, or interest rates go up."

"Those are the characteristics of a really great business for us, and a company must possess all of them for us to be interested. One without the others may make it a good business, but not a great one. And it doesn't matter to us whether the company is large or small, or whether it is categorized as value or growth. We are pretty style agnostic. What we care about a great deal is the business itself."

"We get a lot of Wall Street research," Jim continues, "but that research is completely secondary to our own work in what we call PDR, or portfolio development and research. It's our model, and while a model is only a model or a discipline, not a strict formula, it's still something we pay a great deal of attention to. All of these characteristics greatly reduce the number of companies from which to choose, and we are not going to buy anything just because somebody else likes it."

"What price you pay for that business is the next question," Jim says, "and that's a matter of different methodologies of measurement. Some of it relates to the price-earnings multiple. Some of it relates to historical relationships to markets. Some of it relates just to the company's growth rate itself and what's sustainable and what's not sustainable. We run it all through various models in order to identify what a realistic price is, and unless it has a 20 percent or more upside potential in a given year on paper, we will wait. It's the price you pay that determines your rate of return."

Jim Jr. adds, "One of the major differences between us and other portfolio managers is that we truly do operate as if we were a private equity firm. When we buy a stock, it's not uncommon for us to speak with the management 12 times and to also speak with 15 analysts. We visit the company and find out every single thing we possibly can."

Sometimes investing ideas come from unexpected sources. "My wife is from Thomasville, Georgia," Jim says, "and a few years ago I was out running down there over a holiday. I saw a sign that said, 'Tractor Supply: Here We Grow Again.' This is a relatively rural town, and I figured it was just another John Deere dealership or tractor supply store. For some reason in the next few weeks I saw the sign again somewhere and realized it was a public company. I began to look at it and saw that it had no debt, management owned about 30 percent of the company, and it had a high return on equity. It was not a tractor business, but rather a recreational business for the wealthy gentleman farmer who buys small tractors and does all sorts of work on weekends. Basically, nobody else was in the business. We did the follow-up research work and found that the company was barely covered by Wall Street and almost completely unknown. We bought the stock somewhere around 30 before it went to 70."

"We spend so much time up front," Jim Jr. says, "that it can take us a few months after we think we actually want to buy a stock to get to the point where all the pieces are in place ... and then we actually buy it. Our portfolios are a lot more concentrated than your average mutual fund or third-party money manager's, and that's because we spend so much time up front that once the stock is in our portfolio, we are really intimate with it. We oppose over-diversification. Warren Buffett says, 'A sheik can't get to know all the girls in the harem.'"

"As a result," Jim Jr. continues, "it's not uncommon for us to have a client that remains 50 percent in cash for a full year while we are out there trying to find the right opportunities. It's like a baseball player at the plate. He's not going to swing just because the pitcher pitched the ball. He's going to wait for the right pitch. With most third-party managers and mutual funds, if you give them a million dollars, they press a button and all of a sudden you are fully invested. That's what 99 percent of investors do through mutual funds, but it's crazy, if you think about it, because there's no value consciousness whatsoever. They will shop for clothes and not buy something because it's too expensive, yet by following the styles of the managers and mutual funds they hire they are possibly overpaying quite a bit for their investments. We tell our clients to picture us going shopping. We want to buy that beautiful Armani suit, but we are going to do it when it's on sale, not just throw money at the market. This really resonates with clients, because many of them are corporate executives and business owners. Successful businessmen and women are prudent, otherwise they wouldn't be successful."

How much time does all this research take? Jim says, "I would say it takes probably 50 percent of my time, or something like that. But in my mind, it's 100 percent of the time." Jim Jr., however, says, "I think he probably spends more than 50 percent of his time on research, given how much time he spends on the weekends. He reads stacks and stacks of research, as I do, on the weekends, and then we actually have a full four-hour meeting every Monday morning that is 100 percent devoted to research."

As for what triggers a sell decision, Jim points out, "If you have criteria for why you buy something, you have to have the breaking of that criteria for why you would exit something. But it goes further than that for us. If a company becomes 10 percent or more of a portfolio, we will cut it back, but not sell it completely. I think the single biggest mistake investment managers make is losing a position. People say it's cutting losses, but I think it's losing the position. If we make a mistake, or if we are too successful, then we have to cut something back. It's that simple. The greatest joy is when some large organization comes along and buys the whole company, because that means we discovered something well before everybody else did. We owned Reebok when Adidas came along and bought it and paid twice what we paid for it, and that's been the case for a number of companies. And with the incredible dynamic that went on with private equity over 2000–2002, any one of the companies we've invested in could be acquired at any time because they have the right characteristics. But, of course, if we paid too much for it, nobody's going to buy it from us at the profit we planned for."

THEMATIC INVESTING, ALTERNATIVES, AND HEDGE FUNDS

Jim says, "We've believed that globalization and productivity and the demographics of the Baby Boomers have been the three true overarching themes for the last ten years, and will be for the next ten years." From a larger perspective, he feels that "very few people spend enough time on thematic investing—on the real, true, driving forces behind things." As for which sectors they are likely to invest in most heavily during coming years, Jim says, "I don't know. We'll wait for our work to take us there. We've been out of technology for a number of years, and we are slowly building it up. Again, typical portfolios may include weightings in health care, technology, finance, consumer spending, energy, and commodities."

As for alternative investments, Jim says "We've tripled our money or more in energy and doubled it in gold because of what we thought the dollar was going to do. Clearly, that's not bottom-up investing, but it made a great deal of sense to do it. Like any model, you've got to be willing to override it if there's a compelling case."

As for hedge funds, Jim is increasingly cautious. "It would be easy to put hedge funds into a category where it would seem like too much money chasing too little opportunity or too little product, the same way international markets may be overdone now, or real estate might have been overdone, or Internet stocks may have been over-done. But hedge funds are different in that they are so unregulated, thus I think there is good reason for concern. Lots of advisors are getting into the hedge fund business who don't have experience with it, and who aren't really doing what they are promising their clients. The whole derivatives market is full of risk for those who don't understand it or know how to do it."

"Under no circumstances," Jim continues, "do I indict the hedge fund industry as a whole, because I think it plays a tremendous role in creating more honest-to-goodness efficiencies in the pricing of all sorts of securities. And for those who are good at it, these funds are providing, as the name implies, a hedge to reduce risk. There are some who are way over-leveraged, and the investors didn't really know it. Certainly there are plenty of stories over the years, and there will be more stories this year and more next year, because there are more and more hedge funds and more and more money is going there. But I still believe that for those investors who have already made their money, and whose sole goal is to preserve that money with a fair rate of return, hedge funds make plenty of sense."

"But let's remember here," Jim adds, "that with well over a trillion dollars, you are talking about ten-thousand-plus hedge funds, and only about a hundred of them really control the marketplace. It's that small. That's not to say that number hundred and one isn't meaningful, it's just that only about a hundred or two hundred have most of the money, and most of the talent. And lots of the newer hedge funds that are being formed came out of those hundred."

As for the future of the markets in general, Jim likes to point out that there are generational paradigm shifts in investing that are hard to see in real time. "The paradigm of the seventies was that financial assets were out of favor, and tangible assets were very much in favor, including oil, gas, real estate, and gold, and anything that was an inflation edge. Then the eighties and nineties completely reversed that, and the markets got out of hand, hence the so-called 'bubble' that exploded. I think we are still in the relatively early innings of a reaction to that, and the last few years have gone a long way towards putting a toe back in the water."

Jim smiles, and adds, "If we look around the corner right now, a tremendous amount of liquidity is being taken out of the system. And I am telling you, as odd as it might sound, that I see a scarcity of equities coming. I have no idea whether the markets have to go down first, but I think there's a big bull market developing again in the future. Hopefully we'll pick up this book ten years from now and you'll say you read it here first."

THE FIVE Fs AND OTHER CORE PRINCIPLES

While the Six Pillars underpin The Hansberger Group's financial success, they are not by any means the only set of core principles that Jim lives by or shares with others. For example, even more important to Jim than the Six Pillars are the Five Fs: faith, family, friends (and other people), fitness, and finances. "These are the priorities of life for me," says Jim. "They are not something I try to impose upon anyone directly in business with me. But I am going to push family, and I think everyone here would agree that we really bend over backwards to respect the family and time needed outside the office, and no one takes advantage of it. Friends refers to other people and how you treat them. And fitness—physical and attitudinal—has an enormous impact on energy levels and discipline, including how you feel about coming to work." Jim adds, "It may or may not be appropriate to talk to the client about Faith, but it sure as heck is appropriate to talk to them about their family, their health, and how they look at things and feel about our people and our group."

Interestingly, finance is the fifth of the Five Fs. "It's fifth, not last," Jim notes. "There are plenty of things that are less important to me than finances, even though I have as much ambition and as many goals for this group, our clients, and myself as I've ever had. But to have a successful life, you've got to set some priorities. Finances may be more important than the next hundred Fs. But only when you get the first four right, as I have found in my life, do finances turn upward. Otherwise you end up constantly living in two worlds, constantly being stressed. In one world, there are winners and losers; in another there are only winners. In one world, it's all about success and cleverness, in another, it's only about integrity and kindness. The older I get, the more I choose to live in the second world. So if you can get the foundation right, everything else falls into place. Younger advisors often think that spending time on faith or family or fitness is not going to get them where they want to go, because it's taking time away from work. But I've found that if you spend time on these priorities, you end up having more time. I've written thousands of business plans and investment plans, but I don't see enough life plans. I see a lot of fruits, but not enough roots."

"The Five Fs," Jim continues, "are a personal issue, and in my own life, I know that from the moment my feet hit the ground each morning I am trying to find the balance among family, business, time with other people, attention to health, and attention to spiritual well-being. It's just a constantly spinning wheel. I've got stories on each of those Fs and how they got there over the course of my life. It keeps me centered, it keeps me focused, and there isn't a day that I don't get out of bed thinking about the Five Fs."

Jim Jr. echoes the importance of the Five Fs and the other principles his father advocates. "He's always preached that you have to have a balanced life in order to be successful in any one area of your life. If you are extremely unhealthy or overweight, you are going to be tired and lethargic and unable to work as hard for your clients. If life at home is in turmoil, that will affect everything else. It's balance that he preaches, and that he lives." Jim Jr. says that he's already hoping that his sons, Jim III and Hill, will one day join the group and lengthen this legacy of balance.

Jim tells a good story about how one of the Five Fs—fitness—came about. "I was an All-American baseball player when I was young, so I always thought I was good at baseball. After I had been working a few years and gained some weight, a brokerage and bank league asked me to play on a team, thinking I was kind of a ringer because of my background, even though I hadn't played in a long time. I went out into left field and will never forget what happened. The first ball hit off the bat bounced in front of me and hit me in my stomach. I was so embarrassed. I got off the field and said to my wife, 'This is never going to happen again.' I remember it like yesterday."

"And so," Jim continues, "I started running, started lifting weights again, and became very serious about staying in shape. I changed my whole eating regimen—so much of success is all about *habits*—and I lost twenty-five pounds. I went on to run many Boston Marathons, and I play in a lot of racquetball and tennis tournaments. But my real interests all along have always been running and lifting weights. So today my regimen is pretty set: I lift weights and run every other day, and do some yoga once a week just to remain flexible. The best combination I have found is the aerobic or cardio and the muscle strength. As you get older, you recognize that it's not only for vanity, it's all about energy, and about the bone density and muscle strength you are going to need later in life." Today Jim continues to run about 35 miles a week, and he intends to run the Peachtree Road Race, the world's largest 10K, when he's 100 years old.

In addition to the Six Pillars and the Five Fs, Jim relies on a total of about 20 other principles. Too numerous to review in detail, they include things like HG=P+R (Hansberger Group equals performance plus relationships), A+A (advice plus access), Art & Science ("the art is your communications skill, the way you look, the way you dress, the presentation you make; the science is your substantive knowledge and competency"), USP (unique selling proposition, which for The Hansberger Group involves how they manage money and the level of service they provide), Tyranny of the Urgent vs. Opportunity of the Long Term, and many others, either originated by Jim or taken from elsewhere and restated. Quite a few of the principles, such as POMO vs. NEMO (positive momentum versus negative momentum), State of Mind/Excellence ("you can control your state of mind"), and The Land of the Beginning Again reflect Jim's strong beliefs as to the importance of both thinking positively and taking action on those thoughts, and never judging the future within the limitations of the present. Replace the destructive words "If only" with "Next time," he says, and always "Live the solution, not the problem."

PLANNING FOR THE FUTURE

Complementing Jim's principle-based approach to business and life is an ongoing focus on planning. "I believe that anybody who is in any kind of a CEO or senior partner role must have a combination of big picture thinking and detail orientation. We don't have the luxury of being the big picture thinker and relying on others to fill in the details, yet we certainly can't think long-term and look around corners unless we are really thinking at the global level as well. The role of the CEO or senior partner is to allocate assets intelligently, whether the asset is human capital, financial resources, or time. That's when the principles come into play. I am much more interested in helping people develop their strengths and talents than trying to improve their weaknesses."

Jim takes off the last two weeks of every year and revamps the group's business plan. "Then we'll have a meeting in January to talk about the plan and have everybody reflect on it. They've already been assigned certain questions and asked for certain input, and I'll have all that data before thinking about the plan for the coming year. It sounds ridiculously formalized, but all I am really trying to do is create some kind of an honest to goodness focus."

"Everything we've ever done," Jim continues, "has been based on five-year goals, and I credit this process for our success. One-year goals are too short-term and you can be disappointed too easily. I care about moving forward over chunks of time, rather than judging success or failure in a year."

To augment this planning process, Jim says, "Every year for thirty years, I've sat down at home, alone, on Christmas Eve and written out what's going on in my life at that time. It's a little bit of a New Year's resolution, and a little bit of a business and life plan. It's looking ahead, while looking back. I seal up the document, and don't look at it again until the next Christmas Eve. This is an approach that I would absolutely recommend to anybody, because it points out so many things. In many cases the things that you were most concerned about last year you no longer need to be concerned about, and vice-versa."

Another thing Jim regularly plans for are his charitable involvements. "I think probably my two biggest passions here are children, and men who have somehow lost their way—sort of 'There but for the grace of God go I.' This typically involves the homeless and substance abuse, or whatever it is that might have knocked individuals off track, and giving them a particular program to get back on track.

So we give our time and money to the Union Mission and Trinity House, and through the Peachtree Road Methodist Church, to the Mountain Top Boy's Home and similar charities."

As for the future of The Hansberger Group, Jim says, "I expect it to grow. There are a number of young people involved, including my son, who has a serious 'fire in the belly.' I want the business to grow based on the level of their strength and ambition, and I want to help bring them along and provide leadership. I'd be less than honest if I said that I wasn't learning every day from people half my age. I find our business very intellectually stimulating and that keeps me fired up. Fired up versus burned out. That's the plan."

When asked about retirement, Jim says, "This is not a business that you really have to retire from. I really enjoy it, and I can pretty much do it from anywhere as long as I have competent partners. In the end, for me it's about learning and growing. All the growth in my life has come from some kind of adversity or challenge that has provided me opportunities to grow and change. We all have the power of choice. I tell the story of two sons of an alcoholic father. One had a successful career and a happy family, and the other was homeless and in and out of trouble. Each was asked how he had reached that point, and each said, 'What else could I, the son of an alcoholic father, have become?' I believe in hope and change and growth. My wife and I were in London at Westminster Abbey and were struck by the inscription on the tomb of an Anglican bishop. There's almost never a day that goes by that I don't read this:

> When I was young and free, and my imagination had no limits, I dreamed of changing the world. As I grew older and wiser, I discovered the world would not change. So I shortened my sights and decided only to change my country, but it, too, seemed unmovable. As I grew into my twilight years, in one last attempt, I settled for changing my family—but alas, they would have none of it. And now, I realize, on my deathbed, if I had only changed myself first, then, by example, I might have changed my family. From their inspiration and encouragement, I would then have been able to better my country. And who knows? I may have even changed the world.

Coming from a man who has made a big difference for many by standing out against the norm, this is yet another principle well worth noting and living by.

CHAPTER 4: NCA FINANCIAL PLANNERS

NCA FINANCIAL PLANNERS (ROYAL ALLIANCE)
CLEVELAND, OHIO

(From Left to Right) Melanie Ross, Jasmina Tadic, Kevin Myeroff, Elizabeth Verner, Karey Edwards

Kevin Myeroff has always reached for the stars. "As a child," he says, "I was sure I was going to be an astronaut. I loved astronomy, and even studied it under Carl Sagan at Cornell University when I was getting my accounting degree from Ithaca College." While Kevin hasn't travel into space, he's certainly reached the heights of success. He is not only the president and CEO of NCA Financial Planners, Cleveland's premier financial planning firm with 31 employees and over $1 billion under management, but he is also literally a star himself, having appeared for over 15 years as the financial commentator on the local NBC television station.

To what does Kevin ascribe his success? "I've just worked hard and been lucky," he humbly states. "Truly, I'm one of those guys who, the harder he works, the luckier he gets." But there's more to Kevin's success than just hard work—plenty of financial advisors and financial planners work extremely hard. What really underlies Kevin's success is a simple but profound philosophy: "Never allow yourself to become the victim of circumstances."

"This is something I learned from my father. I never really understood it when I was younger, but he always said that the difference between being good and being great is that great people never allow themselves to become a victim of the circumstances. For example, when I was interviewing with the then Big 8 accounting firms, I would leave home two hours before my interview, just in anticipation of getting a flat tire or having something else happen. If I had arrived late, and been asked why, and said 'I had a flat tire' ... well, that's just being a victim of the circumstances. I would typically sit in the parking lot for an hour, because usually nothing went wrong. But if something had gone wrong, I wouldn't have been a victim of circumstances. I still would have been there on time."

"In my view—and I drill this into all of our professionals— there's no excuse for not accomplishing something because you've become the victim of the circumstances. You have to allow for changes in circumstances in any models you build, any planning you do, and any promises you make to your clients. By doing this, our planners will always figure out a way to solve a problem or accomplish a goal. Being unwilling to be the victim of circumstances is the difference between someone making $100,000 a year and someone making $800,000 a year."

THE FATHER OF SUCCESS

"Even in high school, I knew I wanted to be in some type of business," Kevin says, "but nothing led me to believe that I would become a financial planner one day. In high school I really liked the accounting courses I took, and in college I was attracted to accounting because it was supposed to be very challenging. I was always good at math, and I was up for the challenge."

"In 1983," Kevin continues, "after graduating from Ithaca College with an accounting degree, I went into public accounting and got a job with what's now called Ernst & Young. You worked six days a week, eighteen hours a day, and learned more than you could in any kind of graduate study. It's an unbelievable experience. After three years there, which I absolutely loved, I wanted to take one week of vacation to go skiing in Vail, Colorado. They told me I couldn't go because it was the busy season. Well, I just came right out and quit. I had moved up very quickly, so they came back and said, 'We're sorry, we made a mistake. Not only can you take the vacation, you can take an extra week off.' They even brought in people from the main office in Chicago to try to talk me into staying there."

"But it was too late. I just said to myself, 'You know what? This feels good. I'm glad I made this decision.' I'd already had a number of clients who'd asked me to come and work with them, so I really wasn't concerned about getting another job. I knew I'd be all right. Plus, one of my reasons for wanting to go on the ski trip was to ask my girlfriend to marry me, thus I figured that as long as I was going to get engaged, it might be nice to have a less demanding job. I quit, went to Colorado, and got engaged."

"When I returned, I put my resume out and looked at a variety of opportunities. Then my father called me and said, 'Kevin, why don't you consider working with me?' Well, I was initially too proud to work with him. I said I'd rather do it on my own, and that I was planning on becoming the financial officer of some big company some day. He said, 'Kevin, why don't you just come and take a look at what we do?' At that point I didn't really understand what my father did as a real estate syndicator with two employees, so I came and took a look."

"Well, my parents were very young when they married and had kids. My dad was twenty and my mom was nineteen when I was born. So here I was, twenty-six years old, and my dad was forty-six.

He told me he'd always dreamed of our working together, so I agreed to it. He gave me a phone book and told me to call all the doctors and try to get sales appointments. That was Monday morning. About two o'clock that afternoon I quit, because cold calling just wasn't for me."

"But my father was intent on our working together. He said, 'The real estate business is changing and there are too many big companies coming in, so let's get out of this and let's do something else together and figure out a different way to get clients.' He asked me what ideas I had. Well, as a public accountant I used to teach people in corporations how to use the new technologies. The coolest thing way back then was Lotus 123, the first spreadsheet program to come out. I loved teaching chief financial officers how to use it."

"I told my dad that this would be a great way to get clients, and we could also help people manage their money. He said, 'If you want to go this way, let's do it together,' and unlike many fathers who try to dominate or keep you beneath them, I knew my dad would support me completely. His company was called David Myeroff and Associates, but once I joined we started calling it North Coast Advisors. (Not many people realize this, but Cleveland, which sits on Lake Erie across from Canada, is actually on the north coast of the United States.) A few years later, we moved to a new location and needed to put up a new sign. By then we wanted a more descriptive name for our business, so we just used the initials and called ourselves NCA Financial Planners."

GROWING THE BUSINESS

"Back then, in January of 1986, the term 'financial planning' didn't really exist," Kevin says, "but we soon started teaching people how to watch over their investments. We then became the first customers and biggest producer for a brand-new seminar company called Successful Money Management. Our firm started to grow from there. When my dad left the company in 2000, we had taken the business from three employees and no assets to fifteen or sixteen employees with about $200 million under management. Today we have thirty-one employees and over a billion dollars under management, and are still steadily growing. Our first year, we used to put up a sign in the office to remind ourselves that we were trying to raise $100,000; the year after that the goal was $200,000. This year, the firm raised $120 million."

Asked to explain such remarkable growth, Kevin states, "There's no one single event that's made all the difference. Again, we have all just worked hard and been lucky, and things have evolved over time. In the beginning it was pretty hard to bring on new clients, but we did manage to bring them on, one client at a time. I didn't have the personality to cold call, so our only way to bring on clients was through the seminars. Luckily, I was a ham and used to love doing those seminars, teaching people about the concept of financial planning. Even when I didn't feel like going to a seminar, once I got up in front of the audience, it felt great. Eventually, though, I realized that my seminar days were over, which meant I had to pass on that part of the business to others who still had the excitement."

"One of my very first clients from these seminars is still with me, and his help has proved invaluable. We had planned a seminar at a high school and four people showed up. We were wondering whether we should cancel it or not. I was just starting out, and we had put a lot of money into advertising the seminars, although nowhere near as much as the almost $300,000 a year we now spend. Back then it might have been a couple of thousand dollars, but it was the only couple of thousand dollars I had, so I had to go on with the seminar."

"So I did the seminar for these four people. One was an officer from a local bank who was retiring at the young age of fifty-five. He's a very direct individual. If he sees something he doesn't like, he'll let us know. He recently called me to tell me about a misspelling in a newspaper ad of ours, and said that this was below our capabilities and we should have caught the error. Nobody else would have noticed, but this fellow notices everything because his job was to balance the bank's accounts to the penny. If his account with us is off by a penny, he'll let us know. In addition to being a good friend and a great client, he's responsible for many of our firm's customer service changes and upgrades."

ON WITH THE SHOW!

Relatively early on, Kevin was "fortunate enough to have an opportunity" that has proved to be a marketing masterpiece, one that has turned his name into a very recognizable brand name in the Cleveland area. "Fifteen years ago I had a chance to be on television. Good things happen to people who are doing good things, and I was treasurer for the Ronald McDonald House of Cleveland. We were building a new house for the charity, and in December the NBC affiliate invited me to do an interview on why December is a great time for charitable contributions. I agreed and spoke about the fact that December is the best month because you can write it off the very next month on your taxes and get a quick payback from your donation."

"That was mid-December," Kevin continues, "and then the station said, 'Hey, December 26th, the day after Christmas, nobody's willing to come in and talk. Want to come in and talk about last-minute tax issues?' I was happy to do that for them. It's always a challenge to get your name out there. Newspaper advertising works only on a huge budget over a long period of time; nobody responds to one-time advertising and you just lose your money. Radio and television is possible—you can buy into those—but I realized long ago and early on that it's far better to be an expert, because then you don't have to pay for the advertising. Also, people automatically perceive me as having credibility. Of course, being on TV doesn't mean that I'm any good as a financial planner, but hopefully I back up that perception with some reality."

"It went quite well. Many of my peers are much smarter than I am. But I have the ability to talk in sound bytes, and that's what television requires. Now I actually teach a seminar to my peers on how to do radio and television interviews. It's called, 'You only get one chance; don't mess it up,' because that's how the industry works. When you're asked a question, you have to either rephrase the question so you can answer it in fourteen seconds, or just answer it in fourteen seconds. Luckily, I've got the ability to do that."

"Fifteen years later I'm still the station's financial expert. It's been a great ride—a great form of promotion for the firm and for me—and I would gladly pay to be on TV. Instead, they pay me, and I give all the income I get from my appearances directly to charity. I'm actually an employee of NBC, and I'm on at least a few times a week, Monday mornings and Wednesday midday. But if something happens in the market—if the market were to fall a thousand points today—they'll have a camera out here and I'll be on the six o'clock and eleven o'clock news. If my cell phone rings, and it's either my family or NBC, I take the call immediately."

The number of clients coming to Kevin because of his TV appearances has grown over time. "I told my dad recently that I was lucky and blessed to be able to be on television and create this brand. He said, 'Kevin, you went down there twice a week for three years with no benefit at all.' I tend to forget about that, because I was having fun and it fit in well with my overall life vision."

"So for the first two or three years," Kevin notes, "I didn't get much out of it, and assumed that just my mom and my wife were watching, and that nobody really knew me. Then one day we went to a restaurant here in town and there was a very long line and the manager came up to me and said, 'I watch you on TV; we are ready for you right now, sir.' I thought, 'Hey, this is cool,' and that was really the first time I got any benefit from doing three years of TV."

"But as experts in the media industry will tell you, those three years were really spent building my name, face, and brand recognition. Now I can't walk into any place in Cleveland without somebody recognizing me. It's funny, because if you and I were at lunch, people would recognize me but not come up to the table. But as soon as you went to the restroom and I was left alone, people would come over to the table and say hello. People are very nice about it, and I'm definitely known as the 'financial planning guy' here in Cleveland, although my family, friends, and employees keep me pretty humble by teasing me about my appearances any chance they get."

These days Kevin can also be heard on the radio. "The radio is a weird thing," he says. "It's Q104, one of the top morning shows in Cleveland. Basically, I'm going on a rock/pop morning show to talk about financial planning. It's a strange fit, but it works. They asked me to come in one day and they made me welcome. I can go there as often as I like. They'd like to have me more frequently, but I already have a day job." As with his TV work, Kevin gives all of his actual income from radio appearances to charity.

As a result of his TV and radio appearances, Kevin says that he probably gets "two meetings a week with people in excess of a million dollars in assets, every single week. I sit here and people keep calling up wanting to come in. I do get referrals from my clients, but most of the people they refer have already heard of me. Overall my new business is probably split fifty-fifty between referrals from existing clients and business that comes in due to television, and now radio. Of course, I share these referrals within the firm and spread them around to my other financial planners because I can't service all of them."

Another source of publicity was the book Kevin wrote in 2001, *Countdown to Retirement: Designing Your Financial Future.* "We did signings at Borders and at local bookstores, but I wasn't really out to try and sell a bunch of the books. I was using it as a very expensive business card. In order to leverage it, I called the financial planners who work with me and said, 'Hey, I've got an idea. How would you like to be a part of this book?' So we have something like eight different covers for the book, with me and a different planner on each one. The ton of publicity we got for it has worked out very well for all of us."

A FIRM (BUT FLEXIBLE) STRUCTURE

NCA Financial Planners has four types of employees. At the top of the hierarchy, Kevin says, "are the Senior Planners, who run their own little business within this business. For example, there's my partner Dennis Lehman, who was here when there were just three or four of us. He's been with me for 20 years." Carole Weinberg and Warren Wernick have 18 and 21 years with NCA and are also partners.

"We also have Team Planners, individuals who support a Senior Financial Planner as part of a team. I have three Team Planners—Jasmina Tadic, Melanie Ross, and Karey Edwards—who support me and what I do. Then there are paraplanners, people who would like to become Senior Financial Planners one day and are in effect part of our apprentice program. They train with a Senior Financial Planner or Team Planners for three years before they can start meeting with clients. And finally we have our Financial Planning Assistants, the people who run the back office. They process the paperwork, make the trades, and generally get things done. Roni Smith, who has been with NCA for almost twenty years, is the backbone of our back office. That's mostly a nine-to-five job, and they don't have client meetings, though I am pretty sure Roni has never left at five in the last fifteen years."

"Our CFO and chief compliance officer is Kelly Russell. Leslie Biro, our receptionist, has been with us since 1999. We get more compliments on her than I can possibly relate. She reviews everybody's schedule every day and when a client walks in she welcomes him or her by name. As a single mom, she's one of my heroes. The way she manages to consistently show up at work, take care of her kids, and do it all on her own is amazing. She's just great. We also have an internal technology person, Jeannette Fabian, who works with the outside firm that handles all of our computer needs. She handles little things right away, so we can keep working, and she is also in charge of the twenty-five thousand documents we scan monthly."

"Lastly, we have a marketing person whose job is twofold. First, we have a big seminar business. We do educational seminars at colleges and adult education centers. The only commercial we do during these seminars is at the end, where we say something like, 'Some day, when you need a financial planner, we hope you remember that we were nice and smart and that you think of us.' About two-thirds of the people who attend our seminars actually come in for an appointment, and about half of those are people we'd like to work with as clients."

"The other half of this person's job is marketing the Kevin Myeroff brand. Despite my television and radio appearances, and the top rankings I've received from *Barron's* magazine through The Winner's Circle, my brand is very hard for me to focus on. And it's not that I don't have a big ego. It's just really hard for me to talk about myself, so I have someone else work on promoting my brand."

As for compensation, Kevin notes that "everyone here is on salary, so nobody has to worry about doing enough business or making enough commission." Kevin himself is also salaried, but he and the other planners take bonuses at the end of the year. "Three factors determine anybody's ultimate compensation here. One is how they personally do in bringing in new business and retaining their current clients. The second is how the company as a whole performs. And the third is how well they play in the sandbox with everybody else. I ask everybody here to have his or her own area of expertise and to make that expertise available for everybody in the firm to share in. For example, Dawn Mullinax is our 529 expert, and anybody can go to her for help. If Dawn started not cooperating or providing requested help, that would drastically hurt her bonus."

As the majority owner of the firm and the individual ultimately in charge, it's up to Kevin to make these and many other decisions. "The reason we decided to build the firm vertically instead of horizontally is because our industry has become so commoditized. And while maximum returns are obviously important—they are expected and you simply have to achieve them—the service we provide is more important than anything else. We are the Ritz Carlton, not the Holiday Inn."

To this end, Kevin makes clear the professional expectations of everyone at the firm. "We've made some mistakes by assuming that people know what the partners want out of them, so we've developed some systems. And even though our average employee has been here ten-plus years, every year I still review what I call my professional expectations, a list of ten things that we expect. We expect integrity, and we expect each employee to treat his or her colleagues with respect—I never want to hear anyone saying something negative about a colleague."

"I also expect people to take ownership of client issues," Kevin continues. "I never want a client to call and hear somebody say, 'I'm sorry, nobody here is available to help you.' If you are talking to them, then you help them out. There's no, 'That's Warren's client, not Kevin's, so I can't help her.' If the client has a problem, and her planner is out of the office, you take the issue and figure out a way to solve it."

"Also, I expect people to complete work when promised. If you give a client a date, and you're not done by that date, then call the client and tell them that you are not done. Don't hope they won't notice, because they *will* notice. All it takes is a phone call and you've got to take care of it. I also expect people to immediately contact clients who express any type of dissatisfaction. You can't wait two days. Those are the hardest phone calls. Usually the dissatisfaction is because somebody didn't get back to a client with something when they were supposed to. We're lucky—we've never had a lawsuit here. I firmly believe that if people just talk to their clients, they can resolve almost any issue."

"I also expect employees to feel empowered to make decisions within their job responsibilities. If they don't feel empowered to do things, they've got to come talk to me so I can talk to their supervisor. Everyone here should feel empowered to do his job. Everyone should dress and act professionally. I also expect people never to be the victims of circumstances, as my dad taught me. Finally, I expect them to hold their colleagues accountable for upholding all of these professional expectations. I'm not going to police all of this. If our firm is going to continue to be one of the top firms in the country, then we all have to police it. If somebody is not doing what he is supposed to be doing—for example, if someone comes in dressed inappropriately—then they need to be told about it by whoever sees them and make the necessary change."

WORKING—AND HAVING FUN— WITH THE BEST AND THE BRIGHTEST

Kevin maintains a certain social distance from his employees. "I don't socialize with the people here, and I surely don't try to necessarily be their friend. But I do try to be their teacher and mentor, and back them up whenever I can. If it comes down to a conflict between a client and one of my employees, I'm going to back up my employee, which is something I've had to do a number of times. If an employee tells me that a client was mean or rude to him, I'll call the client and let the client know that's not acceptable. My employees are very, very important to me, and that's one reason they rarely leave."

To promote employee longevity, Kevin makes sure that despite the serious nature of what he and his employees do, they also maintain "an extremely fun environment. For example," Kevin says, "we were going through a period where the markets weren't doing very well. Clients were getting upset and nervous and scared, and there was a residual effect on the planners. If people are depressed, they can actually pass on that depression without knowing it. So I had to come up with something to change the atmosphere. Well, my children and I filled up about thirty squirt guns with water and came in very early one morning and put one on everybody's desk. So we had people who were making a couple of hundred thousand dollars a year crawling army-style down the hallway shooting people with their squirt guns. We try to do fun things like that."

Kevin also takes care of his employees in other ways. "There's a company here in Cleveland that uses a mobile home to sell designer women's clothing. They were doing a commercial at the station when I arrived for my television appearance. Well, the majority of our hardworking planners are women, and by the time they finish up on any given day, the stores are usually closed. So, I asked if they could go over to my office immediately. I gave everybody a few hundred bucks and said, 'Go shop.' Everybody went out to the parking lot to pick out designer clothes from the van. We picked up the entire tab for it. This has to be a fun place to work. We regularly put on events, including our annual clam bake and Cleveland Indians opening day cookout."

Finding potential employees who can meet Kevin's professional expectations, and who are likely to become solid contributors, starts early. "By design, we go out and hire the brightest and best," Kevin says. "If we can, we always try to get people as interns, so we'll have three or four interns some years. And then we pick the brightest of those to come join us. As a financial planning firm, we want to hire people with four years of college and close to a 4.0 average. Grades are just one thing that we look at, but we generally—perhaps unfortunately—don't give people a chance if they're not in the top tier academically, although some of our financial planning assistants who run the back office have been noncollege people, and they have performed superbly."

There is a good deal of flexibility about what route each new employee eventually takes. "Suppose someone comes in out of college and starts out by supporting me as one of my paraplanners. For example, Dennis, after three years with me, had a choice. He could have continued to support me, or he could begin to run his own practice. For a long time he just continued to support me, but now he's a partner and runs his own practice within our firm. Some of our employees have more fun and probably make more money working directly with me or with one of the other senior planners, and some prefer to have their own thing going."

"Ultimately," Kevin notes, "you can go almost any way you want in our firm, and many people move up over time. Karey Edwards was our marketing coordinator, but she came to me one day and said, 'Hey, I see what everybody is doing, and I want to make more of a difference in people's lives and become a financial planner.' She was right that we're truly in a great business: what we do is so gratifying because being able to help people every day is inherently rewarding. Well, she wasn't sharing in that, so she became a paraplanner. Now, you can stay a paraplanner forever; you don't have to move up to being a financial planner. Indeed, Karey thought she'd remain a paraplanner, but then she realized that she wanted to go to the next level. So after three years she moved up and promoted one of our interns, Elizabeth Verner, to replace her and become my paraplanner."

WOMEN PLANNERS AND THE NONFINANCIAL SPOUSE

Most of the financial planners in the firm are women. "We have twenty-five women and six guys," Kevin notes. "What I've found is that, given the way we do business, women tend to be better financial planners than men. The biggest part of financial planning is being able to listen to clients, to understand what they want. Women tend to do a much, much better job of listening. And women tend to do much better at listening to the nonfinancial spouse."

"During our meetings, the nonfinancial spouse (frequently the wife) is often afraid to ask questions because she fears sounding dumb or 'bothering' me. But once they leave here and go home, and the husband goes back to work, she'll call up one of my team financial planners because they are women, and ask tons of questions. These days I often pay a lot of attention to the nonfinancial spouse during meetings, and that's in part because of some very direct feedback I received early on that really changed how I handle client meetings."

"I was doing a review with a couple who were one of my first clients," Kevin relates. "I talked to them about a lot of things, but spent the whole time looking at the husband. I even—while his wife was sitting there—asked him if he wanted to go golfing and made plans to do so the next day. When they left, I thought we'd had a great meeting. His wife soon called me back and asked if I would mind having a meeting with her. Well, she came in and told me what was on her mind. She told me that I had been disrespectful, that I had made a completely wrong assumption that he alone controlled the money, and that in fact she had as much control as he had. She also told me it had been rude to invite him to play golf and not invite her; as it turns out, she doesn't like golfing, but what if she did? Finally, she pointed out that during the entire meeting I didn't look at her once, which made her feel unimportant."

"Well, I apologized, and luckily they stayed with me. And that completely changed the way I operate. If it appears that the female is the nonfinancial spouse, I spend extra time talking to her, looking at her, making sure that she's included. She's the one who can make or break the relationship in the long run, and so this has really changed my business. Today, they are one of our biggest and most successful clients. What if she hadn't cared enough about me, and simply told her husband that I was a creep and she didn't want to work with me? I thank her to this day for teaching me that lesson."

WORKING WITH AND SERVING THEIR CLIENTS

When a client first comes in to work with Kevin, "two things happen. One, they get segmented, and two, they are assigned a team financial planner. Segmentation means that different types of clients get different services. Some get four meetings a year, some get three meetings a year, some get three additional phone calls, and some get two additional phone calls. Some need to be called every month. Some require personal attention from me, meaning that they are invited to special sporting events or other events that we run. We do cooking classes that people, especially CEOs, seem to really love. They bring their spouses, there's wine, and it's a lot of fun and a really good time. My paraplanner keeps track of whom I owe contacts to, whom I talk to, when I talk to them, and whether I need to have additional personal contact with them."

"Second," Kevin continues, "as the senior financial planner, I'm on every client's account, but there's also a team financial planner who's involved with every client. So when a client comes in, three of us—the team financial planner, and paraplanner, and I—sit through the meeting. My job is to look at the big picture, to be strategic, and perhaps most importantly, to teach the team financial planners the business. In fact, these days my job is more teaching than almost anything else."

"Actually, there was a time, many moons ago, when I was the smartest person here. But now, if I look at everyone who works here, I'm something like twentieth down the list in smarts. The clients still want to see me, however, because I have more life experience than many of the younger people who work here. So my role at a lot of these meetings is to provide nonfinancial life experience advice that the clients look to us for. The financial planning part, and the asset management part, has become very commoditized. Clients certainly expect and want good returns, but they're also looking for the other value-adds that we bring."

"We begin by meeting with new clients to gather all the information we need. The team financial planner then takes that information and goes through the process of putting together a plan for the next meeting. That includes estate planning, tax planning, insurance planning, the whole works. Before the second meeting, I review their plan and give them my thoughts: 'Did you think of this? Why not consider this? Why not look at this?' Then, fifteen or twenty minutes before the client meeting, they brief me one more time and hand me the agenda for the meeting."

"My average meeting lasts an hour or less," Kevin notes, "because we get right to work. The first part of a planning meeting—or any meeting—is usually devoted to building credibility, but because of my media presence, that's generally a given. Generally I'll run the meeting, but I'll often pass things off to the team financial planner, because I want the client to know that that's the person they should be calling, not me. If I do it right, the clients are very comfortable working with their team financial planners. Keep in mind, these are very smart people. But I'm still in the picture. If one of my clients winds up going through a divorce or some other life-changing experience, he'll come and talk to me, just because I'm older than the other guys or ladies and I have more life experience."

"The paraplanner keeps a record of the entire meeting. The planner's job is to listen to whatever the client says, write it down, and then document any promises that we make. The team financial planner does most of the actual work, along with me, but it's the paraplanner who's the stage manager and makes sure that the work actually gets done."

EDUCATING CLIENTS AND PROVIDING SPECIAL SERVICES

For Kevin, a very important objective of these initial meetings is educating clients. "Ultimately, the more knowledgeable a client is, the easier it is for us. Some financial advisors are afraid to take really, really smart clients, but I would take smart clients any day because they understand the process and know what's happening. They know that markets fluctuate, and they understand the business decisions we have to make."

"And the more educated the client," Kevin continues, "the more effective our hand holding can be. And almost everyone needs some hand holding at times. Also, right in the first meeting I'll tell the client how we charge, what our fees are, and how we expect the relationship to go. I also tell them that if they're going to be calling us every day, we'll either have to end the relationship, or figure out some other way for them to compensate us for what we're doing, and they all understand that."

Although providing good returns is very important, Kevin is clear that "that's not what keeps our clients here. Wealth management is 20 percent investment," he says, "and 80 percent holistic attention to your clients—helping them with all the other issues in their lives. The clients expect you to handle the assets part, the 20 percent, correctly. When you get on an airplane, you expect to arrive safely at your destination. But when you come off the plane, what made it a good or bad flight was how the ride and service were."

"The same thing is true in our business. Clients expect good returns; the quality of the ride depends on all the other things you can offer them. So what keeps our clients here are all the other things we do in the areas of estate planning, insurance planning, and the concierge services that we offer, things that they can't get elsewhere, including tickets to events. For example, we help our clients get good deals on buying real estate and cars."

"As one of the top one hundred financial planning firms in the country, sitting in Cleveland, which not long ago was the poorest big city in the country, we are a very big fish in a very small pond. We have relationships with all the car dealerships in town—a lot of them happen to be our clients, and given my brand recognition, they know who we are and the types of clients we have—so we can make a call and set things up so the client can go in there and look at the car and drive it without any questions about money or sales pressure."

"If the client wishes, we can negotiate on their behalf and have the dealer send us the invoice. With the paperwork all ready, the client walks in, spends ten minutes filling out forms, and walks out with the keys. This is very easy for us to do, and while we might make some of our clients 20 percent on their money, in their eyes that pales in comparison to being treated like a big shot at the car dealership."

THE INVESTMENT COMMITTEE: STEWARDING "LIFE-ALTERING" MONEY

Along with the overall financial planning they do for their clients, Kevin and all his planners are very aware of the importance of stewarding their clients' resources and making appropriate investments on their behalf. "Returns are expected, and so we have a thirteen-person in-house investment committee that works on all the investments. We spend a lot of money, time, and effort on this."

Interestingly, Kevin is *not* a member of the investment committee. "By design, I'm not on the investment committee, although all of my personal assets are managed by the committee, that is, all my assets are in the same allocation that my clients' assets are. Before we had an investment committee, I would do the asset allocating. I'm a CPA and I like numbers, so when modern portfolio theory came around in 1990 or so, I was thrilled that there were ways that we could make investing more of a science than an art. It worked out very well for me, and I used to really enjoy doing the investments."

"But then I got burned out on it," Kevin says. "I was getting four hours of sleep and couldn't pay attention in meetings. When I started nodding off while talking to fund managers I knew that I needed people smarter than I was doing this. I realized that if the business was going to survive, I couldn't control everything myself, and had to start letting things go. The investment committee is now a very, very big part of the firm. I still get my say, but I don't control the committee."

"All the members of the committee are financial planners," Kevin adds," and while at first it might have seemed that they were wasting their time being on the committee instead of being out there marketing and getting clients—we could have always gone a different route and outsourced the investment choices—they've come back and told me that telling their clients they sit on the investment committee was great for marketing purposes. Nobody on the committee wants to let down the other twelve people who are counting on them, so they are forced to really learn, dig in, and get to the bottom of things. They feel that they are learning more than ever, and that being on the committee has helped them tremendously. So we've decided to keep things as they are, which works great for me."

"The investment committee," Kevin continues, "is split up according to styles—large-cap value, large-cap growth, and so on—and multiple people are assigned to each box. The committee meets twice a month, and also meets in small groups and talks with people such as fund company representatives and economists. They end up creating set portfolios based on risk tolerance, so we have a 100 percent invested portfolio, a ninety-ten, eighty-twenty, seventy-thirty, and so on. We are monitoring and changing these portfolios all the time, and it's been phenomenal for us."a

"They vote as a committee on what investments are added—mutual funds, ETFs, index funds, individual stocks, individual funds—and what are taken out. For 99.9 percent of our clients, we have 100 percent of their money, and the majority of our clients are retired or nearing retirement. So our overall investment philosophy is that we are handling what I call *life-altering money*, and we simply can't mess up. We can't lose 25 percent of a client's assets, because we will literally mess up his or her life. We have a big responsibility and we need to sleep every night. So the committee makes all its decisions with full awareness that they are handling life-altering money."

In part, this awareness results in an appropriately more conservative mix of investments than might be found in other firms managing over $1 billion in assets. "For our higher-end clients," Kevin says, "I don't mind looking at using hedge funds or private equity, and some alternative investments are part of all our portfolios. But I have to understand an investment before I'll use it. We have to see all the pieces, and are not willing to work inside some black box or take some company on their word that they know what they're doing. So we did not use collateralized mortgage obligations, because it always seems to me that in the middle of the process, you just have to trust what goes on. And there were some hedge funds that we used, but when we ran the numbers, we realized that the numbers we were being given just didn't jibe with our numbers. So we pulled those investments entirely."

"Ultimately," Kevin concludes, "we spend very little time talking about specific investments with our clients. They just want to know that we have an idea of what we are doing, that we have a plan and a system, and that we can help them buy a car one day. So they conceptually buy into how we do things, and I normally won't give into demands for specific investments. If a client has a very specific question, then I'll call someone from the investment committee who works in that area and I'll ask them to have a conversation with the client. Ultimately, we're not traders, we're investors. There are always going to be ways to make money and grow assets, and we look down the road and pay attention to those."

"Now, when clients come in and talk to us as financial planners, our job is to determine their risk tolerance, what they are trying to achieve—their goals and objectives—and which of our portfolios is going to best fit their needs. Our job is to figure out not only what our clients are saying, but what's behind what they're saying, what they mean by it. And then we've got to be prepared to either help them meet those goals or tell them that they're not achievable. That's a difference between clients and customers: customers are always right, clients aren't. My clients know that, and know that I'm not always going to tell them what they want to hear. But they've got to hear what they need to hear. It's their money, and in the end they make the final decision, but I need to sleep at night."

"Since we don't time the market with any of our portfolios—timing the market just can't be done—if a client is scared, he needs to be moved, for example, from the seventy-thirty portfolio to the fifty-fifty portfolio. So, overall portfolios are prepared by the investment committee, and then when an individual's portfolio is set, it can be customized. If someone has a grandson who works for a company, the stock of that company can be added to their portfolio if they want."

But Kevin and his planners won't let a client do just anything. "If a client comes in and wants to roll the dice, and wants individual stocks and to really go for it, well, that's not our expertise. All we could do would be either get lucky or really mess things up and create something bad for ourselves. In the past, we've made the mistake of taking clients even though we knew that their assets didn't fit the personality of the firm, and eventually we had to fire them. Now the firm is big enough that we get to choose whom we want to work with and whom we don't want to work with, so I've let tens of millions of dollars walk out of here. We focus on doing what we do well, and on doing it right."

This kind of focus enabled NCA Financial Planners to do extremely well during the dot-com tech bust. "Our worst period," Kevin says, "was 1998 and 1999, when we actually lost some clients because we refused to move away from our philosophy of splitting money between value and growth. We had clients whose friends were making 200 percent while they were 'only' making 50 percent. We couldn't understand how they weren't happy with making 50 percent, and so we always kept within our philosophy. Most importantly, we never deviated from our asset allocation method of managing money based on modern portfolio theory, and that's what saved us."

HELPING THOSE WHO NEED HELP

Kevin notes that of the 31 people employed by NCA Financial Planners, "ten or eleven of us are fully qualified financial planners, and we have roughly twenty-one hundred clients. This is a little under two hundred clients a planner, which is about the right critical mass. I myself have some four hundred clients that I have direct responsibility for, and by leveraging the three team financial planners who work directly with me, I'm able to see them all. These three individuals could go to any firm and be great financial planners on their own, but they'll tell you that they learn more this way and probably ultimately make more money. Some people are great financial planners but not great marketers. This way they can live off the brand I've created."

On the one hand, Kevin regularly assists the bulk of his clients by making sure their entire financial plan is in order, and that they are well asset allocated. "There are the obvious stories," he says, "of clients who worked in big corporations and invested all of their net worth—everything they owned—in the stocks of those corporations. While the companies looked like they were going to continue to grow and do great, prudent financial planning says you've got to have more diversification than that. We diversified lots of clients away from overconcentrated holdings, and those were home runs, because the companies ran into problems and their stocks went down. If we had not done what we did, those clients wouldn't have the lives they have today."

In addition to helping out his regular clients this way, Kevin has found a way to help a variety of individuals who might not otherwise qualify for his help. "Every couple of years someone who is 35 or 40 comes in, sits down, and says he just came from the doctor, has a terminal illness, and will be dead in 18 months, and please will I help him set things up for his family. Well, these people have enough falling apart in their lives, so they need somebody who will talk to them in a very matter of fact way about what needs to be done. They don't need emotional support; they need help. We try to help people like that whenever we have an opportunity."

In a similar vein, the *Cleveland Plain Dealer* ran a contest that included a free financial plan from NCA Financial Planners. "A police officer who had developed Lou Gehrig's disease, ALS, won the contest. He came in with his wife, and he was an unbelievable guy. The first thing he said was, 'Do you want a Duggy hug?' and he gave me this huge bear hug. While he wouldn't have qualified to be a client, we helped him with some very basic things like restructuring his income, assets, and debt. And the newspaper article helped his wife get a job."

"Duggy had one dream," Kevin says, "which was to go to Las Vegas while he was still able. Today he's in a wheelchair. Well, we helped him pull off that trip—a bunch of his friends contributed some money, as did our firm—and he and five or six buddies went to Las Vegas and he had the time of his life. They are all set up now and are running the course, but they still have access to us whenever they need us. Overall it was very, very rewarding for us to be able to help somebody in that situation. There are tons of stories about multimillionaires we've helped to become more wealthy, but anybody can do that."

"We also help out single parents," Kevin adds. "They typically have no time to see a financial planner and think about their finances. All they have time to do is work, take care of their kids, and try to get a few hours of sleep. We ran a contest where people could nominate a single mom, and we sent all the nominations to the local paper, which picked a hundred of them. We took these hundred single moms and their children on a cruise ship called *The Goodtime* for a half a day. There were clowns, balloons, and face painters for the kids. We gave each of the moms a financial plan and helped set her in the right direction. What many of them needed more than anything else was debt restructuring, or advice on how to put money into their 401K plans so they could retire one day.

"What about individuals who can't meet the firm's minimums? As your business grows, you realize that the one commodity you have to guard is your time. In this business, people tend to figure out how to do this in different ways. One of the most common ways is to set a client minimum, because it takes as much effort to work with a $2 million account as it does to work with a $200,000 account, and you make ten times more money with the $2 million client."

"Over time," Kevin continues, "we've raised our standards. I've had to change my criteria because I can only see so many people, and today I generally work with people with a million dollars and up. I will, however, make exceptions if somebody is referred by another client and has the potential to reach a million in investable assets. Also, my overall client retention rate is in the high 90th percentile, so I still have those clients who once qualified but would no longer qualify under the raised minimum."

"We won't turn anybody away from the firm. We'll always find a way to help people as long as they have assets to manage, since we don't typically do debt consolidation or services of that nature. If someone is below my firm minimum, then one of my team financial planners may work with them."

"Another way I help others," Kevin says, "is through what I do on radio and television, where I'm able to reach many people. Then I wrote my book *Countdown to Retirement*, which helps the average person figure out where he or she is in that respect. In that book, we tell the stories of actual clients, with their names changed, and show how their lives were changed by the financial planning process."

Along the same lines, Kevin says that "If there was something I could change in the future, I would love to find more ways to help the average person, the person that's making $35,000 or $40,000 a year and who has credit card debt, is struggling to add to their 401K, and can't afford to hire anybody to get advice. I'd like to find more and more ways of helping these people, because that helps everybody. The stronger we can make the middle class, the less debt and the fewer financial worries people have, the better off this country is going to be."

"So besides growing this firm," Kevin declares, "I'd like to find a better way to help those people who need help the most, but who, because of the economics of our business, aren't being served. Making more use of media, like radio, is one possible way, or maybe I'll eventually clear my calendar one day a month for appointments with anybody who needs help. I'm looking at a bunch of ideas in this area."

FRIENDS OF THE FIRM

Kevin and NCA Financial Planners have found at least one novel way to directly serve a whole category of otherwise unqualified individuals, called Friends of the Firm. "We used to have people come in here with $25,000 or $30,000," Kevin says, "but because of the labor involved to be proactive with them and keep them in line— it just didn't make sense for us to work with them. We'd send these people away and they'd go to some brokerage house, wind up with some young, inexperienced planner, and be put in a terrible fund where they'd lose their money. It wasn't working for them, and we were sending a lot of money out the door. That's when we created the class of client called Friends of the Firm."

"These people work with one of our financial planners on a commission basis," Kevin says, implying that since this is a one-time investment decision, there is no need for ongoing fees. "We tell them up front that we'll find them a good investment based on the goals, objectives, and needs that they outline for us. We tell them we'll put them in a couple of investments, and then they won't hear from us again. If they have questions about their investments, they can call us and we'll be happy to talk, and if their objectives change, they can call us and we'll be happy to change their investments. We'll be happy to have them call us and come in once a year and talk about their investments, but we're not going to call them. So we tell them how to invest their assets, and we earn a commission on that."

"Friends of the Firm also tend to be referral sources for people who do qualify as clients. Now and then we have events for Friends of the Firm. Whereas for our regular clients we'll have a fund's chief economist come in and give a talk, for the Friends of the Firm we'll have a wholesaler come in. So we can still take care of nearly everybody, and we don't have to turn people away. These folks understand how they fit into the firm, and they don't have to stay with us, but 95 percent of them do."

"And if they want a higher level of service," Kevin adds, "they can pay for it. Essentially, our business model has us earning a minimum $5,000 on every account yearly. So if they want to pay a $5,000 fee, we'll give them more of the services they want. But in most cases, in one meeting we can tell them how to allocate their 401K, what to do with their assets, and how to line up their three main goals so they can accomplish them in the next three years. And we make sure that when they accomplish each of those goals—we give them graphs and other monitoring tools—they come back in and see us. So a typical Friend of the Firm will end up fully invested in their 401K, will have all their credit cards paid off, and will have an emergency fund, and then they'll come in and talk to us again."

"What people don't like," Kevin notes, "is being led to expect a level of service and not getting it. We are really honest with them. We say, 'If you get lucky and go to some other firm and find a really bright kid just starting out, you might get way better service and more hands on with your money.' But, in this business, to find somebody of our quality and actually be served, with $50,000 of assets, is unheard of. We have figured out a way to do it, and it's all about setting expectations. Not one of these people has ever complained. Ever. This has worked out really well for us, and today we have about a thousand Friends of the Firm."

THE FUTURE

"Wayne Gretsky, 'the Great One,' always said that you want to go where the puck is going and not where it's been.' Well, my job is to figure out where this firm needs to be in the future to be competitive, to take care of our clients, and to take care of my employees. From my standpoint, this business changes every five years. Fifteen years ago we did all our business with individual mutual fund companies. Then brokerage accounts came around, which at first we were totally against, but now we couldn't do business without them."

"Now," Kevin continues, "technology has drastically changed how we look at things and how we leverage our time. It used to take us a whole day to prepare for a client meeting; now we can do it in fifteen minutes using technology. And we used to be completely commission-based, then we were commission and fee, and now we've moved mainly to fee only, although commissions aren't going away and we do still have some commission business. I fought the fee trend for years, but fee technology and pricing has changed to the point where I now think a fee system makes sense and is very fair."

Over the next five years, Kevin sees the firm itself "growing in a pretty controlled way. We are about to increase our office space by 40 percent, because you can't run a successful business unless you have capacity. Many businesses make the mistake of getting clients before they have the infrastructure or service capacity to handle them. If you make the investment in your infrastructure first, and then everything fills in, it seems seamless to people. We are in the process of increasing our infrastructure because I think our industry is about to go through five or six years like we've never seen before, with more money crossing over from more families and more people needing help. So we want to be ready for it when it comes with new hires, more people going through the training process, and more leveraging of our capabilities."

"Some day," Kevin adds, "this is going to be the firm that manages my personal assets without my involvement, and so I want to leave it with people who have the integrity and skill level to manage my family's assets. So my job is to teach, train, build, and look strategically where the firm needs to be to stay on top of things. Somewhere between five and twenty years from now I'll retire, and meanwhile over time I'll work less. Last year I took the entire month of July off, and when I came back I had no phone calls or emails to return. My team took care of everything, which makes them very valuable to me. I was so pleased by this that when I came back I gave everybody on my team raises. And I'm looking at taking more and more time off so I can watch my kids grow up and spend time with them, because that's what I really enjoy."

A WONDERFUL (AND MOSTLY PRIVATE) LIFE

"I'm a very lucky guy," Kevin reflects. "First and foremost I have a wonderful, supportive wife and three beautiful children. I love my employees, I love what I do for a living, and I feel we add tremendous value to people's lives. We get phone calls from people on a regular basis just to thank us, which feels really great. So I wake up every day excited to come to work, or do whatever I'm doing. I don't spend a lot of time being upset or sad, because it's so much more fun and satisfying to be happy. That's how I live my life. I'm a simple guy. And my philosophy of life is simple too: I'm a big believer in the Golden Rule—do unto others as you would have them to do unto you."

Kevin's philosophy explains, in part, his ongoing dedication to philanthropic activities. "Because my involvement in the Ronald McDonald House got me into television, I give them all of my income from television. But I look for different charities too, and every year my wife and I try to find someone else who needs help. Sometimes the best charitable things you can do aren't through a nonprofit corporation; instead, you find a person or family you can help directly. My wife and I don't need the tax deduction to help somebody."

"For example," Kevin says, "there's a place called Hershey, Pennsylvania, where they make Hershey chocolate bars. It's also a big amusement park area and about a six- or seven-hour drive from where we live. Middle schools around here like to take their kids there to do science projects, like calculating the rate of descent of a roller coaster. For all the local sixth graders, the school trip there was a really big deal. Because of school funding issues they had to start charging the kids $400 or $500 for a three-day trip. Since we'd observed the value of the trip to our own kids, my wife and I offered to pay anonymously for kids who couldn't afford to go on their own. We like doing stuff like that. Nobody knew we did it, and we never asked for credit. For us, that was a better way of making a difference than giving to the United Way."

Another example is a program called Kids in Flight. "This is run by a young woman in her twenties, who has a very serious form of thyroid cancer. But somehow, in a very grassroots manner, she's managed to provide airplane flights for terminally ill kids. Her philosophy is that when you are up there in the sky, all of your problems seem small. I like finding people like her and helping them build their vision. I worked with her for the last few years and helped create an advisory board, including some people from the radio station and TV station she probably couldn't have gotten on her own, who provided her with great advice and marketing assistance. She's a big deal now, getting grants from everywhere and doing great, so I'm looking for my next person to help."

Kevin has three children (two girls and a boy), and he coaches many of their athletic teams—baseball, soccer, football, and basketball. "I left a lot of the charitable boards that I was on because I was coaching so much, and coaching is another way of giving back to the community." Kevin also likes to spend time with his kids in others ways. "I love anything that's active and outdoors, like water skiing and snow skiing. I have a small group of friends, five or six guys from high school who are now all over the country, but we get together a couple of times a year to go skiing. And I love playing sports with my kids. I enjoy traveling too, both warm places and cold places. And I not only love my kids, I love being there for their new experiences, just as I love seeing people the first time they go on a glider ride. I just love being able to provide that sort of thing for my family and employees. It really fills me up."

What makes it possible for Kevin to fit so much in is his absolute clarity about what he values most. "Nothing," he says, "is more important to me than personal family time. I don't miss any of my kids' events. And so I don't create relationships with my clients that involve going out to dinner or parties."

"We will do a few firm things during the year," Kevin continues, "such as getting a suite for an Indians game and invite ten clients to join us. But I'll have my wife with me. That's the way I create my relationships. My clients are very aware of my values, and I think they respect them. I'm lucky because I don't really enjoy going to dinners and social events all the time. I don't like putting on a tie. I like hanging out with my wife and my kids. That's what I really enjoy."

"Of course," Kevin adds, "when I started out I was working Saturdays, Sundays, and whenever a client wanted me. Luckily, I don't have to do that now, and there are other people within our firm who have the ability and the hunger to do it. The reality is, if someone wants to see me, they have to come in between nine and five, Monday through Friday. Most of my clients have my cell phone number if they need me—and if somebody has a real emergency, I'm in the phone book and it's easy to find my home—but nobody uses it. They all really respect my time." Clearly, they respect Kevin as well, a man who knows the value of taking care of others—family members, employees, clients, and charitable causes—and who always stays focused on what's really important.

CHAPTER 5: THE CURTIS GROUP

SMITH BARNEY
PALO ALTO, CALIFORNIA

(Top Row Left to Right) Brian Araki, Thomas McGuirk, Mark Curtis, Ricardo Santamaria, Tom McCue

(Bottom Row Left to Right) Christy Spilsted, Tracey Story, Terry Joerger, Anamika Mandal

Whensuper asked about his success, Mark Curtis—who has consistently been ranked by The Winner's Circle as one of the top financial advisors in America—humbly protests that he's been incredibly fortunate and blessed. He'll refer to his upbringing (his dad was a successful advisor); his early love and great passion for the business; his desirable Silicon Valley location; and the extraordinary longevity of his relationships with clients, team members, and money managers. Mark also says that the only firm he's ever been with, Smith Barney, has empowered him to achieve high levels of success.

At the same time, it's worth noting that this highly energetic advisor and his team have led the way with several important industry firsts, and that Mark's trademark is his propensity for thinking outside of the box. An enemy of complacency who's still not entirely satisfied with his many remarkable achievements, Mark will confirm that he's a dedicated and astute student of the markets, and that his success is based on a combination of instinct, performance, and client service. And he'll reel off any number of success mantras or formulas that he's personally road tested and firmly believes in.

"It's funny," Mark says, "but if you think about successful individuals, there has to be some combination of characteristics that distinguish them. For me, I believe it's a combination of passion, love for what I do, luck, and the good fortune of being in a geographical area like Silicon Valley. Obviously, I love what I do, but beyond that and good fortune, I can't say that there's anything really unique about me." Mark may not be able to state what's unique about himself, but his words and actions have consistently demonstrated the kind of impassioned originality that have propelled him to the very summit of success.

"IT'S A GREAT HONOR TO HAVE A CLIENT"

Mark's interest in being an advisor began very early. "I'm really lucky my dad was in this business. This may sound crazy, but I remember wanting to be in it even when I was very young. Perhaps my earliest memory is when I was four or five years old, driving home from a vacation, sitting in the front seat of my dad's car, listening to him talk about his work. My dad made the investment business sound so exciting."

Mark's views on the importance and honor of being entrusted with clients have changed little over the years. "It's a great honor to have a client—to have someone say, 'I want you to help me fulfill my goals and aspirations, not just for myself, but for my family as well.' It's a tremendous responsibility." But as usual, Mark is not completely satisfied with the status quo. "There's a fundamental importance to what we do. Savings and investment are an important cornerstone of our society. It bothers me that somehow we are not seen as professionals in the same way as doctors, lawyers, or accountants. Because those of us who enter this business primarily to help clients in this way are true professionals, and we need to make sure that we are regarded as such."

After graduating from Stanford University, Mark worked in the music industry for a year, then received an MBA from UCLA. After graduating, he followed his father's advice and pursued the brokerage business, joining E. F. Hutton.

On August 3, 1981, Mark became an advisor, and to this day his feelings for the business have stayed as positive as when he was a young boy. "For me this isn't a job, it's more like an adventure." And it's an adventure that, even more than a quarter century later, he finds as much fun as ever. "In our business things are always changing. I get up most mornings asking myself, 'How much fun can I have today?' Not 'What do I have to do today?' And when I go home, more often than not I'll turn to the materials that I've brought home with me, continuing to work at a business that I love a lot."

FOUR DISTINCT BUSINESSES

Mark's extremely successful practice has four distinct components. "I really have four different client books of business," he says. "Corporate services, institutional consulting, high-net-worth, and third-party business. Each of these four different business models was created by focusing on a business opportunity, achieving success with it, and then recruiting a team that could support and leverage it."

Corporate services refers to the Curtis Group's work with major corporations on cash management, stock plans, deferred compensation plans, and directed share programs.

Institutional consulting covers the team's work with retirement plans, endowments and foundations, and other institutional pools of capital with respect to their investment needs.

High-net-worth, of course, refers to the team's work with high-net-worth and ultra-high-net-worth individuals and families.

Third-party business, perhaps the most unusual of the four, involves the Curtis Group's work with other financial intermediaries who are looking for the kind of products, services, and capabilities that an advisor from Citigroup, Smith Barney's parent firm, can deliver. "We support banks, independently registered investment advisors, financial planners, and family offices with the types of asset management capabilities and services that their clients are looking for."

"For example," Mark continues, "a family office might look to us for access to top-tier equity managers or access to the full spectrum of alternative managers. We work with independent firms that have their own clients and need to choose a firm to provide institutional capabilities including custody, trading, and access to the full spectrum of investment vehicles and products; quite often we can provide them access at lower minimums and with very reasonable fees."

"The benefit of a diversified business," Mark continues, "is that it delivers multiple revenue streams and thereby smoothes out the volatility of any one business. My overall business is more conservative because it is diversified."

It's hard to deny Mark's success with having four businesses, given that he and his team manage billions in assets. Another benefit of having four businesses is that they are "very synergistic." Some of these synergies are easy to see, such as the following example, which helped launch his career.

"In the summer of eighty-five, I had decided to focus on investment consulting and opened my first managed account. I always kept a generic investment consulting presentation on my desk, and everybody who came to see me, even if it was for a $2,000 IRA, received that presentation on managed money. Like a lot of advisors in Silicon Valley at that time, I was forming relationships with officers of emerging companies as retail clients. Many of these clients also had corporate cash management responsibilities and asked me who should manage their cash for them. So I started to specialize in short-term fixed-income manager searches, and soon enough I had a whole cadre of corporations for which I was performing that function. Then CFOs would come to me and ask, 'We have a problem with our stock plans. Can you help us?' I had to quickly find out what I needed to know about that business."

Another example of synergy occurred when Mark and his team were asked to provide educational services to a notable stock plan client and to its participants. They decided to send two junior advisors to go onsite every Friday to offer the company's employees the advice and education they requested. "They were provided with an office, and there was a sign-up sheet so any employee could walk in and spend an hour talking about their issues with no obligation. Within a year we had opened nearly three hundred accounts!"

"Furthermore, the exposure to different types of clients," Mark adds, "has given me a broader perspective on all aspects of our business. It has allowed me to have a larger team with more resources and a deeper bench. Also, I can go from one type of business challenge to the next all day long, and I like it that way. Our business is constantly evolving."

TEAM LEADERSHIP AND STRUCTURE

Mark has structured his team to service the four distinct types of clients who make up his four businesses. "My team members have a great understanding of their direct responsibilities and what segments of the business they are a part of, and are rewarded accordingly," he says. "The team structure has been a major factor in our success."

Mark embraced the team approach early in his career. "I realized that I would need to recruit people with different interests, skill sets, and strengths than I had. From the beginning I tried to recruit the best people available. I hired the best administrator in the branch to join me, and then recruited an associate to focus solely on servicing and maintaining client relationships. I had read a study that said that clients valued relationship above all else, so I structured the team to deliver an excellent client experience."

Mark also recognized early on that he would have to learn to empower his team by delegating responsibilities to them and building processes that would leverage the team's workload. "When we meet a client for the first time, we decide who on my team is going to be the relationship manager and contact person for that client. I introduce the team member and say, 'This is the person you are going to talk to every day. This is who is going to be managing the details of our relationship. This is your person.' This structure allows me to do what I do best and add value to the relationship based upon my own unique skills."

As the go-to person for investment decisions and strategy, Mark compares himself to a piece of artillery. "If we were a military unit, assume that I'm an artillery piece that is not mobile; I'm not automated or mechanized so I can't get myself into place. So the team has to get me onto the field and aim me at the target. Once they've staged me and I'm in the right place, I will fire away and hit the target. But I can't get there on my own. The team has to do that."

Currently Mark has 25 to 30 team members, down from the 50 to 60 he had when some of his earlier corporate services stock options business demanded a much larger work force. The team members who have worked with Mark the longest (in the 20-year range) include Terry Joerger and Tom McCue, who both work in the high-net-worth business and the third-party business. Karen McDonald is Mark's partner in the corporate services business. These three individuals, as well as everyone else on the team, bring unique and specific skills with them.

For one thing, Mark believes that just as with successful sports teams, to build a winning financial services team you should "draft the best athlete or the best talent available. That way you create a deep bench, and hopefully you don't find yourself having to fill a specific need." On occasion, however, Mark will hire someone based on a momentary gut feeling. "Some of the best decisions are made from gut instinct and it may take a while to realize the benefits of that decision."

As an example, Mark says that one of his team members was "not a great corporate salesperson when we first hired him. During a meeting, when it would come time to summarize the features and benefits of the proposal, he would cover his mouth or drop his voice about two octaves. I told him that it seemed as though he was not confident or that he did not believe in what he was saying. Well, for the first couple of years we traveled together, I would jokingly say that I lost a lot of money on him. But today he is one of the finest corporate salespersons I have ever seen. I think and also hope that we will work together for a very long time. You know why? Because we have a lot of fun working together. He is basically his own boss, and he is happy, healthy, and has a balanced lifestyle. We have really great people here, and that's how it all comes together."

In the end, Mark attributes a great deal of his success to his team. "John Wooden, the great basketball coach, once said, 'The main ingredient to stardom is the rest of the team.' I may be highly rated on someone's list right now, but I feel a bit guilty about this because, continuing with the basketball analogy, it's like we just won the game fifty to forty-nine, and I scored just one bucket, two points, but it just happens to be the last shot. So everybody saw me hit the last shot and carries me off the court in celebration when in fact my teammates scored forty-eight points."

Mark notes, "We can't ignore the importance of teams as we go forward. Ultimately, you form a team so that you can grow your business faster than would otherwise be possible. So first, you want to form a team that leverages your strengths and compensates for your weaknesses. Your team should enable you to do what you want to do and what you're good at, and allow you not to do the things that you're not best at. Secondly, you want to surround yourself with good people, people whom you want to work with and whom you care about, and who care about you and agree with your goals and values."

"And third," Mark continues, "you want to be with people who work well with your management style. To be blunt, I'm not a good manager, but I am a good leader. I articulate the objective and then let my team do what needs to be done. Somebody may have a process that makes no sense to me, but if it works for them and the team, and they're successful at it and achieve our goal, then that's fine with me. And because everybody makes mistakes, I don't want my people looking over their shoulders or second-guessing what they're doing. I just want them to work hard and be focused. While passion can come from the bottom up, it also clearly has to come from the team leader, and that's something I try to provide. Maybe in part it's because we're in Silicon Valley, but I really believe we should think, act, and feel like we're in a start-up."

THREE ATTRIBUTES OF SUCCESS

Mark's success is based upon at least three separate attributes:

1. A desire to be on the leading edge
2. A restless dissatisfaction that drives him to further success
3. A thoughtful, honest, and individualized problem-solving approach

First, Mark always strives to be on the leading edge of whatever business he's in. When asked what drives him, Mark pulls out another basketball analogy: "I want to play the game above the rim." Put differently, Mark is fueled by his desire to succeed and reach beyond himself. "You can be motivated by money, by fear, or by desire," he says. "But money is finite, and fear will condition how you think, sap your energy, and distract you. Only passion will drive you to reach your potential and achieve unlimited heights."

Second, despite his successes and pioneering practices, Mark is never quite satisfied, but instead yearns for greater and more complex challenges. "If you get one big account, most people would be happy with that and just sit and focus on that one account. I closed my first large stock plan with one of the biggest banks in the world, and then a couple of years later I had a summer where we gained five companies as clients—in different industries—that collectively were as large as that bank. I think a lot of people might have been satisfied with just one of them."

A lot of people, but not Mark Curtis. Even though he always advises his high-net-worth clients that they should know what "enough" is in terms of money and the ability to do what they want to do in their lives, with respect to his own practice, Mark hasn't yet reached that point. "It's normal to have a point in your life where you are there," Mark says. "You've made enough money or you are successful enough. I'm just not quite there yet, but fortunately we have a platform and a business model that is firing on all cylinders."

Finally, Mark enjoys working on unique challenges. He approaches one situation at a time, with a thoughtful and honest problem-solving approach attuned to each client's individual situation. "I have always viewed myself as a problem solver for my clients. I never defined myself as an investment consultant, or an expert at this or that. Instead, I've told my clients that the business I was in was whatever business they needed me to be in. If they told me what they were trying to accomplish, what their challenges and issues were, I might not know the answer right off, but if they allowed me to, I would go to work on their behalf."

Admitting when he doesn't know something has always been a source of strength for Mark. "Very early in my career I realized that the people who always felt the need to have a quick solution or to know everything, who thought they had to be knowledgeable, were demonstrating a weakness and probably not serving their clients well. What is better, if true, is to say, 'I don't know' or 'I am not sure.' Too often in this business, people are afraid of being embarrassed and want to be seen as having answers to everything. But especially in the high-net-worth market, I think it's almost a weakness to have an immediate response to every problem set you are presented with."

Mark continues, "Suppose you go to an expert with what you feel to be a complex personal issue. The expert says, 'Tell me about it,' and you do. After a few minutes, the expert says, 'Oh, that's easy. I've got a simple answer to that. I've heard ten guys just like you.' Well, your client more than likely doesn't want to hear that. They want you to say, 'Okay, let me see if I understand your issues. Let's spend time on this and figure out a solution.' I believe people want their advisors to be thoughtful and to focus on them."

Mark elaborates further on this point: "One of the things about my approach is that when I meet somebody for the first time, I'll take out a notepad and pen and say, 'Tell me about yourself.' People want advisors who listen to them."

"My biggest weakness when it comes to a new high-net-worth client," Mark continues, "is that I will often sit there and contemplate what to do. What should the asset allocation look like? Which managers should we use for income, liquidity, growth? Often I can't just spit out a recommendation. Some of my peers may think this is inefficient, that you need to have a standard model, and that as people come in, you characterize them relatively quickly and come up with recommendations. But by doing it my way, I develop a more personal relationship with the client. You can't control outcomes. Whatever happens is going to happen, but if you always do what you think is the right thing, your clients are going to know that."

LUCK AND LONGEVITY

Circling back, trying to pin down how Mark became the number one financial advisor in the country, two intertwined themes consistently emerge: luck or good fortune and consistency or longevity.

With respect to luck, on the one hand Mark will admit that, "One of my skills is knowing my business in depth. I'm very quantitative about my business. I come in on weekends and review various metrics related to it." On the other hand, Mark will frequently diminish his own accomplishments: "I don't want to profess that I'm some great business guy when the reality is that I've been able to put myself into highly leveraged opportunities and have benefited from the platform I've built, a platform where lightning seems to continue to strike."

Mark's claim that lightning just happens to continue to strike "over and over again" where he happens to be is reminiscent of a story about Ben Hogan, one of the greatest golfers of all time. After Hogan won a major tournament, a reporter asked him how he was able to hit so many miraculous shots under such pressure. Hogan responded, "I guess I'm just lucky." The reporter said, "But Mr. Hogan, you practice more than any golfer who ever lived." And Hogan replied, "Well, the more I practice, the luckier I get."

Nowhere does Mark speak of his good fortune more than with respect to the longevity of his relationships with clients, money managers, team members, and other people in his life, including his wife, Jackie. ("I was the first person my wife met at Stanford. She got off the bus, sat on her suitcase, and I walked up and met her. We were engaged a week later, and have been together now for thirty years. How lucky is that?") "I have been blessed," Mark says. "You look at my life, and I've had the same team, and the same clients, and many of the same money managers, my whole career."

But there is a pattern to these fabulous relationships. Mark will meet someone, develop the relationship, provide great service and friendship, and stick with that person over time. One example is Mark's first third-party business relationship. "My dad worked with a CPA who sold his firm and took a sabbatical. When he came back he couldn't practice accounting because of a noncompete agreement, but his clients still wanted his advice. So he became a registered investment advisor, providing fee-based advisory services. We began a business dialogue and I gave him access to many of the top money managers. I had my first conversation with him in 1982, and today, decades later, a significant portion of his clients' assets are custodied with me, and he has built a tremendously successful business. In fact he is a Winner's Circle Independent Advisor, and when his son wanted to transition from public accounting to his father's business, he came and trained with me first."

The same pattern of longevity holds with respect to Mark's individual high-net-worth clients. "If I look back at my original retail high-net-worth clients, it's amazing to me that twenty-five years later, I still have them. I'm having dinner with my first individual client and his wife next week. My second individual client is still a client too, and I'll also see him next week. All along the way, I've kept many individual clients. It may be a function of where I've lived, but my clients have all prospered independently of what they did with me, and they brought me with them to experience new and exciting challenges."

With respect to the longevity of his money managers, Mark says, "I met people along the way who I thought were really good people as well as great managers and I've hired them to manage my clients' assets, and they've turned out to be fabulous in the long term. I've been so lucky to have made good asset allocation decisions, and to have hired wonderful, honest money managers with high integrity who have been the best at what they do. This has really enhanced my career."

Significantly, Mark makes good, informed choices and then sticks with those choices over time. "One of the few institutional accounts I've lost," he says, "happened when they fired the head of the institution and had a whole new investment committee come in. The new head of the committee came to me and said, 'You've had this account for thirteen years. You have five managers, and I see you've made only three changes in thirteen years. What do you have to say about that?' I said, 'I'm sorry about those three changes.' He said, 'What do you mean?' I said, "Well, if I had done my job correctly in 1989, you wouldn't have had any changes. But unfortunately, you've got to change things every now and then.' He said, 'No, no. How come we haven't had more changes?' I said, 'I'm sorry, but if I did everything right in 1989 you might not have had to change anything.'"

With respect to his team members, Mark makes the same point. "Something that's unique about me is that many of my team members have been with me for many, many years. Who would ever have known that I would be so lucky? In our business, the longevity of our team is extraordinary, and you can't overlook the impact of such longevity. Having the same people working together for a long time allows us to simplify our processes while increasing the overall level of service that we deliver to our clients."

Mark sums it up this way: "The keys to my success have been the same clients, same team members, and many of the same money managers. If you think about my peer group, they are looking at attribution analyses, asset allocations, alpha, and all the various quantifiable perspectives. Don't get me wrong: I do believe in all of these. But honestly, I would just as soon meet somebody and spend an hour with them asking them what they do and how they do it. I've met great people in my career, and I hate to use the word 'blessed' again, but I'm just being blunt. I've been blessed by great people."

Mark feels that he's been blessed in other ways too. "Today I live in the same house my family moved into when I was just a few months old. How lucky is that?" He adds: "I'm going on three decades with the same firm and I've been healthy the whole time. I also have wonderful family support—my dad was in this business, everybody in my family understands the business I'm in, and they all encourage me to pursue the business and my career wholeheartedly. I've been very fortunate in my life, and there's no doubt that luck has been a major component of my success." (Contrary to Mark's repeated statements that he's been lucky all these years, his success is more likely the result of his extraordinary ability to anticipate clients' changing needs and react accordingly.)

Mark also reflects on one last piece of so-called luck. "Another key to my success," he says, "is that people have wanted me to succeed. I don't know why this is, but I feel people have really rooted for me along the way."

SUCCESS MANTRAS AND FORMULAS

If the other side of luck is practice and skill, then it makes sense that over the years, as he built up his four lines of business focus, Mark would have developed quite a few proven success mantras, or formulas. These include:

- "Your greatest strength is your greatest weakness."
- "View competitors as opportunities."
- "Always think and act like a business owner."
- "Focus on maximizing revenue opportunities, not revenue."
- "All roads lead to retail."
- "Client acquisition is our greatest cost."
- "Simplify the complicated."
- "Identify trends."
- "Deliver the organization."
- "Manage the brand."
- "Take care of your business, and your business will take care of you."

With respect to launching and running a successful business, Mark has three interconnected success formulas. First, he says, "You should always think and act like a business owner. You can't sit around and complain about the firm or this or that issue. The one great opportunity you have in this business when you first come out of training is that you are immediately a small business owner. I have always thought and acted like I own my business." A corollary success formula is this: "Always take care of your business." "If you take care of your business," Mark says, "your business will take care of you. Your business and your career are living things that accompany you wherever you go; so always take care of them."

Second, Mark states that an advisor "should not look to maximize revenues, but look to maximize revenue opportunities. For example," he continues, "I read a study once that said if you sell a client one product or service you have an eighteen-month life expectancy with the client. If you sell a client two products or services, you have a thirty-month life expectancy, and if you sell three or more products or services, you have an unlimited life expectancy. Especially in the corporate and institutional marketplaces, we have found that if you have multiple revenue opportunities with a client you can be more competitive than if you are a point solution provider. So, if you're competing with a point solution provider who is doing one thing and you're doing three things, you can compete more aggressively on that one point solution."

One way that Mark has maximized revenues is to recognize that "All roads lead to retail." Early in his career, Mark says, "I had two mentors. One of them was an institutional consultant, and he taught me first that the whole goal was to make everything simple for your clients. The second thing he told me was that if I was in front of an institutional board and one of the board members later on asked me if he could be my client, I should tell him 'No.' Then my other mentor in corporate services, one of the smartest guys I've ever met, said that I shouldn't do any retail with the plan participants—that if I did, the corporations I was serving would view me as being solicitous and that would put me in conflict with them. Well, *I listened and took what I could from those two mentors in regard to the institutional side, but in regard to the retail side, I did just the opposite.*"

Mark's third business success mantra is, "Client acquisition is our greatest cost. Therefore you have to think about ways to extend the life expectancy of a relationship by doing as many things for the client as possible." For Mark, this means being willing to invest in his business. "I am willing to do whatever I have to do to invest in the future of my business, including investing in a business opportunity for a time. I think it's absurd in our industry that people want a twelve- or eighteen-month payback on an investment. If our clients are willing to invest with us, why are we not willing to invest in our own businesses?"

Mark also feels it's very important to "Simplify the complicated on behalf of the client." "It's one of our ongoing goals," Mark says. "We talk with our clients about a lot of issues with a lot of moving parts. In any kind of decision-making process with lots of variables, it's up to us to simplify the process for the client. We are very good at managing processes for decision making and prioritization, and this allows our clients to make better decisions and help us to manage their complex issues."

A POSITIVE PROPHET OF POSITIVE PROFIT

Mark Curtis is very positive about the future, and not just the future of the industry. In fact, you could even call him a dyed-in-the-wool optimist, which from his perspective is a very good thing to be. "To succeed in our business," he says, "you have to be optimistic. The stock market is not a zero sum game. And I just really think that the difference sometimes between the people who are very successful in our business and those who never quite reach their potential is that the latter are not optimistic. And if you're not optimistic in our business, you'll get crushed more often than not and in more ways than one. I'm very optimistic about the future, and I believe that's one of the keys to my success."

With respect to the future of the industry, Mark sees a "golden age of advice giving on its way if you have an advice model, and you structure your business accordingly. Why? In the past people in our business have thought their role was to supply a product. But what happens when the costs of generating a good product decline? Or when there are fewer barriers for new providers to enter a market? Further, with the number of investment vehicles available today, it's easier to allocate assets efficiently and add more diversification to a client's portfolio than even five or ten years ago. While we are becoming more sophisticated about what we do and how we do it, things should not be getting more complicated for the client."

"As an advisor," Mark continues, "you are helped by the wonderful benefit of new technologies to add more value. So as this continues, as more complex and effective investment vehicles become available, you are going to need to distinguish yourself somehow. If you are on the outside looking in, everything that's available today looks more complicated. But if you are on the inside, and you understand things and can simplify them, then your advice will be highly valued."

Speaking of highly valued, Mark clearly feels blessed by his family, including his wife and two sons. "Quite frankly," he says, "I'm only going to be a parent once in my life, so I focus on enjoying being a parent as much as I can. When one of my sons was a high school senior and the other a freshman, both were starting centers, for the varsity and JV basketball teams, respectively. Between the two of them they played a fifty-plus game schedule. And despite how busy I was with travel and client demands, I made it to forty-eight out of fifty games."

Positive about his business, optimistic about the world, and feeling blessed and lucky in so many ways, Mark Curtis takes nothing for granted. "You can't be a dinosaur," he says. "Always listen to the market so you can try to be ahead of it. That's what creates the opportunity. And ask yourself what it is about your business, today, that you value the most, and what you can do to increase the value of your business to you, to your partners and team members, and to your clients. If you can focus on what you like doing, and on the best ways to grow your business, then you'll have more fun at work, you'll work harder and longer, and you'll be able to enjoy all the good things that come out of your work." It seems that the harder he's worked, the luckier Mark Curtis has become, to the benefit of the many clients, team members, and countless others who've been touched by his efforts.

CHAPTER 6: THE HALBFINGER GROUP

UBS FINANCIAL SERVICES
NEW YORK, NEW YORK

(From Left to Right) Adele Lake, Paula Christiansen, Stacy Seip, Amy Provost, Martin Halbfinger, Kaysian Roberts, Clifford Stober, Gerty Simon, Steven Kleiner, Ron Shapira

As Marty Halbfinger tells it, "My story is a real simple one. Born and bred in the Bronx, I came from a lower-middle-class family of European Jewish immigrants. My parents moved from Poland to Palestine to New York because they heard the streets here were paved with gold. Although their dream didn't exactly work out that way—my father worked as a unionized house painter, a laborer, who never made more than $15,000 a year in his entire life—maybe he hoped that their dream would pass a generation, and that I'd be the lucky one to actually be able to mine gold."

Looking at how things stand today, one would have to say that the father's dream for the son has indeed come true. Marty, his partner Clifford Stober, and the other eight individuals who constitute the Halbfinger Group manage over $2 billion in assets for their clientele, with nearly $900 million in alternatives and the rest mainly in traditional long-only managers and fixed income. But the real gold being mined by Marty and his team isn't monetary gold, it's the *relationship gold* that comes from truly caring about, listening to, and holistically serving their clients.

"What I do that really turns me on," Marty says, "is taking care of people. I really believe that's what I do for a living. My mother wanted me to be a lawyer, and my father wanted me to be a doctor, but I chose another profession where I'm helping people on a daily basis. Every day I'm affecting one of the two most important psychological underpinnings of every family's life, which is money. Everybody has the same problem: 'What do I do with my money? How do I make sure my financial decisions benefit my family?'"

By caring deeply, by remaining incredibly focused, and by being willing and able to reinvent himself, his team, and his practice to adjust to the times, Marty has been able to provide his clients the kind of answers to these questions that have enabled him to build one of the premier financial advisory practices in the country. From his humble beginnings to the deep charitable commitments in which he and his wife are engaged, from his stick-to-it-ive-ness to his cutting-edge alternatives research and client service, Marty has put together a life that is a picture of great success. "I think I'm in the best profession in the entire world," he says, "and I'm the luckiest guy in the entire universe. I came from nothing, and I've been blessed with the ability to be in an exciting industry that never has two days in a row that look the same."

HUMBLE, HARD-WORKING BEGINNINGS

"My parents never really Americanized," Marty says. "I was the youngest of three children, and we all lived in a four-room apartment. All of my friends' parents had more money and were better educated, and I always felt that there was something better for me out there. So you could say that in my formative years, the lack of money was a critical issue in my life. But the issue wasn't money itself; it was about having enough when I raised my own family so that there would be a horn of plenty instead of a horn of want. I wasn't one of those kids who felt the grass was always greener on the other side, but I knew I wanted to be involved in some way in a business that would allow me to share in the American dream."

Marty started working when he was a teenager. "My father's $15,000 a year of earned income wasn't a lot of money to go around, so if I wanted money, I had to go out and work for it. I started working part-time jobs when I was thirteen, literally delivering chickens in the neighborhood for a local butcher. I made quarter tips, and thought I was in heaven. Also, because my dad was an immigrant and never got into baseball, even though I lived only eighteen blocks from Yankee Stadium, I never once attended a game until somebody else took me. In order to go back again, I got a job selling peanuts at ball games. I went on from there to become a busboy at a restaurant, and in late high school and early college—I went to Yeshiva University High School and then Yeshiva University in Washington Heights—I became a waiter in the Catskills mountains resort hotels. All you needed to do was be willing to work fourteen- to sixteen-hour days, and for that they gave you money ... which was an amazing thing when you had none."

"Those were my kind of jobs," Marty notes. "They were all people-related jobs, which was very crucial to my formative years. Although I clearly didn't understand it then, my strong suit has always been people. After finishing school, like every confused college kid of the day in the late 1960s and early 1970s, I was groping for what I wanted to do. But after a certain point I always knew it was going to be related to Wall Street."

Marty knew this, in part, because he had already been investing in stocks. "I started investing when I was a teenager in high school," he says. "I could not tell you that I was a successful investor back then—sometimes I won, sometimes I lost—but I did cut my teeth on it and found it very exciting to invest in stocks. And I knew because of this that when I got out of college, I wanted to be involved in the markets in some way. From the time I was in high school until now, I've never stopped investing."

BECOMING A BROKER: EIGHTH TIME'S THE CHARM

Marty's road to becoming a broker was not an easy one. "I actually went out and interviewed with *seven* Wall Street firms to get into their registered broker training programs, and I was turned down by all seven. I absolutely couldn't get past the application and interview. Basically, it all sounded the same when I listened to their responses: 'You don't have any connections. You don't come from the right family. You don't have the right background. Other than your interest in the market, you don't have any of the things we want.'"

"I did all the things I thought I was supposed to do," Marty continues, "but obviously I wasn't a very good interviewee, and I wasn't very convincing. I wasn't hired because I just told it like it was, and it's very hard to break into this business without contacts. Most people got hired in those days because they knew someone. I had a very limited Rolodex at that point in my life—actually, I'm not sure I knew what a Rolodex was back then. I had no family money and no family contacts. No matter where I went, I couldn't get into a broker training program."

Marty persevered, though, and found his way into the industry anyway. "I finally was hired into an operational training program at a small firm, where I worked in the back office. I did a rotation and learned how to process paper and at the age of twenty-five or twenty-six became a manager of the department that processed buys and sells of transactions. I was inching closer to the business but was clearly on the wrong side of the window. I had a department of twenty-five people, but was not enjoying one minute of what I was doing."

"Still, I held onto my dream. I knew that I really wanted to work on the brokerage end as a financial advisor, or stockbroker, as it was then called. Well, I had a friend who worked in the personnel department at Dean Witter. We got together one weekend and he said, 'There's an opening in a department here that you should really take a look at. You'll have to take a sales test as part of the interview, but you'll do fine.'"

"This was the Dean Witter department where they taught you about the technical underpinnings of the market, and then had you write market letters for the sales force. At times you would also be asked by different regional offices to go out and talk about your view of the market based on the technical movement of money. So I took the test, got a decent mark, and did that job for four years. Then one thing led to another and different Dean Witter managers started saying, 'If you ever want to be a broker, call me.' I said, 'I'm ready.'"

"So I talked to the manager of the Madison Avenue office," Marty continues, "and he said, 'Forget about what we normally pay trainees. I've seen you in operation for years, and you're ready for this firm. Come and work for me for two years, and you'll never need me again.' At that point I was almost twenty-nine years old—I like to tell my kids that I'm a late bloomer—and that's how I started in the business, with basically no money and just the contacts I had started to build up as a young single person in New York."

PHASE I: BUILDING HIS BUSINESS AND YIELDING SUCCESS

"As you go through your career in this business, you reinvent yourself at least one or two times," Marty says. "So I started out, as everybody did, with cold calling. First you go through family—that was easy for me, it took one phone call and two hang-ups. Then you get a list to call, or, in my case, I had lots of friends all over New York whom I told about my new career and what I was now doing on this end of the business. Significantly, one person told me this: You can always talk about the stock market, and you'll be right, then you'll be right again, and then you'll be wrong. So unless you want your career to be about two rights and a wrong, you need to find a better way to do things."

"So, as a raw rookie, what I decided to do was to go out and sell yields. The concept was that people needed more return, which was the case then. Today, the world is about how you can give your clients a good return for lower risk than they need to take or should take. So the first part of my business, the beginning of my career, was all about yield stocks, utilities, and bonds. That was all I ever did. There's a reason why there's a learning curve in this business, and it was very slow going in the beginning."

"What I always enjoyed the most was the client contact. I found that over time, as my business began to build, I was spending as much time counseling people as I was in selling them something."

"My first client," Marty continues, "was someone I met in one of the Catskills hotels where I had worked as a waiter. He was a guest and I was the waiter, but we became friends and stayed in contact. Again, my Rolodex consisted of people I had met in my jobs and people I socialized with as a single guy in New York. I'd like to tell you it was glamorous, but it wasn't. It was paying the rent, and doing the things we all try to do when we start becoming more independent. And while most of my social friends didn't have a lot of money, they might have had the ear of their parents. So I built my career by conservatively advising my friends and asking them if there were other members of their families that I could help as well."

"Importantly," Marty notes, "my personal life and my business life are basically one, and it's been that way from the day I started in this business. My attitude has always been that if I can't manage the money of my friends and family—both of whom I care a lot about— then why would I be able to manage the money of somebody else I don't know nearly as well? Today, almost all of my friends are my clients, and my closest friends all happen to be my clients, which is one of the reasons I enjoy what I do so much."

"I never planned it to be this way," Marty adds, "but that's the way it's always been. A lot of people divide their lives into 'work' over here and 'life' over there. But my answer to anyone who's ever asked me if there's a conflict in combining my life and my work is that 'I do what I do rather well, and while I make mistakes like every other human being, I care more.' And I think it's the caring that really is the essence of our job if we're doing it right."

A BREAKTHROUGH MOMENT

"Back then," Marty says, "I asked my friends to 'Tell your dad what I'm doing and let me sit down with him. Just make an introduction and tell him to give me thirty minutes of his time. You can be there, I won't bore him, and I'm sure we'll have a good time.' I got a lot of 'no's' and then every once in a while I'd get a 'yes.' I began to see that my friends' folks were obviously much older and wiser, and typically had many brokers, so it wasn't about winning all of their business. It was simply about getting a *piece* of their business and earning my way to the rest, which is how I've always grown my business. I wanted to start wherever somebody would allow me to start, and a couple of times it worked."

"Often," Marty ruefully notes, "I'd be asked what my favorite stock was. But I learned very early in my career that that wasn't a good question to answer. You'd either be right or wrong, and if they bought the stock but didn't buy it through you, they'd always remember that, and if they bought it through you and it didn't work out, that's what they'd always remember. That's why I always turned the subject back to yield, saying, 'Here's what I think you ought to do to get a higher return then you're getting elsewhere.'"

"At one point," Marty continues, "I had a breakthrough moment involving a very old, dear friend of mine. Like me, he didn't have any money. But I made the request to him about talking to his father, and he immediately said, 'You want to meet my father? You've already met him socially at our house, but do you really want to meet him on business? He's a pain in the you-know-where. He's really tough, and you're not going to have a good time. He absolutely eats people for breakfast.' I of course said, 'Yes, I really want to meet him.'"

"So one day I met his father, and we talked for an hour about yield, and we talked about bonds, and we talked about how not to lose money. And nothing came of it. Then he called me back a month or two later, and he said, 'Marty, you going to be in the office at three o'clock?' 'Sure,' I said. He said, 'Well, then, I'd like to come in and see you.' So I said, 'Great, I'll be here.'"

"And he comes in—this is a true story—with two shopping bags covered with newspaper, so all you could see was the newspaper on top. We started chatting, and he said, 'Look, do you know what's in the shopping bags?' I shook my head. 'These are municipal bonds. We've been talking about yields and bonds, and I'm too old to be clipping coupons and going to the vault every time there's a coupon to be clipped. I want you to take these bonds and keep them. Where's your vault?' He had twenty years of bonds that he kept in his own safety deposit box. He'd never trusted a brokerage house."

"Well, there was between $1 and $2 million worth of bonds in those two shopping bags, and he had taken the train to my office. Of course, our office manager panicked, because there was $1 or $2 million worth of bonds in shopping bags sitting on my desk. So we took them into a conference room and got the operations person to count them out, bond by bond. Then we deposited the bonds in our vault, which wasn't on the premises.

"It was really a transformative experience, a breakthrough for me, as it was for my friend's dad. *And it was a turning point in my career, not because of the money, but because I really began to understand that I could help people.* We all come to the table with different fears and different anxieties. We're all human, and much of what we are is a matter of what our life has been up until this point. He decided to trust me, for whatever reason."

"I've also realized that over the course of my career there have been moments that really changed me. Here, it was because I found out I could help. I found out I had something to offer. And it was all because *one client believed enough in me and in what he saw in me to give me a chance to help him.* To some degree, the rest of my career has been nothing more than an evolution of that chapter."

"Now," Marty continues, "up until that time most of my client accounts were in the tens, fifties, and hundreds of thousands of dollars. I didn't have any million-dollar clients until my friend's dad came in with the shopping bags full of bonds. He was the biggest client I had ever had, which is another reason it was a mile marker for me. No question, it changed what I was able to think about. It empowered me, enabled me to believe in myself. And while it was a circuitous path to getting there, in that moment I not only knew I could help people, but I had gained the confidence to seek bigger clients and to ask those I was already working with for bigger things."

"By the way," Marty continues. "My friend's dad has passed away, but my friend, whom I've known since I was fifteen, was best man at my wedding. He became a dentist, and while neither of us ever knew that our relationship would evolve into a financial one, I now manage money for him, his two siblings in Israel, and multiple grandchildren all over the country and in four other countries, all to the tune of about $50 million. And this all started with his dad, who never told his kids what he had. They never knew they had money because he kept putting every extra dollar into real estate or municipal bonds."

BUILDING SUCCESS BEYOND THE COMFORT ZONE

"Even though I'd had a breakthrough, this was still the father of a friend, and I knew that for me to really grow my business, I'd have to get out of my comfort zone. The way I did this," Marty explains, "was by working with charitable organizations, where the work that I was doing meant something to my heart. I got involved not because it would help my business, but because giving back to the community was very important in my life and my family's life on an everyday basis."

"Through those communal efforts, I met a lot of people who, aside from the friends that I grew up with, became the core of my world. Many of them were from major New York families that I never, ever would have been able to touch base with on my own given my upbringing. Being exposed to these people enabled me to gain the comfort that I could talk across the table from somebody who then might have had $10 million and who would maybe now have a billion dollars."

"Part of how this enabled me to get beyond my comfort zone was that for any given charity, I always gravitated to being the fund raiser in charge of development. With one particular charity, the way they would raise money would be to have dinners and then read aloud cards that would say, 'So and so family was nice enough to donate. Isn't that wonderful?' I would be the one whose job it was to read those cards, and I'd always add a quip to it like, 'This dynamic duo.' And I would call them the 'dynamic tennis duo,' or say 'two warmer people you've never met,' or 'two of the most sensitive souls on this earth.' To this day, thirty years later, I'll go out to dinner with some of these people and they'll say, 'You were so full of baloney then.' But they never forgot what I said that evening."

"So, the second big revelation for me, after realizing I could help people, was that because of a common cause or a love for a particular charity—by a kind of accident, really—I could find myself in a room with a lot of other caring people who were much, much wealthier than anyone I would ever normally come into contact with. This was a great source of business for me, because it naturally evolved from people's knowing what I did for a living and ultimately wanting somebody with integrity, someone they could trust."

"Really," Marty adds, "this is where much of our business comes from. It's normally not because you're the most brilliant investment person who was ever put on this earth. It's because other people really think of you as being caring and trustworthy, and having integrity. They can just see and feel how passionate you are about what you do, and about doing right by them and their families. That's how businesses are built. For example, there's one man who runs a multibillion-dollar corporation whom I first met at a charity dinner where I called the card for his donation and said something he liked. We became friends first and then started to do business later. So many of my clients come from that early part of my community involvement, and then they refer more clients after that. It's always been about which people I gravitate toward and who gravitates toward me regardless of whether they're business owners, owners of institutions, doctors, lawyers, dentists, or anything else. My specialty, if anything, is that I'm a good listener, but it's never been one particular kind of person who's been attracted to me."

PHASE II: A FAMILY FOCUS WITH
A WOMAN PARTNER

"It was yield only in my early days," Marty says, "but things evolved to the point where I couldn't really rationalize the way I was serving clients. So I decided to take in a partner, Nina Alexander, whom I had met through one of the charities I was involved with." Unfortunately, Nina passed away in 1999 from colon cancer.

"She was with me for twenty years," Marty says, "and she used to be dubbed my 'second wife.' We were as close as any two people could be in the world, and we were very, very early in the game of team formation among the brokerage houses. Now, of course, everybody is all about teams. I'm not saying I was preaching teams early on. Sometimes you just walk into things and they feel right. And if they feel right, you pursue them. That's what really happened with the two of us."

After working at Dean Witter for a few years, and in conjunction with meeting Nina, Marty was enticed by a manager to move over to Rotan Mosley (which was eventually acquired by PaineWebber, which in turn was eventually acquired by UBS). "Rotan Mosley was a twelve-branch, Texas-based firm dealing mainly in oil," Marty says. "We went there because we wanted a smaller atmosphere where we thought we could nurture the team concept."

"Nina and I got together twenty-seven years ago, when I had already been in the business maybe four years," Marty notes. "We started to create a family-focused business, where our main goal was taking care of families. I brought Nina in as a partner because she was so caring and I thought her personality perfectly complemented mine. Everyone loved doing business with her. Some clients were even reluctant to do business with me when she passed away. The opportunity for women in this business is just astronomical."

PHASE III: RESEARCHING ALTERNATIVES
FOR DIVERSIFICATION

"I had another idea in the early 1990s," Marty says, "which brought about another transformation of our business. By now we were with PaineWebber, which was a big, wonderful firm with a lot to offer, but we were dependent solely on their research. So in the fall of ninety-one, I petitioned the powers that be—I've always had the luck of having great people listen to my story—to allow me to go out and interview people in charge of hedge funds and alternative investments around the country. I had a number of friends who were hedge fund managers, and I thought this was a great diversification tool for our clients."

"I repeated that this would be a great way to diversify the business, and the powers that be said, 'Okay, but you've got to make sure that you tell us what you're doing.' We started off by putting $250,000 with one investor in a fund that we found and that was approved by the firm. We had to do all of our own due diligence, so I went to school and learned about the alternatives business by traveling around the country, interviewing managers, and learning what they did, day in and day out."

"I met some of the most talented people I've ever been fortunate enough to encounter," Marty says. "They didn't need any help from the brokerage houses, but as I met with them, I found that they still wanted to raise outside money. So if they managed funds that I really felt complemented a client's investment profile, I started to look more deeply into them and have them approved by our firm."

"From that original $250,000 investment in the early 1990s, today we now have almost $900 million in alternatives alone. At first hedge funds were a new specialty addition, but they became a very valuable tool in a much bigger asset class than I ever envisioned. So, after our nearly two decades in alternatives and many hundreds of manager interviews later, our clients get what I feel is something special. The point, however, is that I didn't get involved just because it was exciting; like everything else I've ever done, it was motivated by what was right for the client. My clients needed to be diversified away from the research of any one firm in order to better withstand the vagaries of the economy and the market. And while nobody was using the phrase 'wealth preservation' at the time, where that was an overriding objective I wanted my clients to have exposure to talented hedge fund managers."

"So while it was another idea during a different time, it was the same rationale—doing what's right for the clients, that is, diversify them and reduce their risk while trying to grow their money. Now we're a team of ten people, and we are providing the kind of total diversification that we felt we needed to offer our clients all along. There's a fixed-income component, an equity component, and an alternatives component. And the equity component now has an international component. It didn't have one ten years ago, because then we didn't think it was necessary, but now we do."

EVOLVING TIMES AND TEAMS

Marty believes that the kind of comprehensive service and focus that today's clients need can be delivered only by a team of highly competent professionals. This explains why every member of Marty's ten-person team is licensed. But when asked how he formulated and built his team, Marty quickly points out that, "I would be lying if I told you there was a road map. Each of the pieces was added in a patchwork quilt, with no initial idea of what the whole quilt was going to look like. There wasn't any model, other than always putting ourselves in the client's shoes and looking at things from their perspective. We've ultimately found that this is the best way to serve the client."

Stepping back in time, Marty notes, "It was the partnership with Nina that really transformed my business into a team. Nina and I went through the normal ups and downs of team building, much of it by trial and error. I'd like to say it's a science, but it was never a science for me. It was whatever felt right at the time. When we became a partnership the two of us had one assistant who serviced both of our businesses. By the nature of our very different personalities, each of us had clients who preferred to talk with one of us. Neither of us cared who the client felt comfortable with as long as we were able to get our points across to them. As you might expect, more women naturally migrated to Nina, and more men to me. Out of that we formed an understanding that we needed to be very aware of what was going on so we could cover for each other."

"So that's how we began running things as a team. There was no other team in the office at that time, but all along I've been blessed with people who've been willing to listen to my ideas and say 'go run with it.' At that time, I think we were one of only five Dean Witter teams in the entire country out of two hundred branch offices. Then as time went by, it became clear to many brokerage houses that teams ultimately made sense, and now the team concept will never go away. At a certain point we added another assistant, so we were a team with two assistants, and then we brought on a third assistant."

"After Nina got sick—somewhere in the middle of her five-year battle with colon cancer—we hired Cliff Stober, who is now the other lead member of my team, as the third person on the team from the financial advisor side. I was doing most of the equity investing and half the relationship tending, and so Cliff was a great complement because he was good with relationships and also had a fixed-income background and could support that side of the business. His broader portfolio management skills also enhanced our overall process. The need was there, and we filled it. And luckily for us, we did so by hiring a professional with institutional money management experience, a competitive advantage that is uncommon in the private client business."

"At a certain point," Marty continues, "we started bringing in more and more clients, mainly through referrals. We soon had the need for additional capabilities in our group, specifically someone who was very operationally oriented. We didn't want to have the basis of our relationships with our clients interfered with by someone misspelling a name on a statement, or a check or income calendar not arriving, or something that was asked for quarterly not being there. There are a hundred items you can check off on a list, and if we fail to do one of those items right, the client will be ticked off. *It's not only about managing the client's money; it's about managing the relationship.* So while Nina and I, and then Cliff, managed the financial end of the relationship, there was a whole other part, the day-to-day operations, which needed to be managed by others. Also, when I don't have to focus on operational issues, I can concentrate better on the management of money."

"In many branch offices the branch staff performs the operational functions. But our managers have, through the years, allowed us to segment our team so that we have people who perform only the operational functions, who concentrate solely on our clients and then interface with the operations of the rest of the office. We've always found that our clients expect great service, so we basically underpromise and overdeliver. Now, if you are one of ten teams, or one of thirty or forty or eighty brokers in a branch office, how could you possibly ensure that what you want done will get done if you are all vying for the attention of a particular operations person in the office?"

"In our view, you had to have the staffing before you had the money coming in. If you didn't, then you weren't going to deliver what you said you were going to deliver to the clients you already had. So we always grew our team by being one staff member ahead of the growth of the business. Whatever it takes in today's world to give the clients what they want, we need enough people to help deliver that."

TODAY'S TEAM

More properly known as The Halbfinger Group, the team is functionally structured as a vertical partnership. "This is a vertical team, where everything emanates down from me," Marty says. "We do tend to sit down together as a committee to make decisions, and I can be outvoted by the majority. But ultimately, I will always do what is right for the client. My bottom line is that the buck stops on my desk and in my hand, and I feel totally responsible for everything that happens to our family of clients, one way or another."

"Today we have ten people on the team," Marty continues. "Cliff works with me on setting and executing strategies for our clients and our business. Ron Shapira assists us on client proposals and business development. Paula Christiansen and Gerty Simon are on the front lines as client service representatives and speaking with the clients all day long on a wide array of issues. Then we have two operations experts, Adele Lake and Stacy Seip, who also work with clients all day long. So between Paula, Gerty, Adele, and Stacy, we really have four people who are in contact with clients all day long. The reason we've separated out Paula and Gerty here is that we've found they can be much more effective if the other two team members handle most of the operational matters."

"Then we've got three analysts," Marty continues, "an area that never existed when I started in the business—Amy Provost, Kaysian Roberts, and Steve Kleiner. They are responsible for preparing all statistical reviews and analyses of client portfolios and presentations to prospective clients. They also support our work in regard to selection of managers and review of hedge funds, an area in which Cliff and I lead our team and to which we dedicate a great deal of our own time."

"Now I would not be telling the truth if I said we didn't struggle with the growth of the team. There were times when we weren't sure exactly how to separate out the responsibilities. But what naturally occurred is that we learned to guide our clients to talk to different team members about different needs."

"Ultimately," Marty summarizes, "we grew the team based on the needs of the client and the needs of the business. Clearly, it's about the team and not about me, and I could not have grown this business to where it is today without the team. The point is that the team delivers the client experience, because that experience is the real cornerstone of our business."

SEGMENTING THEIR CLIENT BASE AND DELIVERING FOUR TOUCHES

"Our top 120 clients," Marty says, "probably amount to 80 if not 90 percent of our business. The evolution of having a top 120 occurred because of client demand. The larger clients simply needed more of our time, and in order to go into life planning, estate planning strategies, and other in-depth matters, we needed larger blocks of time and deeper expertise. Long ago we understood the need to segment our business to take account of this."

"But paring down our client base—which we know that we need to do; everyone in our industry talks about how necessary it is—has been very hard for me. I still have clients from when I started in this business. Some people just need us, and we'll do anything we can to help them. When it comes to new business, most of our referrals are bigger in size and while we make exceptions, we generally have a $5 million minimum. Other team members generally handle our smaller clients, but I'll find a way to get to them one way or another if they want to talk to me."

Even with segmenting, how do ten separate individuals make sure that they do, in fact, stay on top of everything? To begin with, Marty and his team further segment their top 120 clients into two groups, the Alpha and Omega Groups, to make sure they are receiving rapid attention, the best possible service, and multiple "personal touches" each year. "There are two different teams," Marty says, "including one of our analysts, one of our client representatives, and either Cliff or I, or both of us, which handle all aspects of the sixty-odd clients on each of the lists. Of course, our top 120 families might have ten accounts apiece, counting kids, IRAs, pensions, husbands and wives, marital trusts, etc. The individuals on the Alpha and Omega teams become the key contact people for those clients, although if the client calls in the morning and needs something, it will go to one of the operational people."

"The most important thing we've instituted in the last year," Marty continues, "is an action-oriented approach to enhancing the client experience. We demand that every one of our top clients is 'touched' throughout the year. That means that we have at least one highly detailed review per year, or more, depending on the specific needs of each client. Then the two teams are responsible for making sure that other touches occur in between the meetings; we call those 'family touch points.' Basically, we want to know what's new and different in the client's life, what's occurred."

"This idea came about from something that we didn't do very well," Marty notes. "What we don't want is to have the client think we are here managing their money in isolation, because if something happens—if someone died and nobody told us, or if a grown kid needs money to go into business—and we are not understanding the psychological dynamics as well as the movement of wealth, then we are missing key components of the client's need. We had two situations where we weren't apprised of something material that happened to the client between meetings. Not only can this put business at risk, but it goes against our core philosophy of putting ourselves in the client's shoes. And while we were already working at staying on top of our clients' life changes, we realized we had to formalize how we went about doing it. Also, I should give credit where credit is due: I took home ideas on this issue from a seminar I attended at one of the *Barron's* Winner's Circle Top Advisor conferences. Sharing best practices with other top professionals truly helped us improve and institutionalize our approach, to the benefit of our clients. These multiple touches have very much become part of the client experience, and that has enhanced the way our clients feel about us."

"These touches have become a real anchor in our clients' experience," Marty continues. "Our analysts review the data on each client's performance each quarter, so we have real reasons to reach out to the clients to update them at least twice a year, not only on performance, but on any changes we want to recommend. And now we are trying to increase our understanding of what's going on in their personal lives as well. As a result of all this, each of the Alpha and Omega teams is more focused than ever on their sixty families, and each of the sixty families now knows who they really need to go to, and they feel they are getting more service from us than they ever did before."

What about regularly scheduled meetings, to keep everyone on the team up to speed? "We use to just have team members talk to each other, and most items would get discussed," Marty says. "But as our business grew we found out that this wasn't being scientific enough, so we now have one weekly team meeting that everyone attends, normally on Monday or Tuesday afternoon away from the pressures of the market. Then we have subgroup meetings for the Alpha and Omega teams to go over whatever is new and to make sure we are focused on addressing the clients' needs. We also meet with the analyst group once a week to make sure everyone knows what our priorities are and to answer any questions that may come up."

"I am a big believer," Marty adds, "in making sure that we communicate with each other to the best of our ability. We are always working to improve our use of technology, especially to enhance communication within the group. So if anything happens with any client—and something does happen, about twenty times a day—then each of us will receive the email on that client and what's going on. We feel we are better off with more communication rather than less. In the end, this helps us to better coordinate the delivery of services to all our clients."

FULL DISCLOSURE AND THE FINANCIAL X-RAY

When working with a new client, Marty says that he and his team begin by "going through an in-depth analysis or interview period where we learn what their goals and objectives are for their money. The second part of the process is to determine their risk tolerance. Once we think we've got their answers—which may entail a considerable amount of conversation with the client and within the group—we can sit down and begin to put together something for the client that makes sense. In order to do all this, we ask every prospect or client to bring in an 'X-ray' of their financial assets. We don't believe it makes sense to do anything without this X-ray, and if people want to just kind of test us out and not do this, we basically turn them down."

"What we want," Marty says, "is not only a listing of all their financial assets and how they are diversified—as well as what they are doing in terms of estate planning, insurance, and the like—but to see the actual written statements. People have told us they are totally conservative, and then when we look at their statements, we find they own aggressive funds. Sometimes, there's a disconnect in the way people perceive themselves and what they've actually done with their money. So the interview phase for us usually takes a meeting or two, then we come up with what we think the client needs to look at or change in order to start working with us. The most important thing in the world is determining their risk tolerance and making sure we match our investment suggestions to their intestinal fortitude. Everybody's appetite for risk is different. There are some people who feel they really want growth, but the only thing they should ever be in is bonds because psychologically they can't handle a very volatile stock market."

"Most people want balance," Marty continues, "and that's why diversification is the key to our business. The key to investing success is not letting a volatile period steer you away from your long-term investment plan. When we go through tumultuous periods, so many people say, 'Oh, I've got to change everything.' Our main job is to help clients distinguish between reality and their perception, and to help them not let their emotions overrule their investing logic."

"This begins with the financial X-ray, and then continues in our regular reviews, which are very, very important to a client relationship. We have to make sure that people understand that we are up to date on what they are invested in, how it is performing, and that the plan we created for them can still help them achieve their financial goals. It's one thing to have a plan on paper and it's another thing to revisit it six months or a year later, and that's where our dynamic approach of meeting with and touching our clients really takes the relationship to another level. Our clients want to know that we are current on what they own and what's going on in their lives, and that the two are well meshed."

"To make all this happen," Marty adds, "just as our industry needs to embrace open architecture, our clients need to embrace full disclosure. The more our clients share with us about what they have and what their needs are, the better advisors we can be for them. When I started in this business, husbands and sometimes wives often wouldn't tell their partners what they were doing with their money. Today, we like to meet with everybody that's key to a relationship. The closer you get to clients and the more you understand them, the better you are able to serve their needs. So we like to have a couple come in together the first time. Whenever we have a review, we suggest that they both come in. We also want to make sure that, in today's world, if something happens to one mate, the other is fully knowledgeable about where the pieces and moving parts are."

Finally, Marty notes that full disclosure is important because "we have to coordinate each client's investment strategy. You can't have different people in different areas doing things that don't mesh with each other. A client has one life and, hopefully, one set of goals. If we allow different people to do different things for our clients in an uncoordinated way, it's going to take them a lot longer to get to where they're going. That doesn't mean they can't have multiple advisors, but they are certainly best served if they disclose what else they're doing to everyone they're working with. If I don't know everything, it would be like a doctor prescribing a prescription drug without having seen a current X-ray and other medications the patient may be taking. Eight years ago I established this in our practice and today I tell my clients that if they don't give us their full X-ray, they'll be doing themselves a real disservice."

"For some clients," Marty continues, "it is a new idea to tell me what they're doing at a bank, or what they're doing with this or that side-money they have invested elsewhere. Occasionally, a client thinks the only reason you are asking to see everything is so you can advise them to move all their assets to you. I really do want to see the real, full X-ray because that's going to enable me to make sure that all the pieces are actually working in tandem. With some families, we are their sole advisor because we have become almost a trusted member of the family. While we can't do that for everyone, where we can, this close relationship is one of the most rewarding parts of our business."

INVESTING THEIR CLIENTS' MONEY: HOLISTIC DIVERSIFICATION

Underlying everything that Marty and his team do for their clients is what Marty calls a 'holistic approach' to managing money. "So we not only take every client through our X-ray process," he says, "but we look at wealth transfer and tax minimization, estate planning strategies, and insurance planning. Given the great impact of all these things on their lives and their families, we want to encourage clients to think about them. We also want to help them get access to top talent in each of these important areas."

To ensure that clients really do look at all of these things, Marty and his team do their best to focus on the big picture. "We've found that instead of spending time with the client talking about a security that's going to represent 2 percent of their portfolio, we can spend the same amount of time talking about their overall asset allocation. Most of our clients are very busy people, and have a lot going on in their lives. So talking about what in reality will have a very, very small impact on their portfolios is not particularly efficient for them. Instead, we can really help them focus on the larger issues and expand on that by giving them a lot more quality time on things that really matter. Whether it's estate planning strategies or insurance, or anything else they want to talk about, like future retirement, this tends to be a lot more meaningful to them than talking about a specific investment."

When advising clients about how to actually invest their money, Marty notes that "Our real job is to separate what our clients think they should be doing with their money versus what their emotions constantly tell them and pull them to do with their money. When things get rocky, we help guide their boat through rough waters because they trust us. That's why the longer we're in this business, the more the world is our oyster—if we keep giving people advice from the heart, we'll never go wrong."

With respect to specific investments, this advice from the heart starts with Marty and Cliff setting general policy. "But obviously," Marty notes, "every family's risk tolerance and needs are different,

so we work things out according to their individual circumstances."
And while many of the components found in different families' portfolios are the same, these too will differ according to the individual
family in question. "The components are often the same, but based
on their risk tolerance, the allocations will be different. So we will
have certain families who have 30 or 35 percent fixed income, and
we'll have other families with only 10 or 20 percent. As for long-only
equities or alternatives, we use managers we're highly comfortable
with based on our thorough due diligence and on how well they
match up against a client's risk tolerance."

What does that due diligence look like? "If you are a manager, I
want to look you in the eye, know who you are, and have an understanding that I can pick up the phone at any time and find out exactly what's going on. We ask all the questions that everybody else
asks, but we also want to know who their accountants are, who their
lawyers are, and everything else we think is necessary. Basically,"
Marty continues, "I need a communications flow that lets me sleep
at night, that let's me know my clients' money is being managed
properly, and that whatever a fund says they are doing, they're actually doing. Style drift—when you start out doing something and you
then change your discipline when the environment changes—is one
of the biggest problems in Wall Street today. So if I hired you for
doing one thing, and now you've wound up over here doing something else, well, shame on me. This really has to be watched very
closely, because as businesses grow, there is sometimes a tendency to
add other areas farther from one's core expertise."

"The alternatives space is a very specialized one," Marty notes,
"and I'll spend a lot of time with these managers before anyone even
gets on my list. When it comes to long equity managers, we'll certainly use the firm's substantial resources. UBS has vetted and
approved a number of managers. We have developed our own
method of doing a second layer of due diligence, narrowing it down
to a select group of talented, top caliber managers. This is also a
great example of where the depth of the team differentiates us. We
believe that the institutional money management and manager
research experience that resides in our team truly makes for unique,
detailed due diligence and monitoring efforts that benefit our
clients."

Marty and his team embraced an open architecture early on. "It
started with my research into hedge funds and the alternative side
of things. I didn't realize it then—I certainly didn't know the term
'open architecture,' which has since become a buzzword—but I

knew I didn't want to rely on only one source for my investment ideas. I wanted to find the best way I could to access other investment avenues. There are brilliant minds in many places, so why should I look only in my shop? So today we've all gone 360 degrees on this and work to be as objective as we can by analyzing what our firm is offering, what other firms are offering, and then choosing the right mix for our clients."

"Ultimately," Marty continues, "the two tenets on which our business is built is servicing the needs of the client and preserving their capital. This means that in everything we do, we make sure we are fulfilling the ultimate needs of the client through diversification. So we never believe in investing in any single component too much, and we are always second-guessing ourselves. We're also always looking for new or innovative ways to help our clients protect and grow their capital."

Additionally, Marty and his team have come to recognize that the very meaning of the term "diversification" has evolved over time. "When I started in this business," he says, "the idea that we'd be investing outside of America would have seemed ludicrous. But now, if you are looking across the world for growth, this means tapping global growth engines like India, China, Russia, various parts of Latin America, and some of the other key Asian countries."

To bring all of these components together—everything from specific investment and product advice to recommendations on estate planning strategies and insurance—takes more than just one individual, or even one team. "We've had the benefit of bringing in various experts from within UBS, and that's where we use the breadth and scope of the firm to the client's benefit. The key is to bring the client the resources of a big firm, but to do it in a personal way. It's a tricky thing, because you want clients to trust you, the individual, but in today's world you absolutely have to make use of resources beyond your own team. Some independents would say that's not true, but we couldn't possibly do all the business that we are doing if we didn't have the firm's resources behind us. By marrying the firm's resources with our efforts and expertise, we are able to give our clients what they need."

TEAM, FIRM, AND INDUSTRY CHALLENGES

Marty brings a lot of perspective to his views on challenges facing his team, his firm, and the industry in general. To begin with, he's clear that growth is not the be-all-and-end-all criterion against which everything should be judged. "In the future," he says, "the success of our business is not necessarily married to growth. It's married to being the best that we can be. That's what I want to do, in any case. That doesn't necessarily mean we can't be substantially bigger—I don't see any reason why our $2 billion under management can't grow to $5 billion—but I wouldn't want that at the expense of our not being the best we can be. Everything about our business will always be client-driven. This well might require expanding our team just a little more, but I wouldn't want it to grow much larger than it is today. I don't want to alter what I do every day and become only the manager of a team. My passion will always be in helping the client, and I'll never trade that for anything."

Marty's emphasis on not being "only the manager" of a team originates from his experience in managing his team to date. "The biggest challenge for me has probably been in managing my team. I am in my element managing client relationships and managing the investment terrain, but managing the team, and properly creating the right spots for growth, and the right diversity and opportunity, is more challenging for me. When Nina passed away, that was a great team tragedy. Our team was smaller then, perhaps five people, but it changed us in the sense that we became even more sensitive to every relationship. It was a transformation in a way. We all live every day to the fullest now and take nothing for granted. Nina's death was also a real milestone tragedy for many of our clients who knew her. Nina will always be a big part of this business."

The attacks of 9/11 also posed considerable challenges for the team. "It was one of the great tragedies of our time," Marty says. "Clearly, we all pray that there won't be another event like it. It changed the framework and mind-set of the investor. We went from a period of 'how much money can you make for me?' to a period of 'preserve my capital first, and grow my money second.' It also changed family dynamics and people's relationships with each other, and it clearly changed the financial world. More than ever, our clients now want the holistic approach to portfolio diversification that we offer. They want to find ways to seek reasonable growth, but not to achieve it by taking on too much risk."

"Of course, given the recent market environment, investors continue to face new challenges. After a period of some calm that began in 2003, the credit crisis that started in 2007 has reminded everyone about market risks again. And while the bear market of 2000 to 2002 was significant in size and scope, in many ways today's feels much closer to home. After a long, upward climb, clients are seeing that even the values of their homes can go down. They're seeing even the financial institutions where they hold their money go through periods of unusual stress."

Marty and his team appreciate their responsibility, even more so in times like these. "In less than a decade, families have witnessed the tragedy of 9/11, the tech bubble, and one of the worst bear markets in many people's lifetimes, and now a real estate and credit crisis has caused stressed and volatile markets. It's a big part of why clients look to us for the secure, long-term approach we take. They know that we emphasize and are committed to wealth preservation as the key objective for the families we serve."

Marty adds: "It's funny that wealth preservation has become 'hot' again. For our team and our clients, this isn't a new trend, but rather, is one of our core values. While no one is immune from some aches when driving down a bumpy road, we know our clients can sleep comfortably. It's our job to help maintain calm and navigate them through turbulent markets. We achieve this through our focus on risk tolerance, diversification, and our orientation to wealth preservation. And of course, we also achieve it by making sure to take a personalized approach, always remembering to step into each client's shoes. Ultimately, this means that the real key for us is doing what we love to do—taking care of people."

CHAPTER 7: BOGGS WEALTH MANAGEMENT GROUP

WACHOVIA SECURITIES
CUMBERLAND, MARYLAND

Larry Boggs

B y anybody's estimate, as a family man, as a pillar of his small city, and as an award-winning financial advisor, Larry Boggs is a very successful and busy man. Approaching his 35th year in the business, Larry is a managing director-investment officer at Wachovia Securities and the general partner of a wealth management group that will soon reach $1 billion in assets under management. Overall, Larry and his team have relationships with some 1,500 clients; Larry himself has primary responsibility for between 300 and 400 families ("significant client relationships," he calls them). And while he works out of an office in Cumberland, Maryland, the town where he was raised, he also oversees two satellite offices, one in McHenry, Maryland, and the other in Bedford, Pennsylvania, and on occasion works out of another office in Bethesda.

How does he do all of this? With the support of his top-notch team (including two of Larry's daughters), with smart leveraging of the systems and platforms provided by Wachovia (the only firm Larry has ever worked for, if you count certain of its predecessors), and with the help of the work ethic he inherited from his father, it comes together pretty seamlessly. And it all started right there, on a golf course in Cumberland, where many years ago while caddying Larry became interested in, excited about, and then directly involved with the financial services industry.

INTO THE SWING OF THINGS

"My professional background starts right here in town," Larry says, "where my dad was a golf pro at the Cumberland Country Club for fifty years. As a boy of nine, I began working as a caddy and running the retail side of the pro shop. As a youngster I was a pretty good golfer, and occasionally on a weekday afternoon when we weren't terribly busy there'd be three guys who needed a fourth. Well, these guys would talk about business, money, and the stock market, and I found it fascinating. I especially liked the idea that you could be making money on your money even when you weren't working. Essentially, as a young person, I became addicted to the stock market.

"At the country club I met a man named Joseph Dagenais," Larry explains, "who was a partner in a firm then called Butcher & Singer. Joe had a great reputation in the business and was a bit of a radical, and he took a liking to me. Naturally, I gave all the money I made to Joe, who started buying stocks for me when I was nine years old. Early on he suggested that I should get my college degree and then go work for him. Back then I had always assumed I'd be in the golf business, but I began to think I could both play a lot of golf and go into the brokerage business. So all through high school, and then all through college, I knew I was going to work for Joe. I went to the University of Maryland on a golfing scholarship and studied finance. When I graduated in 1973, I went to work for Joe. I didn't even interview anywhere else."

"I started working for the firm in Philadelphia, and spent about a year there. They didn't really have a training program, so they sent me to the back office for six months. I was a margin clerk and worked in the dividend area and in the vault. The operations side of the business was much different back then; there wasn't much technology, and everything was done manually. I did it all, and at the time it was great experience. Then they tried to recruit me into public bonds, but I really didn't want to go into public finance. They basically said they weren't going to hire me as a broker, but Joe went a little bit crazy and they sent me to Pittsburgh to interview with the manager there. He said he'd give me a chance."

"In Pittsburgh," Larry continues, "there was a limited training program. My weekly salary was $150, and if I didn't make it, I had to pay them back. I kept that $300 biweekly draw for the next twenty years. After about a year in Pittsburgh I went to Hagerstown, which was the closest branch to my home in Cumberland." While in Hagerstown, Larry began working at night on his MBA in finance from nearby Frostburg State University. After a few years in Hagerstown, in 1977 Larry returned to his hometown of Cumberland and opened the branch there.

THREE PHASES OF A PRACTICE

As for developing his practice, Larry says, "I grew up in this town knowing most of the wealthy people, but they knew me as the young kid who took care of them at the country club. So when I started in Pittsburgh, and then in Hagerstown, I didn't rely on them as contacts. If they called me, I'd do business with them, but I never approached them. As I was getting back into Cumberland, though, things really started to take off."

"My practice and the way I do business has gone through three phases," Larry continues. "Back in the early 1970s and through the 1980s, what was then Butcher & Singer was predominantly a fixed income firm that focused on bonds, corporate bonds, agency bonds, etc., and that's where you built your base. When I started in the business the Dow was at 570 or 580, and you just couldn't grow a business on equities."

Larry recalls one pivotal client from this first phase of his career. "When I was a youngster in the business, a very wealthy client was referred to me by his lawyer, who was also a client of mine. We talked, and then he called me to his home and eventually invested about $25,000 in five or six different stocks. After that we talked back and forth a lot, and about once a month I spent between seven o'clock and midnight at his house since he was busy all day. He didn't do much business with me, but I knew he was wealthy and that the potential was there. Then one evening his lawyer called me at home to say that his client had just sold his business for $10 million and wanted to see me the next morning. All of a sudden this big opportunity came to me because I had taken a lot of time with him. He's still a client with me today."

As for the second phase of Larry's practice, "Along came the 1990s. The mutual fund business and the trading of equities became our focus. By the time the market reached its top, we were doing a ton of equities, with fairly active trading."

Then began Larry's third phase. "Wachovia came out with their Fundsource platform," he says, "a mutual fund and asset allocation model that is diversified by asset class but also by management style. We started implementing this third phase in ninety-eight and ninety-nine, when the market was rising significantly, and we received a lot of criticism from our clients who perceived that our model was underperforming since it blended value with growth."

"Growth was king, the Internet was king, and emerging markets were king. Of course, by the time we got to 2000 and 2001, we looked like heroes, and the same clients who had thought we were turkeys now thought we were great. Since then we have mostly used money managers and asset allocation models to implement what I call risk management through diversification. These days, because more and more of the investing environment is managed and controlled, it's easier to work with clients than it was in the old days when you were trading individuals stocks or bonds. We serve our clients with an open platform and architecture, meaning we have a wide range of product to choose from with no biases when making decisions, and we've seen really nice asset growth. And we have a great referral base. All of my business now comes through referrals."

A GROWING CLIENT BASE

"A lot of my practice," Larry says, "is composed of clients with $1 to $5 million in assets. We also have a lot of accounts that are in the $250 to $500 thousand range. In my little town, if somebody has a $100,000 IRA rollover who's friends or family with a big customer, I can't chase that away—I'm not going to betray a twenty-year relationship. But I can move the small new account into fee-based, and assign one of our team members to service it. I won't spend an excessive amount of time with it, but I've got enough support here that I can get the relationship going and assign a primary person to take care of it for me. Overall, we are probably at 65 to 70 percent fee based, and about 90 percent of our new business is fee based."

Significantly, Larry's clients are all over the country. "I'm registered in about thirty states," Larry says, "and I've picked up some accounts all over, so it's not just western Maryland. I make a dozen to fifteen trips a year to visit clients around the country. I have many clients who are doctors, including many who were born in other countries. Most of my doctor clients are on the East coast, but they're also on the West coast, in California, in Iowa, all over the country. Doctors are very much into networking, and absolutely refer me all over the place. There are usually some highly respected or dominant people in their social circles, and if one or two of those become clients, they in turn refer a lot more people to you."

Of course, there's also client attrition. "Over time, in a practice like ours, clients eventually leave. You've got to like your clients, and they've got to like you. We have a lot of great clients."

Every now and then, even a large client has to be moved on. "Unfortunately," Larry says, "there are some people who only care about alpha and disregard the investment risks involved. In those cases we just have to walk away. Also, we occasionally have to turn away a significant client account because some clients have their own agendas. After doing this as long as I have, I can eventually tell if I want to work with someone or not. We might meet a couple of times and have several long discussions, but sometimes I know it isn't going to work. It takes me a long time to release a client. Do we do it very often? No. But if we get to a point where we can't seem to meet the client's personal objectives, we move on. You reach a stage in your career when you know your practice and whether someone does or doesn't fit."

THE INVESTMENT PROCESS

When Larry begins working with a new client, he begins by sitting down and talking with them. "It's got to be an engaging conversation," he says, "trying to get them to talk. 'Tell me about your life. Tell me what you like to do. Tell me about your investing. Tell me about your family. Tell me what's worked well with your previous investing. Tell me what's been bad.' I really don't contribute much at all, but instead try to get them to talk about themselves. Most people want to talk about themselves, but in our industry there is a tendency to want to tell clients what to do. I try to just listen for a while. In my experience, if it's somebody with substantial wealth, it's going to take about three meetings before I get to the point where I can come back and make some good recommendations. Sometimes it's quicker, but it can takes months, even up to six months."

"We also spend a lot of time educating clients," Larry continues. "Even some very wealthy clients who are successful in business don't necessarily understand what risk means. So we walk them through the scenarios of the late nineties, and then 2000 through 2002. We explain volatility, and why they need to diversify by asset class. Ultimately, it's our focus on asset allocation and the consistency of the return—not the home run—that keeps bringing money to us. Luckily, in the late nineties we had already started moving in that direction, although in hindsight we weren't moving fast enough. Our major clients definitely have a different mind-set now than they had in 1997."

Larry also reviews Wachovia's proprietary platforms and systems with his new clients. "Envision is a life planning software package that we use. If a client says to me, 'Larry, I'm fifty-five, I want to retire at sixty-two, and I'm going to need $150,000 a year after taxes. I've got two more years of college tuitions to pay, and the wife really wants to have a condo at the lake that's going to cost me half a million dollars. Here's what I can save a year. Am I properly invested? Can I do that? Is it realistic for me to retire at sixty-two?' This software will then run a Monte Carlo simulation and give us a statistical probability of it all working. It's an extremely useful tool for clients approaching retirement age. Of course, these are only projections of various outcomes and nothing is guaranteed, but they give us a road map."

"Envision is product neutral—it has no agenda to provide a specific product. It really asks, 'What are your goals for the rest of your life? Can you do what you want to do? Are you invested properly to get there? Are your dreams too low? Are your dreams too high?' A lot of the retirement planning or estate planning software that I've seen has been geared to sell the client something. Although the end result may be to sell them a product or service, you don't start that way. For someone managing a client's money," Larry continues, "Envision makes it relatively easy to plug in all kinds of assumptions and get a reasonable prediction. We've had some nice successes with this. Even when a family loses a parent or both parents, the kids come in and ask if we can do the kind of planning we did for their mom and dad. Also, whenever a client has new money and they get an investment report, Envision tells them if they are underweighted or overweighted in different asset classes. It doesn't tell you where to go from there, but it does suggest—from a risk tolerance perspective and from what we are anticipating—how to adjust their portfolio."

Larry also makes regular use of Wachovia's FundSource platform. "This enables us to make use of different money managers, different asset classes, and different management styles, and blend them. For example, we can use it with Wachovia's DMA, or Diversified Management Account, where one statement can cover five, six, or seven different managers. The FundSource platform is all nonproprietary. It gives us a lot of flexibility and enables me to tie myself to the next generation."

Larry feels he also enjoys a significant advantage working with the next generation through using Wachovia's trust department. "Fifteen years ago," he says, "you would have a good client with a great relationship, and then suddenly, when they got closer to retirement age, the local banker or the local lawyer would get hold of them. The next thing you knew, the account you built would disappear and end up in someone else's trust department. Well, today I take a very proactive approach, particularly with my larger and older accounts. I talk about our trust department. I work with a number of lawyers in Pennsylvania, Maryland, West Virginia and elsewhere, and at a certain point we bring in Wachovia as the client's successor trustee. When clients already have a trust elsewhere I find that those firms push their own proprietary mutual fund products. Sometimes that's okay, but other times performance lags. If I keep the trust within Wachovia, I can use my premier managers."

In addition to more mainstream equity investments, Larry makes judicious use of alternative investments for some of his clients. "Before alternatives were popular," he says, "I had done a lot of specialty real estate investments—and not just tax shelters, but private real estate deals that have worked out quite well. In the past ten years I've also done a fair number of oil and gas deals, including one natural gas site, that have worked out well. Whether you are talking about private equity or hedge funds, I probably have about twenty-five to thirty-five clients who are good candidates for alternative investments."

"As for exchange-traded funds [ETFs]," Larry continues, "they are another arrow in our quiver, and we've been using them in concert with an internal management service that Wachovia provides. Our use of ETFs will likely continue to grow as they grow in popularity." With respect to international investments, Larry says, "Our FundSource models run anywhere from 10 to 25 percent international, and most of our Envision recommendations are also anywhere from 10 to 25 percent international. If an account is big enough, we use individual managers for international."

TIME WELL SPENT

When asked to describe his practice, Larry says, "I head up a small wealth management group within Wachovia that specializes in risk management. You can think of me as the general partner. It's not that I have all the answers, but I'm a good sounding board. Likewise, I will run things by my team, most of whom have been with me for twenty years. I have very little turnover, in part because of our profit/performance structure through which many of the team members share in the revenues."

To understand the functioning of Larry's team, which consists of thirteen individuals including Larry, you have to begin by understanding his work ethic. And to understand Larry's work ethic, you have to go back to his dad. "My dad was a workaholic," he says. "For many years he was not only the golf pro, but also the manager of the country club. He left home early in the morning, would come home for dinner at four o'clock, and then go back for the evening shift at the club. So as a young person, if I wanted to see my dad, I had to go to work. Even after he retired and I was doing well here, he would call some mornings at seven just to check if I was on the job. As a result, I'm kind of a seven-to-seven guy when I work. Most of the time I'm in at the office by seven, and most evenings I'm still here at seven."

When asked if his schedule has slowed down a bit after 35 years, Larry says, "No, it hasn't changed. I enjoy working early. Now, I do like to take about a week off every quarter and just disappear, and it's also not unusual for me to leave here early on Friday afternoon. I'm not opposed to taking extra time off here and there. But when I come to work, I'm usually in the presence of a client, either on the phone or in person, most every day from about eight to six o'clock."

It was Joe Dagenais, the financial advisor who first hired him, who originally drummed into Larry the importance of spending as much time in client-facing activities as possible. "Joe was kind of old school," Larry says. "He started after World War II, selling cars door to door—literally taking cars to the homes of wealthy people. He became the biggest producer for his firm. Joe's feeling about the business is that if you are not with a client, you are wasting your time. So if you are not on the phone with them, or you are not in front of them in person, what are you doing? You are wasting time. I listened to Joe, and I guess I like being in front of clients. So that's what I did, and it's worked for me."

When it comes to administrative functions, Larry says, "I hate doing 85 to 90 percent of it, and I'd rather be with clients. So after my initial meetings with a new client, when it's time to start doing the paperwork for opening new accounts, I march the client down the hall, introduce one or two of my team members, and say, 'I don't do any of this. This is what they do.' And the team runs with it from there."

With such a heavy emphasis on spending time with clients, and with an unalterable focus on providing high-quality service—"I would suggest to you that from a service standpoint, we are the best; that's not bragging, it's just fact"—how does Larry manage to serve so many clients so well? As Larry will be the first to tell you, a great deal rides on his team.

LAYERS OF LEVERAGE: LARRY'S TEAM

The structure and function of Larry's team can be best understood from two perspectives: (1) those who primarily provide administrative, technical, and clerical support, and (2) those who have their own books and are primarily focused on developing business and serving their clients. At the center, of course, is Larry, who functions as the managing partner and revenue quarterback for the entire ensemble.

One individual who crosses over the line—she has both a central administrative role and her own book of clients—is Patsy Stullenbarger, who is the licensed branch manager and the overall administrative and compliance head of Larry's operation. "Patsy came to me twenty-four years ago as an accounting major at a local college," Larry says. "The college asked me if I'd take an intern, someone I wouldn't even have to pay. I said that if I took them on, I was going to pay them. At the end of the summer I said, 'Patsy, you've got to stay. You can't leave.' So once she graduated she joined us, and she's pretty much moved through the ranks and done it all."

"Patsy has an MBA with a background in tax," Larry continues, "and she is the head of compliance and administration. She really runs the branch on the administrative side, and if anyone in this branch has an issue with anything, she's the person to go to. While I'm terrible on the paperwork details related to compliance, she loves it and thrives on it. She's administratively driven to a fault. The compliance review from our last audit was perfect—and you never get a perfect audit report. The reviewers are like the judges in the Olympics, or the IRS: they always find stuff. But Patsy does a really great job for me."

In addition to her administrative function, Patsy plays another role as well. "Originally," Larry says, "we had a rule that anyone who wanted to become a licensed branch manager had to have his or her own book of clients." Patsy, then, with her own clients, is considered one of the group's four limited or junior partners, along with Steve Stroup, Brian Kelly, and Larry's daughter Mirjhana Boggs-Buck. "Each of them has specific clients to cover, and for the most part they make their own recommendations. They bring in new business, and are compensated according to how successful they are. And we all cover for one another. If one of my clients is in the lobby or on the phone and I'm not available, Brian or Steve or Mirjhana will step in, and vice-versa. Anybody on the team will take care of someone else's clients if needed."

Steve Stroup, who has been with Larry for over 20 years and who works out of the Bedford, Maryland, office, shares a golfing background with Larry. Steve is located full-time in the Pennsylvania satellite office, and along with focusing on clients in this area, brings special expertise on municipal bonds. And Brian Kelly, who is resident in the team's main Cumberland office, does all of the options-related work for the whole team. "In addition to their individual expertise," Larry says, "each of our partners has a group of clients within the team that they support. Steve and Brian, in particular, have both been with me for a long time, do a great job, and the clients love them. They are an essential part of the team all the way around."

The last, and newest, limited partner is Mirjhana, Larry's middle daughter. "My involvement really started during my freshman year in high school," Mirjhana says. Larry notes that, "She's the youngest person on the marketing side at this stage—she's only been doing it since 2006—and she's been asked to take on a lot of service activities for smaller clients, which has been great for her. In today's world, given how much competition there is, it's almost impossible to take somebody who's twenty-five or thirty and just let them loose and have them try to build a practice. You've got to bring them in as a junior partner, and you've got to help them get started. So Mirjhana will work on certain things that no one else has time to do, and it's been a great learning process for her. And, importantly, the clients are getting served better than they would otherwise. I am constantly working on developing her further, and always giving her more and more to do. And the clients have the sense that 'My family is still being taken care of.' It's our family taking care of their family, and in Mirjhana's case, it's literally true."

"Originally," says Mirjhana, "I was my dad's assistant. My sister Dagenais often serves as the first point of contact in the office, and then if my dad is not available (he can't be everywhere at once) I sometimes step in and cover for him. That's been great because it's given me exposure to some people that I wouldn't normally have interacted with. Now I have a split role: assistant to my dad and independent advisor."

While Larry is thankful for the skills and production level of all his limited partners, he's unsure how many more, if any, he'll take on. "I've seen this team a lot bigger than it is now," he says, "and I'm more inclined at this stage to hire support people versus hiring junior partners. I've put my heart and soul into a lot of young people who ended up not succeeding and not staying. Many young people just don't have the work ethic that one needs in this business today."

Directly supporting Larry in servicing his 300 to 400 significant client relationships, with no book or clients of their own, are Brenda Mulligan, Belinda Keller, Joel Harvey, and Robert Henry, who are all series 7 licensed representatives. "They have administrative duties and are also involved in marketing," Larry says. "They basically call clients to give them my standard recommendations or work with them to execute recommendations that I've already made. Belinda came to me from a law office, Brenda from an insurance firm, and Joel started here, worked for Wachovia in Virginia, and wanted to move back here after his mother passed away. I've tried to put my team together with each of them having areas of specific expertise. I use Brenda and Belinda as a way of leveraging sales—and Joel does the paperwork. They are all very good, and they are coached enough to know when it's time to bring me in."

The entire group is supported by Michelle Lucas, the cashier, and Sharon Nelson, the operations and office manager, both of whom have been with Larry for about 20 years. Finally, there are three additional support people on the team, including Larry's oldest daughter, Dagenais, who was named for the man who first told Larry on the golf course that he would come work for him. "Joe Dagenais and his wife did not have children," Larry says, "and were very encouraging, almost breaking my arm to get me to marry my wife, Deborah, because they really liked her. Well, we finally did get married—over thirty years ago—and a year or so later they were ecstatic that our first baby was coming. Unfortunately, Joe died a month before the baby was born, and so we named her after him."

Dagenais "works with the firm as a people person," Larry says. "Her strength is people. She has an extraordinary aptitude for people—their names, their histories, whether they've been on vacation and where they went. When we go to an event, she's the one who remembers the first names of all the judges and lawyers. People know her and love her, so in our office she's in charge of unusual and unexpected acts of kindness—sending birthday cards, Valentines, cakes, cookies, and remembering all of the trivia that I could never remember. She makes sure the flowers are sent, and 85 percent of the time she takes the initiative herself."

THE FLOW OF THE TEAM

With all of these different layers of support leveraging Larry—from his junior partners with their own clients to the support people who directly leverage Larry's activities to the support people who keep the office running for everyone—things can sometimes get pretty complicated. "There are a lot of people to coordinate," Larry agrees, "and we are getting better at it all the time. It's definitely a work in progress. But we know who's out when and who's on vacation, and we are always trying to make use of everyone's strengths. Most of my team has been crossed-trained; for example, I have three people who can do the cashier's job. We all cover for one another."

To make sure things run smoothly, two all-hands meetings are held every week. "Once a week we hold a big meeting on a big theme with the entire office," Larry says, "including our assessment of how the market is going, how various market sectors are doing, and what product direction we are heading in. And then we have another meeting on the administrative side to take a look at every-thing that's going on, good or bad. I try to miss the administrative meeting when I can," Larry says with a laugh.

Additionally, because he always has so much on his plate, direct-ly across from Larry there is literally a "hot seat" in the office, the occupant of which can be expected to always have his or her hands full in supporting Larry. As Mirjhana says, "The information you gain in a month sitting across from my dad is incredible. From a learning perspective, it's great to be in the hot seat."

"It's both great and awful," Larry says, "because all day long, every time I've got a situation, you'll be called on. Brenda has that seat now, and much of the office has been in it at different times. Brenda is really my delegator now, and whatever needs to be done— if she can't do it or if it's not something that she normally does—then she'll find someone to delegate it to." Larry agrees with Mirjhana that the hot seat is a great place to learn. "I always work with an open door, unless I have a client in my office, since I have nothing to hide when I talk to people. So Brenda gets to hear the conversations about the market, about products, about the situation at hand or about whatever else we're doing."

Even with all the support he has, it's remarkable that Larry is able to both keep it all running smoothly and serve his own clients as well. Keeping up with all of his clients' situations is, Larry agrees, "hard at times, but I have a pretty good memory, and I try to take good notes. Also, my team is good at keeping me set up all the time. Probably half to two-thirds of my day is prescheduled a week or two in advance, but there's always some space in there, by design. I'm kind of like the doctor who all of a sudden meets with the patient, but before that the nurse has already taken the patient's history and another doctor may have done some preliminary work too. When I'm with a client I make it a point not to take phone calls, but I will always call a client back the same day if he or she needs me."

A FAMILY AFFAIR

In addition to having his oldest (Dagenais) and middle (Mirjhana) daughters working for him directly, Larry's youngest daughter, ZsaKiara, has also spent some time at the office and may some day come back full-time. "My youngest daughter worked for me dur-ing summers all the way through high school," Larry says. "ZsaKiara graduated from Georgetown with a degree in finance and accounting. She worked at the World Bank her freshman year, obtained the series 7 registration as a sophomore, and then worked for me that year in the Bethesda office. She interned at Barclay's Bank in New York in 2006, at a private bank in London, then she's going to New York. She has personality, and is extremely intelligent. I can visualize down the road, if she doesn't like New York, that she'll be back. It's a possibility that's always in the back of my mind."

But it's not just the fact that his daughters work for Larry that's worth noting; it's how he treats them and, probably more importantly, how they treat him and the other people they come in contact with, from team members to clients. As Dagenais—in charge of unexpected acts of kindness—puts it, "I've done everything. You can't tell me something I haven't done for clients. I have gone to one client's house and covered her mirrors because she didn't recognize herself as her Alzheimer's started worsening and she began calling the police because she thought there was an intruder in her home! I've taken clients to buy chairs and cars; I've found their keys; I've picked them up at the airport. It's been fun, I've met some very nice people, and I've done some very interesting things that I never thought would be commonplace in a stock brokerage firm. I guess it all comes down to client service."

Dagenais also plays the important role of making sure her dad doesn't work too much. "He shouldn't be working twenty-four hours a day, because he needs to enjoy himself. If you don't sit and watch TV with him, then he sits and he does work. And I'll push my baby son Treyden on him a little bit, and I'll say that it's great because my son has someone to play with and Dad has someone to play with. So I get Dad when he's in a good mood, and I get him when he's in a bad mood. I get him when the stock market has crashed or someone has messed up something. I get the best, and I get the worst. That's what family members do for each other."

As for Mirjhana, "I guess I can say that I'm proud of my dad," she says. "I'm glad that now I can appreciate what he does. When I was a senior in high school I was asked what my dad did and said he was a financial advisor, and then I was asked if he'd like to come and speak. I thought people would make fun of me and it would be awful. But I kid you not, there wasn't a person in the room, not even the class clown or the class troublemaker, who wasn't interested or who didn't say that he did a good job. That was the first time I really knew that there was more going on with my dad than I gave him credit for or had been aware of. And my awareness of how much he does for people has only grown since then."

"UNCLE LARRY'S" FAMILY TAKING CARE OF YOUR FAMILY

In 2006 Larry was given the Wachovia Way Award for Exemplary Professional and Personal Success. At the award dinner, a brief video on Larry was shown. According to the subsequent press release, "A common theme for all who spoke on the video was Larry's deep and abiding commitment to his family, friends, community, and clients."

Larry is well aware that this is how he and his team are perceived. "We've tried to reinforce the theme of 'Our family taking care of your family,' he says. "A lot of my older clients have watched my girls grow up, and really like the idea that they are now part of the team. They see me with them socially, and my girls represent the family at a lot of fund-raising dinners or golf tournaments, either writing checks, volunteering, or participating in whatever the event is. And when it turned out that my grandson, Dagenais's son, was facing some major health problems, one of my clients put us on the church prayer list. Much of my life is family. For most people, when their kids grow up, they leave. Two of my girls are still here, and we all get together two or three weekends a month. I guess we've all grown up this way, focused on the importance of family. I take that theme seriously, and I think my clients know that."

"Now," Larry continues, "we're a little town, of only twenty-five thousand people, so you get to know or at least recognize almost everyone. There's even a group of my clients who have nicknamed me Uncle Larry, and any time there's a family problem, whether it's the grandparents, the parents, or the kids, who do they call? They call Uncle Larry, even though I'm no relation at all. The other day one of my clients had a first grandson. I sent cards and a little present, and the thank you that I got back was to Great Uncle Larry. It was kind of neat."

"Being constantly recognized is very nice," Larry notes, "except when I'm off duty. So I would much rather spend time off either at our McHenry location, which is a resort area, or in the city (Washington, D.C.), where you can go to dinner and you don't have to talk about the market. Or you can go into a restaurant and you don't have to make the rounds greeting everybody. At home, I'm on duty all the time, which is both great and not great."

The perception that Larry is always around, and always making a difference, has not arisen by chance. "I am definitely available," Larry says. "I don't get a lot of calls on weekends, but I do get some calls. When there's a significant client family with something good or something bad going on, I'm usually there. I've bailed out a client who got thrown in jail for contempt of court. If there's a wedding, I'm going to be there. I can't count the number of weddings and funerals I have attended. I'm almost an extension of the many families we work with."

"If there's a death," Larry continues, "I'm going to be there. I didn't want to, but two weeks ago I drove two and a half hours each way to a funeral. You've got to be there for the family. Sometimes I don't think I'm that close to a client, and then there's a sudden death and the wife comes in and says, 'Bob told me that whenever something happened, you would take care of me.' She needed to know that she was going to be okay, that I was going to take care of her or someone in my group would take care of her. That's what she needed to hear. We try really hard, and this kind of thing makes me feel very special. At the end of the day, I can say that I've changed people's lives and that people can count on me."

In fact, Larry's presence is so powerful that in some cases it's the lack of his presence that can cause problems and make adjustments necessary. "Something we've done forever," Larry says, "is send out family Christmas cards, the kind of Happy New Year and Happy Holiday cards where you thank people for all they've done for you and wish them a prosperous year. Well, one year I was sending out cards with pictures of my kids to some close family friends. One of my clients who did not get this card happened to be in the Florida home of another one of my clients who did get it. He called me up and said, 'Larry, I thought we were really close. How come I didn't get a picture of your family?' It was a wake-up call, and now I spend a fortune on Christmas cards, with pictures. I mail a couple of thousand cards the day after Thanksgiving, and my card is the first card that everybody gets every year."

"Recently," Larry continues, "a client passed away. I met with his kids in Hagerstown as they were tending to details and doing a lot of paperwork. Somebody said, 'I think you might like to have these.' It was every Christmas card that I had ever sent this client. He had saved them all."

"I think it's hard sometimes," Larry concludes, "because we don't always know how other people perceive us, and how much of the relationship is friendship and how much is business. When I first went into the business I made the very naive statement that I didn't want to have any of my friends as clients. What I came to realize over time is that many of my best friends *were* my clients. You get involved with clients and go through their happy times and their sad times, their good times and their bad times. They just need to know you are there, and there's a natural evolution of the relationship from client to friend. Ultimately, I think that anybody in our business who's successful learns to develop that kind of relationship with their clients. Of course, you get closer to some clients than others, and sometimes you just don't realize how close you are."

THE FUTURE OF THE BUSINESS

"I'm nearing a billion dollars in assets right now," Larry says, "and I think my minimum goal within the next several years is $1.5 billion. That sounds like a lot, but it really isn't. When you set goals, you need to set goals that make you run."

"A lot of people say, 'You need to have X number of big relationships.' Well, I sit down and come up with a new theme or concept and I work on that for a while. I'm always out there touching people, and if it happens, it happens. We try to find a million dollars a week of managed money. Is that hard? Is that easy? Some weeks you can't do it. Some weeks you find five. My feeling is that if I keep doing what I'm doing, our assets will grow. And my experience is that if the assets come in, then revenues go up."

"Barring a market meltdown, I think we'll reach our goal," Larry continues. "A correction would be fine, but we don't need another 9/11 or another 1987, where the market gives back some huge numbers. Our money flow has been really good so far this year, with revenues up over 25 percent. We've already had some nice successes, and there are many significant accounts that I think will be on our books between now and the end of the year. We've been blessed. It seems that every time we turn around the phone rings and we begin the court and dance for a new relationship."

THE NEXT GENERATION

Larry consistently focuses on working with the next generation of his client families. "In our business right now, with the aging of the Baby Boomers and our clientele, it's critical that we make the next generation feel as comfortable with us as their parents are. You've got to establish a good relationship early on with the kids and grandkids, and keep working on maintaining your relationship with them. We do a lot of estate planning and trust planning, and I often bring up the topic with clients before anyone else does. And of course, when the client goes to see the lawyers, I go with him."

Moving on to the next generation is also a critical issue for Larry with respect to his own retirement and what happens to his group at that point. "I'm in my midfifties, and at this point I have a great person in Patsy for the administrative, compliance, and service part of it. She knows more than I do and more than I'd ever want to know. She can do anything and everything. But I am not sure who the person is who can become the quarterback on the revenue side. Right now, I'm missing that link on my team. Over the next ten years I have to either develop Steve or Brian or Mirjhana, which would take time, or bring in another partner for when I'm not available or want to go away for a month at a time."

"I struggle a little bit with what happens when I'm no longer here," Larry continues. "I think about it every night. You've got to make sure that you're safe, the clients are safe, and the team is safe, and that things keep on going along if something happens to you. I don't think our industry generally does a good job of thinking about the future. I've even talked to some other teams about maybe putting together a merger agreement in case of death, so that if something happens to one of us, we trust one another to be able to step in. I'm in good health, and I love the work, but you never know. Ten years from now the girls will have grown and matured, and I would love to retire and work part-time. With today's technology it's easy to work in Florida for a couple of weeks or a couple of months at a time. If I want to work from the lake or from the city, I've got my laptop."

ONGOING CONTRIBUTIONS

Again, if one phrase sums it all up for Larry, it's "Our family helping your family," and if you count all the people whom Uncle Larry regularly touches in a significant way, that's a pretty big family indeed. Not surprisingly, he has made significant contributions of money, and more importantly time and energy, to a number of philanthropic causes over time. He says, "When Deborah and I came from Hagerstown to Cumberland, we virtually split up the town between us and we got on boards all over the place. I was involved with the Chamber of Commerce and was president of the economic development agency, and Deborah was involved in the ladies group. I was on one hospital board, and my wife was on another. But as the kids got involved in the business and my practice kept growing, I limited myself to three civic organizations."

"Currently," Larry continues, "I'm on the board of a hospital foundation and I'm also on the board of the Allegheny League for Crippled Children. It's been around for a hundred years, and we provide clinics for disabled children who don't have insurance. We get no assistance from the government, and we run about twenty clinics a year with a full-time speech therapist, and see a thousand kids a year. I've been on that board for twenty-plus years now and I'm the treasurer. Also, a few years back the State of Maryland asked me to be on the State Systems Foundation Board, which oversees all the public colleges in the state. I've really enjoyed that, and they've also asked me to be on their investment committee, which has been wonderful. There are eight of us with different backgrounds on the board, and it's purely voluntary. In addition, once or twice a month Deborah and I go to fund raisers for different causes and make decent-sized contributions."

"I've been very involved with our church too," Larry adds, "and I give a golf scholarship to the University of Maryland every year. They gave me an education, and I feel obligated to give back to them. As for my clients' philanthropic interests, I have a potential conflict. I need to make sure that I don't direct them where my interests are versus where their own interests are. Recently, I did an Envision plan for a client in Hagerstown. After making sure that she could afford to do all the things that she wanted for herself and her family, we set up a personal foundation for her. She named Wachovia as the trustee, and we will manage that forever. She's decided to pick out a half dozen charities in Hagerstown, most of them geared to helping children. And that all came out of Envision, because after we answered all of her other questions, we helped her answer the final question of who gets her money. I've had three or four other philanthropic clients of that magnitude."

With so much going on, from serving his many clients to managing his team to spending time with his family to continuing with his philanthropic pursuits, does the man who once thought of becoming a professional golfer still have time for golf? "I play some," Larry says. "I played a lot of golf in my early years in the business. But then the children started coming along and I became more active in their activities. Golf became less important, and family became more." While Larry may have mostly given up golf for now, it seems likely that one day in Florida—laptop or iPhone by his side in case a client or his family needs him—that's just one more thing he'll get back into the swing of.

Chapter 8: The Oberlander Group

Merrill Lynch & Co., Inc.
Chicago, Illinois

(From Left to Right) Annette Seaberg, Lauren Moore, Sharon Oberlander, David Villalobos, Chris Kasamis

In 1978, after working at a community bank for seven years, Sharon Oberlander became a financial advisor for Merrill Lynch. One of her first clients was an architect and engineer who owned his own construction company. He had just turned 60, and although he had some money in the bank, he told Sharon that he would *never* invest in the market because his father had lost a great deal of money in the Depression and had spent his whole life paying back debts.

Sharon sat down with the man and his wife and listened carefully while they explained their situation, their needs, and their hopes and fears. Then she explained the importance of diversifying their holdings. They opened an account, and Sharon eventually became quite close to the couple, as she does with virtually all of her clients.

Time passed. The husband became quite elderly, and the wife had a stroke. A family friend and lawyer who lived in the community and belonged to their church became very involved in the couple's affairs. He urged them to sell their lovely home—which had been designed by the husband to feature splendid Japanese gardens—and move to a senior care center.

Confused and not knowing what to do, the couple went to Sharon. After reviewing their account, she told them that their investments had grown so that they could easily afford to stay in their home as long as they wanted, even if they had to hire 24-hour-a-day help.

They asked Sharon if she would meet with the attorney. "Look at the assets," she calmly and straightforwardly told him. "Look at the income. I've run the numbers fifteen different ways, and, given their age and life expectancy, if they really want to stay here, they can afford to. All they need is some help." The attorney relented and the couple remained in their beloved home. Even after the husband passed away five years later, the wife was able to stay on and enjoy her Japanese gardens for another five years.

Sharon also helped the couple with their wills. When the wife died, she named Merrill Lynch as her successor trustee, and, having no children, she left the entire estate to charity. A few years before she died, the wife asked Sharon what some of her favorite charities were. Upon her death, the wife left money to similar kinds of charities as a way of honoring Sharon for all the help and support she had given the couple throughout the years.

Sharon's friendly, frank, and effective manner, as well as the deep concern she feels for everyone she works with, is only part of the explanation for how she has earned her spot on The Winner's Circle list.

PERSISTENCE PAYS

Sharon Oberlander is a determined person. Born, raised, and educated in Winnipeg, Canada, she often credits her success to her brother, who is six years older and "very strong and determined about what he wanted. I learned a lot just from being around him, and I developed a tremendous tenacious streak. I just never give up."

Sharon's brother, now a successful attorney and businessman, was also very gregarious, while Sharon was initially very shy and quiet. "But over the years," Sharon says, "I have grown and changed, as many shy people do. What happens is that you persist and compensate. So you end up succeeding in a field where you must overcome your shyness, and I think I have done that."

Sharon's persistence came in handy when she applied for her first job in the United States after moving from Canada to Chicago to be with her husband. Jobs were scarce, and although Sharon had no interest in banking or finance—she was taking social work classes at night—she applied for a position with First National Skokie, which had a training program.

But there was a problem: "To get the job I said I could type, even though I couldn't. Every night I went to my husband's office and taught myself to type with the help of a book, so that by the time I was done with the training, I *would* be able to type." Needless to say, proficiency at the keyboard has proved to be a very useful skill for Sharon over the years.

At the bank, Sharon rotated through a great many positions and functions—service clerk, personal banker, purchasing municipals bonds, working with international letters of credit, assisting the bank's manager—and quickly rose in the ranks.

As fate would have it, Sharon often had reason to work with stockbrokers from different firms. "But none of them provided good service," she says, "and I was very aware of this. I had business for them and they weren't calling me back promptly. At the bank I provided great service to all of my clients, and I had a real following. People would come to me with all kinds of issues and problems and I would never stop until I helped them, even if I had to go outside the bank to get the answer. If people had a situation they didn't know how to handle, they came to see me."

Although Sharon had become an assistant vice president at the bank, a seed began to germinate in her mind. She had read an inspiring story about Paula Hughes, a top woman producer for a successful brokerage firm. "I started thinking that even though I knew nothing about the industry, I might be able to do well in it because I'd be willing to go the extra mile." It took another two years before Sharon applied for a position at Merrill Lynch, which she heard had a great training program.

Sharon, along with hundreds of others, went to an open house, filled out an application, and was called back for an interview and an aptitude test. "Then I didn't get called back again," Sharon says, "so I called them. And I called again. I kept calling the manager's secretary and eventually was invited back for more testing, and I did the best I could."

Following another interview with the manager, Sharon again heard nothing. "I had to keep calling, calling, and calling." Persistence pays: eventually Sharon was called back and invited to enter the training program. The rest is history.

BUILDING HER PRACTICE

At Merrill Lynch, Sharon started off strong. "I worked really hard," she says. "I worked six days a week. I worked fourteen hours a day. I was never on the train going home before eight-twenty in the evening. I really lived it and breathed it, and I loved working with people and providing quality service."

To get new clients, Sharon says, "I tried everything they told us to try. I tried cold calling. I did networking. I joined a women's group called 'Women in Management.'" She became president of the group, which over the years led to many new accounts.

Given her banking background, one place where Sharon excelled was in relating to businesspeople. "Before I left the bank," Sharon says, "I was in corporate business development, and I really related to the entrepreneur. When I got to Merrill Lynch I called business owners and talked to them about their business accounts, about money market funds, and about working their money harder. I would mail information to accountants and attorneys. I would educate them. I would send them kits before the tax season started. 'Let us help you,' I would say to them. 'We'll do all the legwork.' Basically, I would do anything I could do to get my foot in the door and start a relationship."

Sharon had several additional sources of clients early on. Her husband, who was a contractor, provided her with a directory of architects, engineers, and contractors. She also had access to a list of North Shore retirees, and made good use of all of the contacts that came to her from the Women in Management group. Clients also came to her from the bank where she had worked; today the grandson of the man who was chairman of the bank is one of her clients. "I was able to make an introduction to an interested party who then bought his business," Sharon says. "Being a resource like that was pretty cool."

Another source of business has been Sharon's daily commute. "I've been a commuter for twenty-five years," she says, "and I've opened up a lot of accounts on the train." Many of these clients are also her friends. "My whole social life revolves around clients who have become friends," Sharon says. "We go to the symphony. We do group activities. We do all kinds of things. I know and like these clients as people, and they like me. I really feel that we have become essential partners in our clients' lives, and many times we become confidantes who learn about and help advise on personal family issues."

Another source of business came from a set of Fashion & Finance seminars that Sharon put together in 1980 with Ann Benson, mother of the actor Robbie Benson, who worked for Merrill Lynch as a consultant. They held an evening session for women who worked during the day and a daytime session for women who were free in the afternoon. Sharon arranged for an all-women panel, including herself, an attorney, and a CPA, and Ann served as moderator. Many elderly women were in attendance during the afternoon session, and one took her card.

"Her husband had passed away," Sharon says. "She was disorganized and didn't know what she was doing. She wanted to make an appointment and bring her accountant, who had been looking out for her." Sharon's advice impressed the accountant, and he started to refer clients to her. "He did that for many, many years," Sharon says. "I initially got three or four great referrals from him, and then those referrals started referring others. The next thing I knew, the accountant's partner was also making referrals. That's how it mushrooms."

Referrals have constituted the core of Sharon's new business for over two decades now. In fact, Sharon hasn't actively solicited new clients or done cold calling since 1981, when she had her first child and stopped working those 14-hour days. "For referrals to come in like this," Sharon says, "you just have to do a great job."

While she worked very hard, Sharon often worried about how she was doing during the early phase of her career. "We didn't know what we needed to do to really get our business off the ground," she says. "All they told us was to open up new accounts."

After a couple of years, however, she attended a networking event with one of her managers, who introduced her in a surprising way. "Meet Sharon," he said. "She is one of our top young stars and she is our top woman advisor." Sharon was quite surprised, because up until that point no one had told her how she was doing. "I learned then," she says, "that everybody needs some positive reinforcement."

BUILDING HER TEAM

One type of reinforcement that every financial advisor needs is a great team, and Sharon focused on creating a team soon after arriving at Merrill Lynch.

Early on in her career with Merrill Lynch, Sharon knew that she needed more and better help. Her first client assistant (CA) was not very enthusiastic or skilled, and did not really engage clients when they called. Sharon knew from her experience at the bank that there must be people out there looking for a job who were more like her— potential employees who were hard working, loved people, and would not shy away from substantial client contact.

So Sharon spoke to her manager, in her usual direct yet diplomatic manner. She told him that she needed to find someone who was better. He replied that there were no such people out there, and that even if there were, they wouldn't be affordable, and that Sharon should just forget it.

Sharon politely disagreed. "I told him that I'd done jobs like this, that everybody has to start somewhere, and that you *can* get the right people. All you have to do is try." Sharon's manager wished her good luck in finding that person. Shortly afterwards, Sharon met Annette Seaberg, a bright hard-working young woman. Their personalities clicked, and Annette has been with Merrill Lynch and Sharon since 1979.

Annette was originally hired to work not just for Sharon, but for a total of five advisors. "Annette and I would go downstairs and have coffee," Sharon says, "and I would write down on a paper napkin some of the things we were trying to accomplish. This was the beginning of our business plan. As time passed, we accomplished those things. I said to Annette that if we could do a better and better job for clients, we could get more clients, and then she wouldn't have to be working for five people. We could get to three-on-one. We could get to two-on-one. Then we could get to one-on-one. And we did."

Then came a personal watershed in Sharon's life: the birth of her first child. "I was a real pioneer having a child and being in the business," Sharon says. "I'm sure it had happened somewhere else in the country, but not to anybody else I knew, and not to anybody I knew at Merrill Lynch."

It was 1981 when Sharon went to her manager in the sixth month of her pregnancy and told him that she was starting a family. She would send her clients a letter explaining that she would be on leave for three months, and that with the help of her client associate Annette, and another broker who was her phone partner, everything would progress as usual—and it did.

When Sharon came back, her business was growing steadily. Given the importance of her family priorities, Sharon had dropped a number of other outside involvements. Still, she knew that to continue to truly serve her clients the way she wanted to, she would need even more support at the office.

So Sharon once again approached management, and explained that "in order to get to the next level, in order to provide superior service to my clients, I would need even more help." In particular, Sharon had her eye on an assistant named Chris Kasamis, who sat near her in the office. But her manager said she couldn't have Chris, so Sharon hired a woman from outside, who did not work out.

Sharon went back to her boss, and again asked him about Chris. He said that if she talked to the other two advisors Chris worked for and made sure they were not unhappy, Chris could work for her also. Sharon had already been made a sales manager, and was aware that two private offices had become available. "I spoke with the two other advisors," she says, "and asked them, given a choice between having private offices or working with Chris, which they would prefer. They said, 'the private offices, absolutely,' because they really didn't care who worked for them. They were very happy to let her go and work with someone else as long as they got their private offices."

"So we worked it out," Sharon says, "and Chris began working with Annette and me. We clearly got the better end of the deal, because Chris is a very smart, talented person who was being underutilized by the two other advisors. We were giving her real challenges. I've always been a believer in delegating and leveraging to an individual's maximum capacity, and I never felt that the support roles on teams couldn't include a lot of challenge, responsibility, and constant learning. How can someone find out what they are good at if all they are supposed to do is greet visitors, answer the phone, and do a little administrative paperwork?"

In addition to Sharon, Annette, and Chris, the team added a fourth position around 12 years ago, which was to be the first point of contact with clients. "Lauren Moore now holds that position," Sharon says, "and the three people who previously filled this role have all been enabled to launch themselves successfully into other things. Lauren answers all the phone calls, screens them, makes appointments, and takes care of administrative problems for clients. She's doing a beautiful job of fitting into our long-established, tightly knit circle."

Finally, for the last five years Sharon's team has also worked with David Villalobos, a young financial advisor who is also a CPA. "We have a pool that we work on together," Sharon says. "He doesn't work with us on business that existed prior to five years ago, but we work together on business since then. That is, all of his clients are part of the team's clients, but not all of the team's clients are part of his business. And all the same people back him up, so he really is part of our team, our fifth person. His role is to drive acquisitions and to identify people we'd like to do business with. He introduces the team to these people, and if we get a meeting, then he and I go in and meet with the people and see if it's a good fit."

Summing up how the team now works, Sharon says, "I am the team leader. I'm the one who meets with old and new clients, and who does most of the in-person client reviews. Chris does all the scheduling, and it's her job to make sure that all of our clients get their portfolio reviews in a timely fashion and that we meet with them on a regular basis. She and Annette both work on the port-folio reviews, and Annette does a lot of the legwork on research and on bringing new ideas to the team. She also does a lot of the community outreach with different organizations we are involved in. (She happens to be the honorary consul from Sweden to Chicago and is very active in the Swedish community.) But in addi-tion to having clearly defined roles, we have a ton of overlap because we all back each other up, including David. With a small team like ours, we have to make sure that when somebody is out, somebody else can jump in."

SUCCESS AND REWARD

Once Chris and Annette began working with Sharon, the team quickly began to grow its clientele and develop a variety of useful systems. Both Chris and Annette became registered, and the three of them, together now since the mid-1980s, would meet together on weekends to analyze their business.

"We developed a discipline, a process, and a plan for looking at our clients as people and serving them, really giving them whatever they needed," Sharon says. "Our clients were disorganized, so we organized them. We had them bring in their stocks from their vault boxes, and their checks and other paperwork. That was really great fun. We always had a lot of fun doing what we were doing as a team."

Along with the fun came substantial success. Although it was less than ten years into her career, Sharon and her team now had over $100 million in assets under management. "I remember being back at First National Skokie in 1976 or so when they had their fiftieth anniversary and celebrated reaching $100 million in assets, and that was a very big deal. We had a party for a week." Now, with just her own small team, Sharon had reached that same milestone. "That was a real eye-opener," Sharon says. "Clearly we were in a very different world."

Sharon and her team are pleased with their success—they now manage approximately $700 million for about 300 clients—yet they are careful not to rest on their laurels. "We have long-term relationships with many clients, and people don't stay with you that long if you are not delivering," Sharon says. "You always have to look at the accomplishments and the achievements and celebrate the good things. If really great things are happening, though, it's easy to become a little complacent. So at the end of the year, we always spend time going over what we have done, who the clients are, and what we need to do better. We are really pretty humble as a team."

In addition to humility, Sharon prizes fairness and always gives credit when credit is due. Although she has a vertical team, she readily acknowledges the accomplishments of her team members, both verbally and economically. "My team members are all consummate professionals," she says. "I treat each of them as a part owner, and pay them a percentage over and above their salaried income, based on how well the whole team is doing and on how they've done as individuals."

Sharon also gives a great deal of credit for her success to her husband, Lee Oberlander. "I've never really looked for a mentor within Merrill Lynch," Sharon says, "although I've had a number of managers over the years who were very helpful. But my husband, who runs his own company and is much more skillful than I at handling certain business situations and negotiating solutions, has always been very supportive of my career, especially when I changed from banking to working at Merrill Lynch. So he's really been my 'business advisor,' the one I would always go to when there was a difficult situation or something I wasn't quite sure how to handle. He has a great sense of humor, too, and has always provided balance, which is important to someone as competitive as I am."

CARING LEADERSHIP

One of Sharon's favorite things about being an advisor is the many skills it requires and the opportunities it offers. "Advisor, manager, time efficiency expert, marketer, and confidante—you do it all. It is extremely entrepreneurial. You have the opportunity to exercise your whole range of capabilities. And if there is something you can't do, you rely on your team, including your extended team. It's important to know what you do well and what you don't do well, and to fill in the gaps in the most efficient way possible. We have a great team, and we all have our roles."

Underlying all these different capabilities, however, Sharon feels that "to be a successful advisor you have to provide leadership. That's the intangible quality that makes people feel confident in your judgment, and that makes them want to follow your advice. If you aren't a leader, it backfires. Clients follow your advice too late, or they follow some but not all of it. Or they follow it a year later when it's the wrong time."

One of the most gratifying groups of clients Sharon has worked with are retirees who need sound advice, especially with respect to diversifying their holdings. "Everyone is nervous about retiring," Sharon says. "Some people admit it, and some try to not show it. But everyone has to go through a transition."

When Sharon was still new to the business, an International Harvester retiree came to see her. "Ninety percent of his money was in Harvester," she says. "He had a small pension, but I told him that his situation was really dangerous. He told me it was a wonderful company, that he'd been there his whole working life and that in fact it was his whole life. I told him that I knew it was a wonderful company, but that common sense says you should not have all your money in one place, and we needed to do some diversifying."

Five years later the company went bankrupt. "He was so grateful," Sharon says. "I told him it wasn't because I knew anything special, had the inside scoop, or knew how to look into the future. Diversifying was just the right thing to do."

Another couple approaching retirement met with Sharon just a few years ago. "Their portfolio was almost 100 percent equities," she says. "I said, 'Oh my gosh, you want to retire in a year and you are all in equities? You can't do this. Where do you think your income is going to come from, and do you know how much volatility you are going to be exposed to?" With her help the couple rebalanced their entire portfolio before the bear market started in the early 2000s. "It was just lucky that they came in to see me when they did," Sharon says. "But they were very grateful."

"In the bull market before the tech collapse," continues Sharon, "many people thought they had portfolios, but what they actually had was a sector bet on technology. These people had a very bad experience. Our philosophy is to help people achieve their goals with the least possible risk." With respect to the future, Sharon says, "No matter what the forecast is, we always stick with an approach that says 'anything can happen.' This just comes with experience in the business. You realize that no expert is always right, and the world is unpredictable. Therefore, we always hedge."

For example, one recent client had large positions in three extremely popular stocks. "They refused to sell any of it. They thought we were in a new world, a new paradigm, and they only wanted technology companies. We said because they were taking such large risks, if they wanted to keep working with us then at the very least we wanted them to buy some puts—some insurance—that would give them the right to sell their stock at a specific price at a specific time." When the stocks took a huge tumble soon after, the client's losses were minimized.

In some cases, Sharon has turned down potential clients who wanted to operate outside the scope of her expertise. "When I was new in the business, I tried to be everything to everyone," she says. "But once you are in the business for ten years, you know who you are, what you are good at, and how you can help people. There are some people you realize you don't even want to take on because you know they want something you can't deliver. If somebody says they want to trade hot stocks, well, forget it. I can't help them. I don't do that." As a result, Sharon says, "We did not have any horror stories about the early 2000s market. We didn't have anybody who had to change their lifestyle or postpone their retirement."

At this point in her career, Sharon also turns down people who don't meet her minimum for investable assets, which is $1 million. "We started having a minimum back in 2001 or 2002, when the tech bubble was crashing. Our clients didn't suffer too badly, because we had well diversified portfolios. But it was at that point that people began to ask if we had minimums, so we set ours at one million, although we will make an exception, for example, for a couple who are both high-earning professionals who have $800,000 and who are regularly saving money. We certainly wouldn't turn away a couple like that because they are exactly the kind of client we work well with. We'll also take somebody if they are part of a family household relationship. If it's a child or a relative of a client, we will work with them even if they only have $200,000. We just consider them part of the household, although it often does take a lot more time since they are really a separate entity."

"On the other hand," Sharon continues, "if it were somebody who just retired and was starting to draw down their assets, we would be less likely to waive our minimum because we have to protect our time. We never used to have minimums, because I used to think that it would be a terrible thing not to be willing to help somebody. But then after a while, I realized that I was creating a disadvantage for my other clients by taking on anybody and everybody and not protecting my time. And, interestingly enough, sometimes it's the smaller clients who expect the most and appreciate you the least. When that happens, it's really a blow. That's another reason it makes sense to have a minimum."

A CUSTOMIZED APPROACH

Sharon and her team go through several steps when they take on a new client. The first is to profile the client, both formally and informally. The formal component is a profile form that is used to collect detailed information about the client, including his or her assets, future goals and desires, family information, and so on. At the same time, the team makes sure to get to know the client personally, a kind of attitudinal profiling.

For Sharon, "the most fun thing to do still is to meet with a new client. I just absolutely adore doing that. We find out what their past experiences have been, and what their feelings have been about these experiences. By hearing a client's stories we can help create a plan that will make him more successful. If there are things that haven't worked out in the past, either because their expectations weren't managed properly or they weren't educated enough about what they were doing, we want to know about it."

The second step is to create a customized plan for the client. "I read a book by Faith Popcorn about the future trend of customization," Sharon says. "That appealed to me as a consumer. I don't want to be treated just the same as everybody else. I really don't like the idea of advisors just plugging people into whatever platform they happen to use."

"So what we strongly believe in is customizing a plan to the client. When people come to us, we talk to them about their past experiences as investors and we explore what they are all about. Then we'll talk to them about all the different ways we can get them from Point A to Point B and what's going to be best choice for them. Should they have their money managed? Do they really want a stock portfolio with proper weightings? Do they want individual bonds or mutual funds? Will they be Nervous Nellies if they own individual stocks, having anxiety attacks every time they hear the news?"

Based on the many wealth management tools, best practices, and recommendations that Merrill Lynch provides, a plan for the client emerges. "We have different models to recommend, but no client will fit exactly into any one model at any given time. That's where the personalization comes in. We are very disciplined about the amount clients need to save in order to reach their goals, and we rebalance our recommendations, and revisit and meet with them, and assess their progress, on a regular basis. There really is no one way to get there. We want to make it comfortable for the client."

The real key, Sharon says, is "to always start with the client, his or her experiences and risk tolerance, and how we can customize the most suitable plan. We must know the total picture, including what their goals and dreams are and what we are trying to achieve for them. What is it all about? What do they want? What do we need to help them accomplish? Then we use the tools that we have to decide what discipline we are going to put in place for them. Is it going to be just a discipline of reviewing and rebalancing because they have already accumulated wealth? Or is it going to involve a discipline letting them know how much they need to save to get there?"

"Ultimately," Sharon notes, "the key to our success, and what separates us from other advisors, is our service model and willingness to customize to the client's situation. Really, there's not too much that's exclusive to particular advisors or particular firms, because so many of us have access to all of the same things. So what we have to offer that's different is our service model, and I'm very willing to share that model with others because even though nearly anyone can say they have a service model, only a few people can actually execute on one. Other advisors might think these are a lot of great ideas, but acting on them—and doing it consistently—is hard. We have to make sure that if somebody becomes a client, he or she actually gets what we promise."

"What happens is this," Sharon continues. "When people come to us, they generally are in their peak earning years and have tried different things throughout their investing lives. They've tried different advisors, different investment companies, and different products, and they've often accumulated an unmanageable situation that they can't get their arms around. I often refer to this as their 'financial baggage.' It's very unusual to have a person walk in the door and say, 'Hello, I just sold my company, here's my big check, tell me what to do.' Instead, people come in and have their pile of statements. There's no rhyme or reason, no one acting as their quarterback, and no one helping them oversee everything. So what we do is help them make sense of what they have. We pull it all together, organize it with our software, and by the second meeting we say, 'Here's what you have and here's where you are.' And then we help them move forward."

At this point, Sharon and her team come up with a portfolio that is custom designed for the client. "We use Merrill Lynch research," she says. "We use our strategists' ideas. We use our economists' suggestions. And we are always looking forward. We put portfolios in place that are right based on the client's risk tolerance and objective. The objective might be income if they are closer to retirement, or it might be growth if they are younger. It varies, but we are always customizing. If someone comes in and says they have an inherited stock position or a concentrated stock position that we have to work around, we help them begin to diversify and find ways and techniques of doing that."

"After a plan emerges, we then use probabilistic forecasting to do a kind of 'stress test' to make sure there's a high probability the client will achieve his goals with our plan. If it looks like he might not, we'll come up with different solutions. It might be that the client needs to find ways to save more money. If that's not possible, we might adjust the targeted date for the client to retire. Or we can always reduce their spending level. Some of these changes may be feasible, and some may not be. We look at all of them and make recommendations for what we think is the best way to attack the problem in accordance with what the client thinks will work."

"In fact," Sharon adds, "we'll even customize to an individual client's subjective feelings. Suppose a client has tried something in the past and it didn't work well. Even if we think it would still be the best solution now, if she really feels strongly that she doesn't want to go there again because of the previous experience, we won't push her. We'll find another solution, partly because we recognize that there isn't one perfect way to get the same good results with investments. We have access to such a broad array of products and solutions that we can always find something that will keep almost any client comfortable and happy and get the same good results over time. So even though it involves a lot more work for us, we work to find a platform that the client is comfortable with; we don't feel we need to push just one platform that works for us."

CLIENT EDUCATION AND FOLLOW-THROUGH

The third step is client education and follow-through. "If people are insufficiently educated, they will sometimes pull the plug and change direction at exactly the wrong time," Sharon says. "Educating clients takes a lot of time, but it pays back tenfold. When your client is more informed, you become much more efficient."

"The importance of education became clear to me when I was very new in the business," Sharon notes. "Occasionally I would inherit a client from an advisor who had left, and I would sit down with that client to try and gauge where they were and what they'd been doing so we could talk about what they needed. I might ask some questions about their portfolio, and typically their answers would indicate that they had little idea of what they and the previous advisor had been doing—they just didn't know what the rationale was. And I would think to myself, 'If I got hit by a truck tomorrow, and somebody was talking to one of my clients, and they had no idea of what was going on, it would be terribly embarrassing.'"

"So, at every client meeting and especially at every review, I revisit a lot of the same things. We talk about what we're doing, why we're doing it, and how we've done. If someone just wants to hit the high points, we'll do that. I've learned to tailor my presentation to what the client is really looking for. I can always tell when somebody has lost interest. His eyes glaze over. I know then that it's time to either shift gears or say, 'We're about done but I just feel it is so important to explain this to you.' One client actually said, 'Sharon, I really don't want to listen to the long explanation. A ten-minute meeting is good enough for me. Tell me how we did and how the benchmarks did. Get right to the point. That's all I want.' So that's what I give him now. Usually I'm pretty good at reading signals, but I can certainly always improve. That was a very humbling but instructive experience."

As an example of the kind of educational experience that Sharon and her team deliver, she describes what happened when she recently "met with some new people, a husband and wife and their daughter. Now, the daughter had previously worked for Merrill Lynch in investment banking, so she was quite knowledgeable and was helping her parents find the right person since they were going through a life transition. The parents were very, very nice people, and, as they were leaving, the husband said to me, 'I want you to know that I have learned more from sitting down with you for an hour than I learned from my previous advisor in ten years.'"

"What I had done was to pull out what I call the 'period table.' It's a visual that shows you which sectors and styles of the stock market relatively outperformed or underperformed other sectors and styles over the last twenty years. How did large-cap growth do? How did international do? How did bonds do? In any given year the results are quite different, and this visual presentation makes it clear why it's so important to have a diversified portfolio that contains different styles of equity investing. It enables the client to reduce volatility and to perform more consistently, rather than just having great years, then terrible years, then great years, then terrible years."

"I go on to explain that if you perform with more consistency and less volatility, the tortoise will beat the hare in the long run. For example, I ask new clients, 'If you are down 30 percent one year and you are up 30 percent the next year, where are you?' The average person will say they are even, but if you do the math, and you start with $100,000 and are down to $70,000 and then go up to $91,000, you are still down 9 percent."

After educating clients and agreeing on how to move forward, Sharon and her team always help clients to execute their plans over a period of time, rather than just delivering the plan and leaving the follow-through to the client. "In the old days, a lot of people did what was called 'financial planning.' They'd come up with a book, give it to the client, and say, 'Here's your plan.' But what happens after the client gets the plan? Someone has to be there to provide the discipline, to make sure things are being tracked, and to see how well we're doing in getting the client to his or her goals."

"Part of our service model, then, is that we regularly monitor the situation with our clients. Some of them don't want to meet with us four times a year, and tell us that's too frequent. Instead, they want to meet three times a year. So we meet however many times they want to meet, but we insist on having meetings and not skipping them. We want to make sure they know how they're doing, how things are going, and why we are recommending certain changes."

"For some clients," Sharon says, "especially competitive ones, it is hard to change direction, so we have developed intuitive techniques for helping people overcome their tendency to do the wrong thing. If someone has a losing investment in her portfolio but is reluctant to let it go, or just can't bear to sell it at a loss, I'll say something like this to them: 'OK, knowing what you know today about this stock, and pretending you don't own it, how much would you be willing to buy it for now?' I'll often get an answer like, 'Are you crazy? I wouldn't buy any now!' I respond, 'Well, by holding onto it you are in effect making a decision to buy it, and since you feel so strongly negative about it given everything you know today, why are you hanging in there when you could be going into something you have positive expectations about?' This may be simplistic, but sometimes reframing things gets the point across and helps the investor do the right thing."

Sharon is always frank and honest with clients, even if it means telling them they can't afford to purchase certain things for themselves or their children. Recently, a client told Sharon that she and her husband went to Colorado on vacation. "They told me," Sharon says, "that they stayed in this great place, and that her husband wanted to put in a bid on it. They were in euphoria, but I pointed out that they would have little opportunity to use it because the husband worked so hard, and that they probably couldn't really afford it if they really wanted to reach their financial goals. I brought them back to reality."

Sharon notes that this happens with clients all the time. "What I tell them," she says, is that "we are going to keep you out of trouble. We are going to keep you on the right track. This is what the disciplines and the processes we have agreed to will accomplish. And sometimes when you absolutely want to do one thing, we may tell you to do something else." Smiling, Sharon adds that "during the tech bubble decline, when people wanted to move their portfolios heavily into tech and get rid of their other holdings, we said, 'You can't.'"

"Recently," Sharon continues, "I read a great book by Jason Zweig called *Your Money and Your Brain: How the New Science of*

Neuroeconomics Can Help Make You Rich (Simon & Schuster, 2007). I loved reading it because it confirmed, based on scientific studies with both people and animals, what I've always known both anecdotally and through experience. For example, when something happens to a person or an animal two times in a row, they begin to feel they can predict it. So if you want to know when money will flow into certain investments, you predict that the highest money flows will be in the third year it's making money because after two years—after two times—people begin to feel they can predict it. At that point people have such conviction and confidence, even if what they are predicting is a completely random thing. This is why, in part, people buy the fund that was the top performing fund for the last two years instead of taking a look at the size and style and what's undervalued right now."

"It also turns out that the possibility of making money stimulates the same part of the brain as cocaine. So judgments become clouded and people sometimes make poor decisions when they get very excited about a potential money-making opportunity. So we, as advisors, have to help our clients take a step back and ask some questions to counter the clouded judgment that results from the pleasurable feeling about the possibility of making money. Over time, then, you begin to understand how to handle certain situations. You begin to know who is going to call you when, and what they are going to say when the market is up or down. And you learn how to calm them down or how to convince people that when the market is down, it's a great time to invest money, even though our brains want us to invest when things are up and we're feeling good."

GOING THE EXTRA MILE

From getting her first banking job, to developing her team, to making sure that she connects in a deep, emotional way with each of her clients, Sharon Oberlander always goes the extra mile. For example, she and her team have always been very organized. "I brought my discipline with me from the bank, and we've always kept impeccable records. Twenty-five years ago nobody had client files, but we did. From the beginning, every client of ours has had a file, and anything relevant to that client goes in the file. If we ever need anything, we have it. It's a little intense, but it works."

A few years ago a client came to Sharon and asked her if she remembered a wire transfer relating to a real estate deal. He told her that he needed some evidence of the transfer because he had to go to a Florida court and prove it. Sharon had her team retrieve a records box from long-term storage, and they eventually found a hand-written approval of the wire transfer. "My client could not believe I came up with this, and it turned out that the piece of paper I was able to find was worth $200,000 to him. Today, of course, we scan everything and our files are electronic, but back then everything was on paper."

Similarly, a doctor client was mailed an odd looking insurance certificate that completely baffled him. "He called me up," Sharon says, "and I asked him a couple of questions. He sent me a photocopy and I gave it to Chris and she started tracking it down. I have always trained everybody on my team that if there's anything you can't get an answer on internally, just keep going and don't stop until you get an answer. If you want to get an answer, you can, if you just keep working on it." Eventually, thanks to Chris, the team was able to track back ownership of the insured property, and Sharon's client received a windfall.

Sharon's willingness to see things through also came into play when she spent a three-year rotation on Merrill Lynch's ACTM (Advisory Council to Management), where she helped design the firm's Client Review Center. "I was on the ACTM during a difficult market time," Sharon says, "and the fellow who was chairing the committee that year said that what we really needed was to be able to push a few buttons on the computer and show our clients how well we were doing for them and how we were protecting their interests on a relative basis."

"As it turned out," Sharon continues, "all of the top advisors had figured out their own review process. So I was doing it one way and another guy was doing it a different way. Well, as part of the ACTM we all submitted our own processes and a few of us sat down, looked them all over, and found that 80 percent of what we were doing was the same, and 20 percent varied somewhat. For example, my clients were more interested in knowing what their annual income was and somebody else's clients weren't interested in that. I worked on the committee for three years to perfect the Client Review Center, and now every advisor at Merrill Lynch can use it."

"I use it every single day to do my client reviews," Sharon adds. "I can look at things in terms of size, style, and sector analysis. It slices and dices everything a client owns, categorizes everything, and gives us a beautiful way of looking at a portfolio or looking at a prospective client's assets and knowing exactly what he or she has. It also helps us rebalance portfolios and to tweak them to the client's customized needs. We are very disciplined about rebalancing, and we don't let clients talk us out of it. Investor psychology, human emotions, and often an individual's personality work against successful investment. Given my experience and understanding of behavioral tendencies, I'm able to give clients explanations and the necessary structure and discipline for proper rebalancing to go forward."

After the three-year rotation, Sharon contributed to Merrill Lynch's revised client investment statement, and she volunteered to chair a regional ACTM. "There were some growing pangs at first," Sharon says, "because often not everyone on a committee is willing to work." But, as usual, Sharon persisted, and today a solid core group is making important contributions toward refining best practices and increasing productivity throughout Merrill Lynch.

Sharon also serves Merrill Lynch in a more public capacity. "For a good fifteen years, I've officially been a media relationships representative for Merrill Lynch in Chicago. There are five or six of us who do this. If a call comes in and the media want to interview somebody about the market, I'm available. Usually something pops up about once a month. TV makes me really nervous, but it's also a lot of fun."

KEEPING STRONG AND GIVING BACK

"Recently," Sharon said, "a new client told me that he could really tell that I enjoyed what I did. I said, 'Yes, I do, I love it.' Then he asked me whether I might not be getting to a point where I want to retire, and I said, 'I'm going to be around. I don't even think about retiring. What would I do with myself? I love doing this work, I love meeting with new people, and I love the challenges that come with constant change. That doesn't mean there aren't some aggravating days, since anything worth doing has some aggravation associated with it. But, yes, I really do enjoy this work, including having days that are very packed. To me, this is a dream job."

Keeping up with the high standards and demands that Sharon has set for herself in her dream job takes a lot of energy. "I have a friend I ride the train with," Sharon says, "and he always says to me, 'I don't know where you get the energy to do all that you do.' And while I said, 'I don't know, I really don't think about it,' I will also say that I've come to recognize the importance of keeping physically fit."

"I neglected my fitness for many years. When I was younger, I was a regular tennis player, but I gave that up along with a lot of other things when I had my children. People always thought I was fit, because I happened to be slim. But in my sedentary occupation—as advisors, we sit around a table with clients, we sit while we're on the phone, we sit while we're on the computer—I was really out of shape."

"But somewhere along the way, about ten years ago, I woke up and said, 'I better do something about this' and resolved to get on purpose about being fit. I started with yoga, and I still do yoga at the local park. And I do cardio at home and use weights as well. I do it all, but I have to squeeze it in at eight at night."

With her son graduating from New York University's School of Law and coming back to Chicago to work with a law firm, and with her daughter (who's spent time traveling in Israel, Turkey, Jordan, and Italy) now a junior at Tufts University, Sharon has more time for community pursuits as well these days. She is involved with her synagogue, and she supports the Lyric Opera of Chicago and the Chicago Symphony.

Most recently, Sharon has become "quite involved in focusing on the businesswomen's community. In particular, I'm involved in the WBDC—the Women's Business Development Center—a not-for-profit that focuses on certifying women- and minority-owned businesses. It's a very complicated process for a business owner to get through on her own. Merrill Lynch is a sponsor, and I was very instrumental in arranging that sponsorship. We attend their annual meeting, which lasts several days, and participate in workshops on doing financial statements and making business plans."

Another place where Sharon demonstrates her commitment to women in business is the Executive Club of Chicago. "This organization," she says, "sponsors something called the Women's Leadership Breakfasts. It's an organization of two thousand or so members, about 20 to 30 percent women, but they are planning to grow that percentage. I'm the cochair of the Women's Leadership Committee; we put on four breakfasts a year focused on women members and women panelists. These breakfasts are fabulously popular and well attended—we had a thousand people at the last one. Imagine getting that many people to an event at seven-thirty in the morning!"

"The topic was 'How Can You Be an Entrepreneur in a Corporate Setting ... or Do You Need to Get Out?' We had speakers from Aeon, Illinois Took Works, and New Age Transportation. The next one is going to be on 'The Power of the Purse,' because women as a group tend to neglect their purses. They are often such perfectionists at making financial decisions that they end up procrastinating until they gather every bit of relevant information, which means they start later than men and then have a hard time catching up. And, of course, even though the situation has improved tremendously, women are still not earning as much as men for equivalent work in many areas. So we'll focus on how women can take care of their own purses and in this way get to the point where they can live life on their own terms, possibly change careers, or effect political change or change in the community through philanthropy or personal involvement."

"Basically," Sharon says, "if you've taken care of your own purse, you can support the things you want to support. I'm going to be a panelist along with a wealthy entrepreneur and philanthropist, and a corporate executive who took many jobs abroad. Also, the Executive Club is very focused on growing future leaders. We have a mentorship program, since our audience includes a lot of women in their twenties and thirties who are in the early years of their career. Right now I'm mentoring someone, and it's very fulfilling."

Sharon is also involved with the Principal for a Day program in Chicago's public schools. "I've participated in this for the last few years and was part of a group focused on a very disadvantaged community. Several of us spent time in different classrooms with different age groups. Sometimes we even got to teach. Last year I was in a sixth grade classroom and the kids were asking me questions about my job and about going to college. These kids don't get much of a chance to get out of their community, and they have very few role models. Recently I was with a group of gifted first and second graders, and I was amazed at what fantastic readers they were. I did an assignment with one of them on following directions and counting and coloring, and in another class I read a story that asked them to predict things as we went along. This was all a lot of fun and very rewarding."

Sharon is also a long-time supporter and board member of the Gastro-Intestinal Research Foundation (GIRF). "This wasn't a personal interest of mine originally. Most people are on the board because they or a family member have issues—anything from colon cancer to Crohn's disease to inflammatory bowel disease. I have been fortunate so far—knock on wood—and got involved only because a long-time client had been on the board for a long time. He said it was very enjoyable and educational, that lots of nice people were involved, and that they needed some high-level, intelligent, professional women on the board."

"I went to a board meeting," Sharon continues, "and found that everybody was very nice. I had a little extra time about then, and I thought, 'Well, this is very interesting, very educational, and I'm learning a lot.' So I got involved. I attend monthly meetings, am chair of a committee called the Friends of GIRF, and am helping to raise money for a research facility at a new hospital."

Ultimately, Sharon Oberlander's persistent, caring leadership makes a real difference in the lives of many people. "I love this job," she says. "It's entrepreneurial. It's challenging. It's both financially and emotionally rewarding. It's constantly changing and evolving along with the market, and you can choose your niche. You can work with every client who comes along, or you can pick your clients— we're very much into working with nice people. You get to structure portfolios and discuss sophisticated macro- and microeconomic issues all day long. And you can change people's lives while helping them to accomplish the things they want to ... while keeping them out of trouble. You are the CEO, the marketing department, the business planner, head of operations, and the event planner. I have the best job in the world." No doubt, many of Sharon's clients feel that they have the best advisor in the world.

CHAPTER 9: 545 GROUP

MORGAN STANLEY PRIVATE WEALTH MANAGEMENT
MENLO PARK, CALIFORNIA

(Top Row Left to Right) Daniel Soares, Ryan Kennedy, Jason Bogardus, Gregory Vaughan, Mark Douglass, Robert Dixon

(Bottom Row Left to Right) Michelle Thomas, Phoebe Zhang, Donna Sunada, Jennifer Thomas

As individuals, Greg Vaughan and each of his three partners—Bob Dixon, Mark Douglass, and Jason Bogardus—are smart, dedicated, competent, and personable. On his own, any one of these men could have started a successful business as a financial advisor. But by combining their individual strengths into one entity with a uniquely fluid structure—an entity consistently ranked by The Winner's Circle as the nation's number one horizontal team—they have created something truly remarkable.

Nearing $10 billion of assets under direct and indirect management for 100-plus mostly Silicon Valley families, the 545 Group, as they are called, is one of the largest and most successful advisory businesses in the country. The unique structure of the group and its trust-based decision-making process serves as a powerful and inspiring example of how financial advisors can do better for their clients and themselves by embracing the true meaning of teamwork.

BUILDING THE TEAM OVER TIME

The 545 Group did not spring up all at once. Instead, it evolved over time as the partners wove together their unique backgrounds and experiences in response to the evolving needs of their ultra-high-net-worth clients.

Longest in the business is Bob Dixon, born and raised in Idaho. His parents were farmers and ranchers. "Although nothing in my youth was directly related to the investment business," Bob says, "my father gave us a good work ethic and made sure we were up working every morning." After graduating from the University of Idaho, he spent five years in a PhD program in finance at George Washington University and worked for the U.S. Senate Budget Committee. Before finishing his dissertation he became interested in the financial services industry, and interviewed with a major national firm. Bob went through training in New York City and was registered in 1976. Returning to Washington, D.C. with that national firm, he would cold call at night and open accounts. Later, he took a job in San Francisco with a firm that would eventually become part of Morgan Stanley.

Greg Vaughan came to Morgan Stanley through a somewhat different route. He was born and raised in San Francisco, where his mom raised the family and his dad had a janitorial service along with some real estate interests. As he explains, "My dad did everything it took to get his kids through life. He had a good strong work ethic, and when he retired he figured out how to enjoy life."

Although Greg did not follow the stock market in high school, when he was at the University of Arizona, studying for his business degree, his dad gave him ten shares of a security. "That sparked an interest in me, which stuck."

Greg started in the industry in 1979 and began building a business "the old-fashioned way, getting on the phone and cold calling, one stock at a time." He then came to Morgan Stanley through what he calls "dumb luck." "A recruiter called one afternoon," Greg says, "and later that night he happened to walk by the office when I happened to be there. He called me the next day, and three days later I moved over. It was apparent that Morgan Stanley was a better franchise that offered a much bigger opportunity. Once I met the people there, I knew that it was a different kind of organization."

In 1981, Greg and Bob were both working in the same San Francisco Morgan Stanley office. Greg was working by himself, supported by a single assistant, when his manager came to him with a fateful proposition. "He said, 'This is not going to work long-term. You've got a lot of energy, but I want you to bring Bob in and work together.'" "From the beginning," Greg continues, "it worked out just fine. We had different strengths—he did things differently than I did—and combining our efforts worked better for the clients. I didn't mind going out and marketing and picking up the phone, and Bob was very detail-oriented and got things 'just so,' and clients really liked that."

"We were just associates then," Bob adds, "and there were almost no other teams within Morgan Stanley at the time. I was excited about our partnership because it's hard to get traction in this business alone. It's nice to have someone to bounce ideas off and create some synergy with. You can create a lot of energy with a partner, especially somebody who has a different skill set than you do. Greg is a master marketer, and he filled that void. The total package fit together."

Working together, they began to build their book. "At that point," Greg says, "we only knew enough to be dangerous, so we made a lot of mistakes along the way. But we did do much of what we still do today—building relationships of trust, one at a time. Even then we focused on Silicon Valley, where we had a presence because Morgan Stanley happened to be the lead manager of the deal when a well-known company went public. While Morgan Stanley was known as a New York–based firm, we did have some people on the West Coast. Silicon Valley was a big attraction, so we tried to make our way around there. Our typical clients were business owners, entrepreneurs, and venture capitalists. Much of our business hasn't changed, and we still have many clients from those days."

Ten years later, in 1990, Mark Douglass joined the team as a partner. "I was born and raised in California," Mark says. "I was the youngest of five, so very early on I knew that I had to fight for all the scraps—which were few and far between. I put myself through UCLA undergraduate school as a waiter. I then did my graduate work in business at Berkeley, and joined my first firm in 1983. I was pretty much a cold call cowboy back then, harboring the traditional retail investor. I amassed a number of interns from Berkeley who came over and cold called for me, which is how I tried to scale my business. But I realized I didn't want to stay on the traditional retail side of the business, and in 1990 I had the opportunity to join Morgan Stanley. I met up with Greg and Bob in 1990. Initially, I was the business development person who was out there trying to source new opportunities for the group. And then as the business and the relationships grew, I also developed client relationship responsibilities as well."

The last member to join the team was Jason Bogardus. "I grew up in Portland, Oregon," Jason says. "Coming out of college I realized that I had been given a lot of opportunities as a kid, and in order to provide those opportunities for my own future family, I would have to build a career. Eventually, I stumbled into financial services. I got a job with the Citibank transaction services group, based in Paris. We provided back office support to a treasury center within the firm that provided Fortune 500 companies with a host of equity, fixed income, and interest rate derivative structures. I then moved to Singapore and was a regional relationship manager for commercial banking clients until 1998. Then I went to the University of North Carolina business school, and joined the team in March 2001."

"We talked a lot about the wealth creation that happened, in Silicon Valley and globally, leading up to the events of 9/11," Jason continues. "It was clear to me that this was a hard business to start in by yourself, and I was very impressed by Greg, Bob, and Mark—particularly by Mark's ability to remain laser-focused on structuring investment solutions that kept clients out of harm's way when there was a lot of market turmoil. The year 2001 was a challenging time to do business development. For example, during a cold call I had one prospective client who started crying on the telephone because he realized for the first time as he spoke to me that he didn't have any money although he had been a very wealthy person on paper. It was a humbling time for everyone, all the way through October 2003, when the U.S. equity markets started rebounding."

Although Jason is between 15 and 20 years younger than his three partners, this chronological difference actually strengthens the team. "It's great," Greg says, "because certain clients want a room full of gray-haired, experienced people and others want people who are younger and more technology savvy. Also, I think that clients think, 'If I am going to hire these folks, when partner A retires, there's still going to be someone here who knows my situation and whom I can feel comfortable with.' So there is a deep bench here, and we'll continue to develop that bench over time."

Jason's analytical capabilities also strengthen the team. "Jason and I just had a meeting with a prospective client," Greg says, "and Jason did some unbelievable analytics. The prospect, who hired us, really wanted to talk about risk and risk-adjusted returns. Jason spent several hours today doing the work needed to quantify the answers to his questions."

In 2000, after around 20 years in San Francisco, the team moved some 35 miles south into Silicon Valley. More precisely, it moved to Menlo Park's Sand Hill Road, the very heart of the nation's venture capital industry. The team, including the four partners, now totals just 11 individuals. "We have fewer clients with larger pools of capital compared to other teams," Greg says. "We just moved into new office space," Bob says. "It was built for us and is beautiful."

One feature of the new space is a large table, known as the turret, that the four partners all use as their main desk and personal workspace. "I want to emphasize the importance of working in the turret," Bob says. "The synergies of the four of us sitting around a table this size all day are tremendous. It's not a matter of having to get together once a week, or once a month, to do this. It's a constant free flow of ideas that makes the whole thing work well every day. We feel that if everyone goes to a separate corner of the room, then you're not really a team. We think of ourselves as a team and try to behave like a team. Even though we're in sleepy Menlo Park, California, it's as if we have a trading desk environment where everyone understands what's going on."

VENTURING INTO SUCCESS

The team's success started to build early on, soon after Greg and Bob became partners in 1981. "If there was one big event," Bob reflects, "it was what happened on the venture capital side." Greg explains further: "It was just dumb luck that we happened to be here during the initial wealth craze in Silicon Valley, and we tried to take advantage of it and remain focused on it. The venture capital community was funding companies, so there was a cash management opportunity. The venture capitalists themselves were doing quite well, as were some company founders. Even at this point in time, it was a very closed marketplace, with almost a country club exclusivity. You had to fight your way into that club, but once you did, and did a good job for people, the momentum fed on itself."

One way Greg and Bob "broke into the club" was by developing a different kind of relationship with one of the major early venture capital firms. "None of us had any real money," Bob says, "but we had the opportunity to invest in a side fund. This was a great opportunity. Not only did we get to know the venture capital firm, but we got to know their portfolio companies, often before anybody else even knew about them. We continued to make those kinds of investments, and now we are involved with at least ten or fifteen different firms. So we went to partner meetings and got to know the companies long before they went public, sometimes before they even had a telephone number. Often Greg and I would go to these partner meetings and be the only people there from our community. Other institutional investors would be there—which was a great opportunity for us—but there weren't other investment banking firms in the room. This, as much as anything else, is what helped our momentum in the first ten years."

"Morgan Stanley had started to build a big presence in technology and investment banking," Greg further explains. "That helped our cause in a big way. We had an army of investment bankers upstairs and they'd been around for a long time. Connecting ourselves to those folks, and providing services for their clients, centered us right into the venture capital community. Over time we transitioned from a kind of general corporate services model into more of a private wealth management model. We were less interested in the partnership activity in regards to serving the firms and more interested in the individual partners."

When Mark joined the team in 1990, things continued along the same track. "Mark joined us when we were really starting to grow," Bob says. "We were fortunate enough to be right in the middle of the whole thing. We had gotten some traction in Silicon Valley in our first ten years, and it just exploded from there, from the mid-1990s for the next five to eight years. Our basic model never changed."

For his part, Mark explains that, "We were acting on behalf of Morgan Stanley as a relationship manager to these private companies and their management teams, leveraging the Morgan Stanley franchise. That was our calling card. And this was helpful to the general partners at the venture capital firms who were therefore willing to introduce us to some of their other companies. Ten years ago, you just didn't have the kind of information flow you do today because the venture capital community was really closed. We were able to network with the venture capitalists and gain the trust necessary to talk with their companies. Even if Morgan Stanley decided not to do business with the companies, we had developed enough rapport and enough of a relationship to work with them later on."

Greg describes how the process actually worked with respect to "a telecom equipment company north of San Francisco that we invested in eight or ten years ago. We were able to make a small equity investment because one of the venture capitalists was nice enough to let us in. As a result, we were able to attend meetings and got to know the management team. We also got to know the CFO, and we were able to introduce the company to our firm. Morgan Stanley ended up bringing the company public, and then ended up doing a secondary offering. We still have three founders and two board members as clients, and we do 100 percent of their business."

RESPECT AND RESPONSIBILITY, FAITH AND FRIENDS

To get a real feeling for what underlies the group's success, it's necessary to go beyond notions of dumb luck or the advantageous positioning that they've strategically cultivated for 25 years now vis-à-vis Silicon Valley's venture capital community. On a deeper level, the group's success can be explained by how the partners feel about their clients and how they work on their behalf.

As Jason puts it, "From my perspective, the greatest story is that of Silicon Valley over the recent decades. So many of our clients are self-made, hard-working entrepreneurs. Many of them get up every morning at the crack of dawn, get dressed, and work long days. For some it's working in an operating capacity with a private or public company, and for others it's more focused on giving away their wealth, which many of our clients cite as more enjoyable than having made it. What's humbling about so many of our clients is that they have somehow been able to stay true to themselves and remain well grounded, despite the phenomenal wealth that they have created for themselves, their families, and their communities. It's fascinating for me to see people with large annual salaries maintaining a moderate lifestyle. Obviously, there are exceptions, but by and large it's been extremely humbling to see these people take their incredible wealth with a grain of salt and realize that money, at the end of the day, isn't the most important thing to them and their families."

Working on behalf of these individuals and their families gives the team a great sense of responsibility. As Bob says, "If there's one thing that I've come to realize, it's the responsibility that we have toward each of our clients because most of them have given us all of their wealth to manage. They have put their fortunes and their families' futures—maybe for generations—in our hands. They put a lot of faith and confidence in us, giving us an incredible amount of wealth to manage and then not bothering us a whole lot about how we do it. We work closely with them to understand their situations—what they want to do and not do—and follow their guidelines in a responsible way. We all take it very seriously. The client always comes first. We are service-oriented, people feel comfortable with us, and we don't lose clients."

Greg wholeheartedly agrees. "We take our responsibility seriously, and our clients know that. While we do have some new clients, we have many who have been with us for years. We've gotten to know them and they us. They've put a lot of faith in us, and we execute on that faith. Not that every investment we make works out exactly as we'd hoped, but we always have their best interests at heart. As a result, our business has flourished."

Or, as Mark puts it, "It all comes down to being a people business. Although we definitely bring an institutional process to the investment management side, it really all comes down to a people approach where we try to keep it simple. We don't overcomplicate. We can be very sophisticated about how we process investments, but the clients, sitting on the other side of the table, simply trust us. Together we are building an advisory relationship, and it becomes a partnership. There is a fine line between business and friendship, and over time we develop strong friendships with our clients. One of the things that has always impressed me is the number of intergenerational referrals we receive, which shows that our clients have trusted us down the line. Many ask us about things that are esoteric or totally out of the blue, which just amplifies how this really is a people business. I think we're pretty consistent. We try to do a good job of getting close to our clients and understanding not just their investment side, but all the other aspects of their lives."

Greg continues along the same theme: "We are fortunate to have clients with big balance sheets, and all of our clients seem to become our friends. They are clients first, but over time, even though you are always in a service position, you build a relationship of friendship. It starts in a presentation early on, and fifteen years later, you have a pretty good understanding of them and they have a good understanding of you. And you develop a common respect. It's fun to work for people this way."

"Ultimately," Greg continues, "we are in the business of helping people run their business, and their business happens to be their balance sheet. So, as businesspeople, we try to give good, solid advice. For example, when people receive large amounts of money it can be a real struggle, because money can have either a healthy or an unhealthy effect on their lives. We try to bring a commonsense approach to these situations. Conversations go towards, 'What should I do for my family today? What should I do for future years?' We are not in the estate planning business, so it's more of a conversation about being realistic. 'If you allow your children to have too much money, too quickly, it's going to change their behavior and their life, and that's probably not a good thing.'"

INDIVIDUALIZED SOLUTIONS AND THE INVESTMENT PROCESS

"All of our clients have made their money," Greg says. "Our goal is to maintain that wealth with reasonable rates of return and over long periods of time, without a lot of volatility for the return, and without a lot of taxation along the way. People who have a big net worth want that kind of diversification, so our job is to allocate their portfolio correctly and then find the best way to implement that allocation."

To achieve the right allocation, the team starts out by delving into each client's unique situation. "There's no black box or cookie-cutter approach that we follow," Jason says. "Rather, each client receives a customized solution. To get to the right allocation for each client we usually meet with a new client at least three times."

We have an introductory meeting," Greg says, "where we tell them who we are and hear them talk about their situation in depth. At a second meeting we come back to them with our suggestions, and then we have a third meeting for them to sign off on what we've come up with. Then we implement it."

To make sure that there is common agreement as to what direction to take, the team usually crafts an individualized investment policy statement (IPS) for each new client. "Our view," Greg says, "is that if someone is going to give you responsibility for money that took them twenty or thirty years to make, you had better have a solid business plan. That business plan is the investment policy statement, and it's a document we refer to over time."

While the team has access to virtually all types of analytics and simulations, Greg downplays the ultimate importance of these. "Monte Carlo simulations and efficient frontiers are part of our discussion, but I find that these are only somewhat relevant. They're great to talk about, but the fact is, they've been marginalized. Everybody in our business does them. What we really try to do is get a sense of how much risk people can really stomach and try to build out a portfolio based on that. I always say that the three most important bullet points are how the clients want their money to work for them. You have to have a good understanding of what's going on in the client's head, or they are going to be disappointed and not stay with you."

Having understood what's going on in their clients' heads, the team works hard to craft the kind of individualized solutions that high-net-worth individuals are looking for. Jason notes that recently "a Silicon Valley Internet company had a public offering that resulted in lots of newly minted wealthy individuals. We spent a lot of time looking into building customized solutions that would fit what we thought would be of interest to these individuals. We worked with an outside vendor to create a cost-effective system that enabled these clients to dial in the amount of correlation they wanted with respect to their concentrated stock positions. They could also dial in the amount of social or responsible investing the portfolio had exposure to, and all of this was done with a focus on tax efficiencies."

Sometimes there is a need to create customized solutions that differ even within one wealthy family. As Bob explains, "Mark, Greg, and I have had a relationship with a family for a dozen years. It started off relatively small. They had $25 million and wanted to give $5 million to five different managers ten years ago. We refused that opportunity because we thought we could do a better job if we had the full $25 million, and they gave it to us. The company turned out to be very successful, and Morgan Stanley just sold it to a strategic buyer for a little more than a billion dollars. So now we have family members that, all of a sudden, have substantial individual wealth as well."

"They've always been rich," Bob continues, "but now there's been a big distribution. So Mark and I have spent a lot of time individually with these family members developing their own portfolios. They are similar in a lot of ways, but different in others. Some of them want to spread their wings and be fairly artistic in what they are asking us to do. Others are extremely conservative about what they want, saying 'This is the way Dad would have wanted it.' So now we are in the process of developing an individualized investment policy statement for each of them."

With respect to the members of this family, Mark adds, "They really look to us not only to preserve what they have—they are already very, very wealthy—but to make sure that they are thinking through the whole process, including leveraging the global platform, looking at alternatives, and looking at international. So we have to be up to speed on the estate and tax side, and make sure we are all on the same page."

Although the four partners work hard at coming up with the right individualized solution for each client, they also strive to be consistent and to work smart. As Jason says, "While the ultimate mandates and the direction of the individual policy statements are entirely different for individual clients, the processes by which we evaluate suitable investments, allocations, manager selection, vehicle selection, and tax strategies are very consistent across our different clients. Also, a lot of the hard work and analysis that goes into the solution for one family can be used in other ways, shapes, and forms with subsequent families. Our ability to constantly evolve the robustness of our capabilities and continue to deliver innovative solutions to new clients over time has been extremely powerful."

Significantly, the team has been called to develop different types of individualized solutions as their clients have evolved over time. "Ten years ago," Bob says, "our prospect might have been a twenty-five- or thirty-five-year-old person, maybe married, maybe not, and probably without kids—or with little ones. Now we often have mature families with a patriarch in his sixties or seventies along with multiple layers of second and sometimes third generations. So the focus has changed from really young guys without a lot of complexity in their personal situations to patriarchal clients who each have three or four children, and those children each have three or four kids. We've had to change our focus to arrive at more complex solution sets. It used to be just stocks, bonds, and cash—figuring out when to sell your stock or how to sell it in accordance with its restrictions, and what to do with the money. Now we are talking about much more complex solution sets: stocks, bonds, cash, and a whole bunch of other things that make sense to our clients."

The need to arrive at these more complex solution sets is actually a big advantage for the team. As an example, Greg points to a recent new client. "A family went to New York and every day spent a full day at a different firm. It was a competitive situation, and we were thrilled when they hired us. Everyone else's response was 'stocks, bonds, cash, and we'll do a great job for you.' We took a much more thorough approach and looked at their whole balance sheet, and because of that we were able to shine. As with other relationships that we've taken on, a lot of the work is done before we walk into a meeting, and what attracts the client is the thorough analysis we've done. The more complex a situation, the easier it is to shine, and with the marginalization of the securities business and the investment business, we need to find opportunities to shine."

MANAGING MONEY, INSIDE AND OUT

Taken together, the team manages a total of nearly $10 billion. Of that, they have discretion over a total of about $4.1 billion, with the rest in concentrated stock positions and other nonliquid investments. And of that $4.1 billion, they directly manage about $3.1 billion. The other $1.0 billion is managed by outside managers with specific expertise relating to private equity, real estate, hedge funds, international equity, distressed debt, non-U.S. fixed income, and other alternative investments.

Part of what makes it possible for the partners to keep tabs on all of this is the way they work as a team. "First of all," Greg says, "we sit out in a room on a trading turf, around the turret, so we share ideas all day, every day, which I feel is healthier than being alone in an office. It's a better environment because we can share ideas, and all day long we are interacting, and among us we have assistants who help to take care of other activities." Bob agrees. "I want to emphasize what Greg said about the importance of working in the turret and the synergies of sitting around a table this size, the four of us, all day. I know exactly what Jason is talking to Greg about, and what Greg is talking to Mark about."

As to exactly what's in their clients' portfolios, Greg says, "We sit within four or five feet of each other all day, so we have a pretty good sense of what's on everybody's mind, for better or worse. And portfolios evolve. If you looked at the portfolios of five of our clients, they would all look somewhat alike. The allocations would be different because each client has some individual customization for his or her needs. But generally they all look somewhat alike. And that doesn't happen because we walk into a conference room and go to a white board and say 'Let's rearrange the allocation.' We each have strong opinions, so it evolves over time as we build a consensus amongst the four of us. We've been doing this for a long time, and instinct and good old-fashioned common sense take you three quarters of the way."

Mark adds, "Two or three times a week we get together in the conference room, away from our turret, so we can strategize. We also have a quarterly review where we ask ourselves what we are doing, what changes we need to make, what we are not thinking about, and what our competitive landscape is like. It's a constant, ongoing, and evolving process."

As for how they actually invest their clients' money, Jason says, "Not to oversimplify things, our investment process can be broken down into two components. One is putting new money to work, and the other is the ongoing tactical rebalancing. When putting new money to work, given our client profile, there tends to be a focus or concentrated position at the portfolio's core, either in the form of an equity holding or something else, like real estate. We tend to develop a multi-phased approach where we will execute against a long-term allocation, but we start by deploying money towards asset classes that have the lowest correlation to their core holding or the lowest volatility in the overall portfolio."

"Often," Jason continues, "common sense wins the day. So in terms of tactical rebalancing, we won't rebalance a portfolio just because a spreadsheet tells us we need to reduce exposure to international equities from 14 to 12 percent. We discuss whether that is, indeed, the right thing to do based on our constantly evolving views of the capital markets. In our industry there is a tendency to rebalance for the sake of rebalancing, and we respectfully disagree with that."

Bob adds, "When we build a portfolio, we try to have a pretty clear vision of what we are trying to build over a long period of time, because creating liquidity is generally an expensive process. So if you are going to go through it, you had better have a pretty clear vision of what you are trying to build and why, and what you want it to look like three or four years from now. Attractive entry points are also important. Buying things at the right price accounts for about 90 percent of the success rate you're going to have. Finding an attractive entry point allows you to take a long-term perspective in building the portfolio."

STRUCTURING SUCCESS THROUGH TEAMWORK AND TRUST

While the four partners all have titles—Greg is managing director, Bob and Mark are executive directors, and Jason is vice president— the overall structure of the team is surprisingly fluid. "Do we have a structure?" Greg muses. "If you asked me for an org chart, no, I wouldn't be able to give it to you."

How, then, does the team make its decisions? "Everybody has his strengths and weaknesses," Greg says. "You just have to trust your partners' decisions. If I want to buy a certain equity for a group of clients that's going to affect our business overall, I don't necessarily ask for permission to go buy it for a hundred different families. I buy it for better or worse. I live with that decision."

When pressed as to what happens when there is a disagreement among the partners, Greg points to the fact that the four partners are constantly within earshot of each other. "I think disagreements are good," he says. "We don't have fistfights, but we certainly have differing views. We don't all just nod and say, 'OK, we're marching to the left.' We take our cues from Morgan Stanley, discuss things on the margin, and then make changes based on a good healthy debate among the four of us. But the fact is that at the end of our discussions, we'll have built a consensus and we'll all feel pretty good about it. While our debates are daily events, someone ultimately takes ownership of every decision. Whoever feels strongly enough about it takes ownership of it."

Bob similarly emphasizes the need for trust, as well as the need for partners who complement and know how to work with each other. "Obviously," he says, "a great team means you have to have great teammates. You have to know how to work together, and I think we've been fortunate in that we do work well together. To be sure, we have our disagreements, and from time to time we have conflicts, but it's never been anything that was ultimately detrimental to the partnership or to the way the team works."

TEAM STRUCTURE

How, exactly, does the team work? Do the different partners have special areas of focus? Or does everyone do a little bit of everything? The answer is, a bit of both.

Certainly, the partners have specific strengths. If you ask Bob about the team's structure, he'll start out by talking about Greg's marketing capabilities. "Greg shines when it comes to marketing," he says. "I give him all the credit in the world for getting us in the door. One reason he's so good at prospecting is that he genuinely cares about people and wants to help them. People immediately recognize and appreciate that. He's great at what he does."

For his part, Greg is philosophical, humble, and pragmatic about his success as a marketer. "Silicon Valley," he says, "is an incestuous market place. People here know each other. The Bay and San Francisco area has 6 million people, but in Silicon Valley there are five hundred people that really make things happen. If you do a good job for the first fifty, then the next fifty will hear about it. So we make a big effort to make certain that we do a great job for those first fifty, and over time, they've brought us the next fifty. We've been really fortunate in that way. Marketing to me no longer means getting on the phone and cold calling. It's just constantly providing service, without selling something to someone. Over time you will earn their respect and their business."

Greg continues: "It's the little things. As an example, today there was an interesting report on an important company, so I shot an email to several people saying 'I thought you would be interested in this.' It shows the prospective or current client that you are actually thinking about them."

Bob agrees that, "We don't have much structure here. Over the years we have all migrated toward the part of the business we enjoy doing the most. I think we've been in the business long enough that it's evolved to the point where we all understand what we enjoy doing and probably what we do best. That hasn't changed a lot over time. What Greg, Mark, and I do overlap a lot. Still, we have different skills. I spend virtually 90 percent of my day managing our clients' money, but I also work with clients themselves every day and on the management side. Greg and Mark both manage some of the money, but they do other things as well."

Mark—who considers himself a generalist whose duties range from business development to asset allocation to alternative investments—points to how the partners step up to being the point person with a particular client based on personal chemistry. "After being in the business for twenty years, we have complementary skills. We understand that it's a people business, and that different types of personalities fit better with different people. So if I'm in a relationship and I get the sense that Greg or Bob would be the better point person for the best interests of our group, then one of them will take over."

Greg makes the same point. "It does all come down to personal relationships, and some people are more compatible with one team member than another. And it's in everyone's interest to make certain that the client works with the right person from the beginning. The reason to have a team is to get leverage from each other's abilities. You can't be all things to all people."

Bob describes a client relationship that started in 2002 or 2003. "Greg brought him in," Bob says, "and the initial meeting was with Greg and Jason. It was a very large situation that needed a sophisticated kind of solution, and Jason prepared a lot of the material and played a big part in developing that solution. Greg then brought me in and we presented to the client in New York. We ultimately ended up getting the business, and today I am the primary point person on the account. I have day-to-day contact with them and do most of the investments and decision making for them. But Greg and I will be on our way to Florida in a couple of weeks to see the client; Greg is absolutely as big a part of it as I am. So Greg found him and brought him in the door, then Jason and Greg cultivated the field for us, and then Greg and I went to New York to get the client. Now I have the primary day-to-day responsibility for managing that money. But they always ask for Greg and how he's doing."

Jason's view of the team's structure matches what his partners have to say. "Through our Morgan Stanley network and by leveraging the firm, we can get access to true specialists in any geography or asset class or expertise. So again, we are all generalists, and in terms of daily responsibility, we all wear a business development hat, we are all doing client relationship management, and we are all managing money. My focus, from a product perspective, is on our third-party equity managers. Also, since we are set up not unlike an investment banking team in terms of multiple layers of professionals, we have an analyst who does a lot of the heavy lifting in terms of analytics, presentations, and client portfolio analysis investment metrics, and I help coordinate all of that."

Mark points out that what's most important is that the way the team functions is *the way their clients want the team to function*. Mark says, "Over the last five years we have seen a number of Wall Street firms go to teams where each individual has a vertical strength or specific expertise. But given the number and complexity of our clients and their assets, we've found that what they really want is a team. If something happens to Greg, they want to know that Bob and Mark are there, equally qualified, not just in one niche, but across the entire range of asset management. We've found a number of other teams where each guy has his own silo and that's all he or she does. Personally, I don't think that's intellectually as interesting. I think we have just as much experience as they do; yet we bring a lot more to the advisory role. No matter what happens, there's a point person here, there's a backup person here, there's someone who will fill in regardless."

"You have to trust each other. You may have personal pride at stake. But you have to be smart enough to delegate, to offload responsibility to other people when you don't think you are the right person. You have to know what your personal strengths and weaknesses are. These are both probably more obvious to your partners than to yourself, so you have to work with them to get an understanding of who you are. If you put it all into perspective, things seem to work out over time. Take a long-term perspective and have a long-term financial orientation as a team, and don't get hung up on the day-to-day, month-to-month, or year-to-year finances, and you will end up having quite a bit more success than people who divvy up the firewood as often as they want to. I hate to say it, but it's almost like a marriage. You have to trust each other until you are proven wrong."

Mark echoes Greg here. "It's a commitment to the long-term success of the team, and not just to yourself. And it's being able to contribute the complementary skills you bring to the team. It's a willingness to put the team first and not let your ego get in the way. There will be stressful times, but the bottom line is you've got to work together. You are committed to each other, and you'd better have a little fun along the way."

Jason sums up what makes a great team. "You have to be collectively aware of what makes you unique, and make optimal use of that awareness to best serve your clients and deliver best-in-class solutions. And you have to have a great platform, ideally, a global platform. We are fortunate to be able to reach across our organization to tap some of the best and brightest minds in the world in the capital markets on behalf of our clients."

Finally, as for distributing the rewards of their highly successful practice, Greg says, "The four of us have been together for up to twenty-five years, and compensation is based on total contribution. Let's use our most recent partner, Jason, as an example. So far, he doesn't bring new clients in as often. But the fact is, when we have a relationship, he's very helpful. When I go out and meet with someone, he has done a good part of the prep work. And he does a lot of the follow-up. I may be the face to the client, but he does a lot of the in-between, the day-to-day, and the quarterly reviews. He adds a lot of value. So everyone has an understanding of what's fair, and it just works out. Some years, some people may feel short-changed and other people may feel better, but we decide as partners. Over time, it works out, and we don't adjust the equity distribution very often."

ON ANY GIVEN DAY

"On any given day," Greg says, "there are four partners here along with seven support staff. As the two most senior guys here, Bob and I have the role of driving investment direction and how the business operates on a daily basis. This relates to how we are organized as a business, but it also relates to managing clients' portfolios. We regularly spend time among ourselves talking about portfolio allocations, and where value is versus risk. Right now risk aversion is very expensive, which makes U.S. Treasuries very expensive, so we're implementing a swap out of Treasuries into municipal bonds."

"We each have client responsibility," Greg continues. "Bob, Mark, and I have the most, and Jason has somewhat less because he's the newest member of the team. But our efforts certainly overlap, and no one takes full responsibility for all of the accounts. We do things on a client-by-client basis, and the person who's primarily responsible for a client will implement the specific changes in that client's portfolio."

"But I have a good sense of what's happening in all of our client's portfolios, so if the phone rings," Greg continues, "and one of my partners is out, I'm able to answer the client's question, have a conversation, or at least make certain any questions get answered that day. While we all think slightly differently, we try to represent each other the best we can, and so when we talk to clients our responses are consistent."

"Bob, Mark, and I mainly worry about portfolios," Greg adds. Jason, as an investment representative at the vice president level, coordinates a good deal of the team's analytics projects. We also have two sales associates on the team—Ryan Kennedy and Dan Soares—who help Jason with the analysis and reporting. We have a vice president, administration/support named Jennifer Thomas and two senior sales associates—Michelle Thomas (unrelated) and Donna Sunada—who are collectively responsible for overall client service and for making certain that the business runs properly. Donna tracks all the inflows and outflows of money. She's basically the wire person whose number-one responsibility is client service and making sure that cash gets to where it needs to be in a timely manner."

"To make sure things run smoothly," Greg continues, "each of the partners has an assistant who sits right next to him in the turret. So Jennifer Thomas is my assistant and helps me with my client base. Michelle Thomas is Bob's assistant, and Phoebe Zhang is a sales associate who directly supports Mark. One of the reasons we are successful is because we have great assistants. When any one of them is out of the office, another can pick up the phone because the clients are basically all of our clients. We can all hear each other's discussions all day, so everybody has a good understanding of what's going on. Someone might say, 'I heard you talking to client A today and you mentioned municipal bonds. Something you might want to think about is such-and-such, and I can help you follow up on that.'"

"Essentially," Greg summarizes, "we have an eight- or ten-hour meeting every day we are in here, where we're either talking with each other or with clients. If someone on the outside were watching us, they might think we were disorganized. But we're not. Everything we need to get done gets done without sitting at a white board and assigning tasks. Everybody has a good, strong understanding of what their responsibilities are, which is key. And everybody feels that he or she could ask the person to the left or the right for help if they couldn't get something done."

MEETING CHALLENGES TO CREATE A STEADY FUTURE

Notwithstanding their success to date, the team faces a variety of ongoing challenges. "The business has become very commoditized," Mark says, "because of the increasing number of players, not only on Wall Street, but outside vendors as well, at a time when clients are becoming increasingly technologically sophisticated and able to access information from across the competitive landscape. So if you are a financial intermediary, you better be in a position to show your value add, because a lot of people are out there meeting potential new clients with big pools of money and talking about overall blended diversification and asset allocation. You had better be able to coordinate with tax and estate counsel, think for the clients, and customize what you do for them. You have to help them preserve their wealth, but also make them money. You need to be constantly educating yourself on what's happening. Since we are generalists who go deeper and deeper, this plays to our strength."

Jason adds that any team offering wealth management must keep up with general industry trends towards more broad-based investing. "Even in the early and mid-nineties," he says, "we saw an evolution away from portfolios of primarily stocks and bonds to ones that were much more broadly diversified and incorporated hedge funds, private equity, commodities, and real asset investment solutions like timber, structured products, and real estate opportunities. Also, there's been an increased emphasis in global investing, all of which has called for additional layers of analysis."

"One of the great challenges that the industry faces now," Jason continues, "is that we are all effectively in the business of managing uncertainty. Especially with clients where there is a fiduciary or trusted agent involved, there's a burden on that individual to defend what they are doing on behalf of the client. We need to be able to prove that we understand the potential outcomes, but, as Greg likes to say, our crystal ball is no clearer than anyone else's. So to manage this uncertainty, we've really had to focus on and develop our capabilities in terms of investment policy statements and game plans that help a fiduciary and a client understand what their range of outcomes and potential risks are. We've had to leverage the firm's quantitative resources to analyze how portfolios would have performed in specific time periods or given a hypothetical set of assumptions compared to what might now happen in the capital markets. You have to maintain a balance between what the historical data and analysis tells you and good old-fashioned common sense. This is a hard formula to get right, but we've done a very good job at it."

Of course, every now and then the team does make a mistake. "Certainly, with the benefit of twenty-twenty hindsight there are certain investments we all wish we had avoided," Greg says. "Fortunately, they have been few, given our team's generally conservative approach over the past twenty-eight years. However, eighteen or twenty years ago we did make a mistake relating to client acquisition. It was a little company that has now grown into one of the biggest in the country and gone public. We were there early, and we had an opportunity to get to know these guys on a Saturday morning in Los Angeles, but we didn't follow up as we should have. We thought we were bigger than that, and we didn't see the opportunity that actually was there. And now, twenty years later, it is clear that this would have been a business opportunity that would have made any of our careers. But we went right by it, and someone else logged onto it. You want to learn from your mistakes, and we learned that we weren't focused enough, and that you can't try to be everything to everybody."

Sometimes, remaining true to themselves has meant parting ways with a client, as Mark retells. "There was an individual founder of a company that Morgan Stanley took public. He had a billion dollars on paper, and thought that he was not only an expert at managing his business, but also in managing his own assets. So, by default, he wanted to be very hands-on and run his own money. He used us primarily for trading activities, and we kept saying to him, 'Look, you are worth a billion, so for the sake of your family, your children and grandchildren, why not at least take $25, $50, or $100 million off the table and invest it in a conservative manner?' This was in the mid-1990s, and while we maintained this relationship for quite a few years, stocks kept going up. It was difficult for us because while we were saying he should be more defensive, his stock picks kept appreciating. When someone's own stock is going up 50 percent a year and you are saying, 'We're going to generate 9 to 12 percent,' your story isn't very compelling. Well, we agreed to disagree, and we kept telling him that he needed to hedge a big piece of that stock and take it off the table. He never did, and, lo and behold, that billion probably went down to $25 million. So he's still a wealthy individual, but we no longer have a relationship. We were willing to see it go because we agreed to disagree. We kept telling him what we felt was in his family's best interest, and he disagreed and moved on."

Today, most of the team's new clients come from referrals. One way the partners get new clients is by leveraging Morgan Stanley's retail side, which was greatly strengthened when Morgan Stanley merged with Dean Witter in 1997. "They have a lot of touch points on the retail side that we realized we can leverage," Greg says, "so we have proactively gone out and tried to partner more and more with advisors on the retail side. We will go to a local manager and say, 'Here's our situation. This is whom we are trying to go after. Are there touch points here? Does someone happen to know any of the family members or that individual?' Or we see whether we can put ourselves in a position where, if someone on the retail side stumbles across or identifies some very-high-net-worth individuals and doesn't have the confidence to go after the business themselves, they will come and partner with us."

"We've developed some great business this way," Greg notes. "Usually the retail person will proactively come to our group. We'll discuss the situation, go through the parameters, and profile it. Sometimes we might say, 'You know what? This is what we would do, but it's not significant enough for us, so you handle it.' But quite often they feel they are in a better position partnering with us."

As an example, Greg says, "Recently we were hired by a family that had just sold a portion of a business, and they had a twenty-plus-year relationship with someone in the local office. Because of the sale of the business, the family became higher profile, and it became a more competitive situation. This advisor in the local office reached out to us and asked for help. We are now partnering with him. He's really the quarterback of the relationship while we act as the chief investment officer for the assets, which is perfect, because he has a lot of history with them. He knows all their flaws and quirks, which would take us years to figure out—and we bring a different skill set, different products, and different experiences."

While the team does spend significant time and energy on client acquisition, Greg notes that "the majority of our time and energy is spent on investing and making certain that our current clients' assets perform as advertised or as they expect. We spend most of our energy trying to do well for our current clients, assuming that if we do, the right new clients will find us over time."

But what does "doing well for our clients" really mean to the team? Is it making better returns or achieving "alpha," a return that is greater than comparable indices? "People who are in the ultra-high-net-worth category," Greg notes, "aren't necessarily looking for alpha, believe it or not. I think they're looking for consistency and a reasonable rate of return. To generate alpha you often have to take more risk than you might like. And so to me, owning a portfolio that generates an 11 percent compounded rate of return, not paying a lot of taxes along the way, and not having a lot of volatility might be a better result than having a manager who creates alpha and advertises that he's four hundred basis points above his benchmark, year in and year out. People who are very wealthy have the same emotions as most investors, good old-fashioned fear and greed. Thus a big part of our job is to get our clients thinking right down the middle, because both fear and greed can overwhelm them at exactly the wrong time."

"During the Internet phenomenon," Greg adds, "being in the middle of Silicon Valley, we were present while a massive amount of wealth was being created very quickly. It was a very interesting time and emotions were high. Greed quickly overwhelmed fear, and we brought in a perspective that helped people manage their concentrated positions. We put ourselves out and said, 'This is the advice that we believe in and have conviction in, and here's how to execute it.' Those who took our advice saved big parts of their balance sheets."

"Just now," Greg adds, "I'm looking at a letter from a client who wrote us out of the blue to let us know that he appreciates everything we've done for him. This is a guy who's very, very wealthy and very high profile. And he wrote us not because the markets are up, but because he knows that we care about him. If we just treat our clients' money as if it were our money—which everybody says they do, but we actually do—good things will happen over long periods of time. So we've been together for a long period of time, trying to do good things for people. Not every investment we make goes up, but generally we are doing what's right, and as a result our business has grown."

"Ultimately," Greg concludes, "we are very steady. We have one of the largest businesses on the street, and we've been doing it for a long time. And clients don't leave. When clients hire us, they stick around for a long time. We get to know them well. We visit with them, we often go to quarterly meetings with them, and we have a very good sense of what they're all about. Whether you walk in today or walked in years ago, generally the story will be the same: You've made your money, and now you want to keep it. You've hit the American dream and, particularly here in Silicon Valley, we're not going to let you get backed into a corner chasing returns. It's consistency we strive for, and that's something you really should want if you are a client." That, and four partners who are smart enough, skilled enough, and mature enough to blend their talents and experience to produce the kind of results that reliably satisfy some of the wealthiest investors in Silicon Valley and beyond.

Chapter 10: Hudock Moyer Wealth Management

Wachovia Securities Financial Network
Williamsport, Pennsylvania

(Left to Right) Holly Tagliaferri, Joe Moyer, Barbara Jennings, Wayne Dieffenderfer, Jason Moyer, Michael Hudock, Barbara Hudock, Dee Gephart, Jane Hawkins, Jennifer Reynolds

Mix one part down-home Southern-born Girl Scout, one part persevering mom who knows how to tackle adversity and bootstrap herself up through the ranks, and one part life and investment planner with a focus on generational wealth transfer, and you begin to get a feel for the depth, warmth, and strength of Barbara Hudock. "My secret mission," she says, "is that when people walk through our doors, they are magically transported to a world that is kinder and gentler, warmer and friendlier."

As managing principal of Hudock Moyer Wealth Management (HMWM) in Williamsport, Pennsylvania, a great many of Barbara's career-related dreams have certainly come true. For example, she was recognized by The Winner's Circle in *Barron's* as one of the top 100 Women Advisors in the nation two years in a row, and Barbara's firm—which she founded with her team in 2001 after spending 26 years with a wirehouse—received the prestigious Forbes Enterprise Award. And Barron's has recognized Hudock Moyer as being one of the top 100 Independent Advisors in the country.

Clearly, Barbara's business is on track. But even more importantly, now that she and her two partners—one of whom is her son, Michael—are fully in the driver's seat and are back in their home town after a challenging move to another city, they are more free than ever to serve their clients and give to their community in ways that are most true to who they are and therefore most satisfying. "In a nutshell, my philosophy of life, as I paraphrase author Mike Dooley is: 'To give beyond reason, to care beyond hope, to love without limit, to reach, stretch, and dream in spite of your fears. These are the hallmarks of divinity, the traits of the immortal, your badges of honor, and your ticket home.'"

With her own career ticket home purchased through hard work and a talent for building profound relationships, Barbara Hudock has traveled quite a distance from college student to mother to wirehouse secretary to financial advisor to award-winning founder of her own successful firm. "She is so well deserving," her son Michael says, "and a hero. To see the impact that she's had on other people's lives, both financially and in other ways, is just incredible."

BECOMING AN ADVISOR, STEP BY STEP

Born in Charlotte, North Carolina, Barbara was attending a local college when her new husband, Mike, was offered a job in Williamsport, Pennsylvania. Barbara resumed her education at nearby Lock Haven University, but soon transferred to Bloomsburg

University, a good hour-long drive from Williamsport, to major in business. By this time Barbara and Mike had a child, Kim, and things became a little stressful.

"The commute was about an hour, and gas prices had skyrocketed. We were living on a $10,000-a-year salary and paying a fulltime babysitter. I participated in a work-study program, so that I was leaving for Bloomsburg at seven a.m. and coming home between four and five p.m. We ate a lot of pretzels and popcorn and actually used pretzel canisters as our chairs."

"If I had taken pen to paper and tried to calculate how we were going to make it, it would have been mathematically impossible," Barbara says. "There's just no way it could have happened. But there was a miracle in there, as there are so many miracles in my life. You just can't document them all. But I really believe that if we take two steps, the universe gives us a break, and we get ten steps free. My daughter gave me a plaque that said, 'When you come to the edge of all the light you know and are about to step off into the darkness of the unknown, faith is knowing one of two things will happen: There will be something solid to stand on or you will be taught to fly.' There were many times when that plaque kept me moving forward in faith."

After graduating from Bloomsburg in 1975, Barbara turned down a teaching position in Lewisburg. "I wanted something closer to home. I wanted to spend time with my daughter." Serendipitously, she took a position as a nine-to-five secretary with a major securities firm. She worked there until January of 1979, just a few days before her son was born, and then worked at some part-time jobs, including assisting an accountant during late hours.

"When I left the firm, I really didn't have an interest in going back, except that I sincerely liked the people there and my manager." But after a year, Barbara realized "that it was going to be very hard living on my husband's teaching salary alone because we had a mortgage and two children. So when I got a call from the manager asking if I'd be willing to come back, I said, 'Yes, I'd be willing to come back as long as I can get licensed, because I don't like working and not fully understanding the business.' He said that would be fine as long as I did it on my own time, which I did."

After a year of serving as a registered sales assistant, Barbara became the office's first client services representative. "Within some offices, the firm created a small accounts division. All of the account executives in the office were encouraged to cull their books, take their lowest producing accounts, and give them to the Client

Services Department. It was really a service position, and my job was to call the clients and take care of them. I did that for a year, and then a new manager came in and wanted me to become an account executive. He encouraged me to take that next step, although I really loved what I was doing."

With this encouragement, Barbara audited the firm's training course in New York City. "I was on a different track and never officially enrolled in the training, but it was the same course and the same training. I wanted the opportunity and the experience, and they said 'This is the way we're going to do it.' I said 'Fine.' Actually, my unconventional career path turned out for the best, because when I left the firm in 2001, it turned out that I didn't actually have an account executive's contract, which would have prohibited me from contacting my clients."

Looking back, Barbara says, "What I really liked about my progression—from secretary to client services rep to account executive—was that I did it in baby steps. Instead of simply being thrown in with a phone book, I was gently encouraged over time to go to the next level." That evolution has been helpful to Barbara in creating the structure of her current practice.

EARLY SUCCESSES: ONE THING LEADS TO ANOTHER

Returning to the office after training, Barbara was in fact now an account executive, and she started building a book. "My gosh, I hated cold calling, but I did it. I remember my manager buying an industrial directory for me. It listed the owner or principal's name and telephone number, and I just started calling. Miraculously, I actually got a few accounts that way. For the most part I would call at seven or seven-thirty in the morning, when I found that the principals would answer their own phones."

"In the beginning, I gave a lot of seminars on cash management accounts, IRA rollover accounts, and other topics of interest to investors. I found that potential clients could attend the seminars— what we now call educational events—without feeling any obligation and decide for themselves if they wanted to talk further with me. It was a low-pressure way of meeting potential clients without being intrusive."

Barbara did not mind working hard or tracking her progress. "Before deciding to go through the training program and become an account executive, I had a very serious meeting with my family. I told them I was going to have to work very long hours for a number of years, and I needed them to support me. We agreed that they'd take care of the house and meals so that when I was home, we could spend the time together. They were so supportive of me and still are. I am truly blessed with a wonderful family."

It was important to Barbara to continue to learn. Because she knows that the world, the markets, and the opportunities available are constantly changing, she's participated in hundreds of conferences, workshops, seminars, and educational courses. "I always loved learning new ways of helping my clients. I still do. I'm a learning junkie, and my entire team is committed to learning and being better." Most team members attend at least one conference every year. Jason Moyer, Branch Manager, Deanna Gephart, Operations Manager, and Barbara Jennings, Wealth Consultant, are all CFPs® (Certified Financial Planner Practitioners™), and Barbara herself is a CIMA (Certified Investment Management Analyst).

Barbara notes, "Acquiring these certifications required a tremendous commitment and also additional annual credits must be maintained. But that's good, because it's one way of keeping our knowledge current. *Kaizen* is the Japanese word for 'constant and never ending improvement,' a concept used by Dr. W. Edwards Deming after World War II in working to rehabilitate Japan. If you'll remember, prior to that, 'made in Japan' was synonymous with 'cheaply made.' Dr. Deming was able to convince the Japanese that they didn't have to invent new things to be successful, they only had to take what had already been invented and make it slightly better, *constantly*. So, they started with transistor radios ... and you know the rest of the story. This is one of our guiding principles: constant and never ending improvement."

"My biggest challenge in the business early on was that management wanted me to measure my commissions daily. I had no trouble working long hours and making a lot of phone calls, but I was never able—willing is probably more accurate—to keep track of my commissions. I know it works for some people; it just didn't work for me."

Once Barbara acquired a few clients by inheriting them from account executives who retired, by cold or warm calling, or through seminars, she was committed to taking excellent care of them. Barbara didn't care how big or small they were; instead, she cared about whether her clients felt that she added value for them. "There had to be a mutual respect and a genuine liking of the client," Barbara says. "My philosophy has always been to treat clients like trusted friends—to treat them the way they *want* to be treated— and to treat them like they're special and unique, because they are."

The real turning point in Barbara's career came with the arrival of a new manager in the early nineties. (Barbara gives a lot of credit to the great managers, coaches, and mentors she has had throughout her career. "Without their support and excellent guidance, I never would have made it.") Until then, Barbara had been moderately successful, but remained in the middle of the pack. The new manager insisted that Barbara do a business plan and then follow that plan. He spent hours working with her and mandated that she write down in detail exactly how she was going to grow her business.

Although Barbara looks back on this as a grueling experience, it was the magical key to exponential growth. A predominant part of the business plan was for Barbara to do investment plans on every client, making sure that she was taking care of all parts of their financial goals, creating a road map that could be followed in both good and bad times. Such investment plans were completely in accord with Barbara's philosophy, which has always been to "start with a client's life and plan his or her money around it." Following the business plan, Barbara's business doubled in one year (seen as impossible), and then continued to grow at a terrific rate.

In 1989, when fee-based investments became available, Barbara embraced them with a vengeance. "Fee-based programs are not appropriate for all clients, but I believe fee-based money management puts the client and the advisor on the same side of the table. I feel it's a win-win for everyone." Once again, for Barbara and her clients, one thing simply led to another.

BUILDING HER TEAM

Barbara's team resembles Barbara in more ways than one. On the one hand, her team is composed of dedicated professionals with a wide range of in-depth skills and extraordinary dedication to the well being of their clients. On the other hand, far more than most successful small firms, Barbara's team feels like a family, with people who really and truly care for each other and who are grateful for the opportunity to work not only with each other, but on behalf of their clients.

"We have team meetings every Tuesday morning at seven-forty-five," says Barbara. "The first thing we start out with is that everybody has to say something that they are grateful for. Sometimes, because of what's going on in somebody's life, that's a challenge. I don't care what they say—it can be that they're grateful to have ten toes on their feet—because it all works, and we all need that momentum. We need to be grateful for what we have, no matter how much or how little that is."

Barbara clearly is grateful for the entire team, from the newest employees to her two partners. Today, the team includes seven individuals who serve as client relationship managers. In addition to Barbara, they are: her partner Jason Moyer (the Moyer of Hudock Moyer Wealth Management), Barbara's son and other partner Michael Hudock, wealth consultant, Wayne Dieffenderfer, IT coordinator (who handles the team's technology needs and also specializes in insurance), Deanna Gephart (who also serves as operations manager), Barbara Jennings (who focuses on clients in eastern Pennsylvania and New Jersey), and Vicky Bartlow, wealth consultant (who has twenty years of banking and trust experience). The team's administrative assistants are H. Joseph Moyer (Jason's younger brother), Cheryl Appleton, Cynthia Hall, and Marcia Pauling. Holly Tagliaferri is the team's communications specialist, and the final team member is Jane Hawkins, coordinator of first & lasting impressions. Impressively, the financial services experience of the team members comes to well over 200 years.

Jason, who serves as branch manager and senior wealth consultant, specializes in portfolio management and estate planning. He originally applied for a job as a financial advisor at the wirehouse firm Barbara was with but was turned down. The manager who interviewed him felt that because Jason was quite reserved, he might have difficulty in attracting clients but did note that he had terrific analytical skills. Barbara says, "He's very analytical and very brilliant, and could pass all the tests in a heartbeat." Jason soon successfully interviewed again for an administrative assistant position, and after three months in the office the manager put him with Barbara.

"It was like we hit the autobahn at ninety miles an hour," Barbara says. "As soon as he joined me, there was a huge acceleration. He was organized, effective, and efficient. He started taking my calls and began to organize and implement the investment plans we had been doing, making sure we were following up as needed. He had a real knack for details, always followed up, and was just the best administrative assistant I'd ever known. Now *that* is synergy! It was truly a match made in heaven! Looking back, what I learned here is that when a new team member joins and it's working effectively, within a very short period of time all the team members feel it. Everyone on the team should feel an ease, a 'whoa!' kind of thing, as you find that things are in sync. When it isn't working, there's a 'thud'—now you've got an anchor holding you down, and you've got to cut it as quickly as possible."

As Jason puts it, "We just really clicked. I was actually working temporarily with Barbara for three months, after which time I was supposed to go into the management training program, but we just took off together. Our hardest struggle was replacing me after I started evolving relationships with clients to the point where they would call and talk to me, and not always have to ask for Barbara. We went through about four people, trying to find the right fit, so I was always straddling the fence, two different things in two different worlds, until we finally left to form our own firm." Jason and Barbara have been together since April of 1997.

Barbara continues the story: "We went through numerous administrative assistants as Jason started to become more of a relationship manager. One manager came over to me at the copy machine and said, 'I just hope you don't break his back,' which was somewhat hurtful. But I've always had high expectations of people who are working with me. When you're paying for your own support, as I was paying for Jason, you feel totally different about your expectations than when the firm is paying. I wasn't willing to accept mediocrity. When you're paying the bill, all of a sudden you become much more aware of the person's performance, and are more willing to say the things that need to be said. Unfortunately, many big firms are not willing to fire people; instead they just move them around inside an office."

The importance of investing in her business by paying for top-flight assistants was a lesson Barbara learned long ago. Early in her career Barbara shared administrative assistants with other account executives but at a certain point, she told her manager that she wanted ed a one-on-one administrative assistant. "It was really important to me," Barbara says, "because if I was sharing an assistant with anybody, then the assistant had to consider that other person a priority as well. But if I had that person alone, then it would be my/our clients' priorities that would always be important. So I told my manager I'd pay for it—which I did—and it took a huge portion of my income at that time."

This brings Barbara to one of her most important principles. "It's the rule of giving back something of what you are getting, and being willing to invest your own money in your business. Until you're proven, the big securities firms are not going to invest in your business and put any money into you, so you have to do it first." Not surprisingly, as soon as she had her own assistant, Barbara's production began dramatically increasing.

Barbara's other partner, her son Michael, came to work with Barbara in January 2003. "With previous experience in advising clients as to financial matters—Michael had moved up the ranks while working at a big bank—he was able to hit the ground running with us." The team recently added Vicky Bartlow to work with Michael and help him manage his relationships. Vicky has over twenty years of experience with banking and trusts. "We've structured our practice into advisor teams. The goal is that no advisor has more than a hundred and fifty relationships. This helps to ensure that clients receive the level of service and attention that we feel they're entitled to. We work as one team—one for all and all for one."

With respect to her son, Barbara concludes that "Michael is doing well. I was concerned that being my son, it would appear that I was favoring him over others. So he really had to work twice as hard to gain the respect of the team, and I believe he's done that. He makes me laugh, which is very good. He gets here at seven in the morning, and many evenings he works quite late. He's more than doubled his assets under management since joining us and receives a lot of referrals. We consider it a great honor, and we take it quite seriously, when clients send us referrals of their family, friends, or colleagues. I think it was critically important for him to work somewhere else and prove himself before he joined our practice."

UNIQUE TALENTS AND HIGHEST PRODUCTIVITY

As for clients feeling the team's magic, the team's first point of contact—and the person who has worked with Barbara the longest (nearly 34 years now)—is C. Jane Hawkins, affectionately known as the coordinator of first & lasting impressions. Jane was the receptionist when Barbara started at her first firm, and over 20 years later, just about when Barbara and her team left to form their own firm, she had reached retirement age. "They actually were going to force her to retire because of her age, but I knew how valuable she was, so I asked her to come with us." Today, when you call Hudock Moyer, the friendly yet unflappable voice that greets you is Jane's.

Once again, a focus on people, on giving back in order to receive, and on making sure that the highest possible value is derived from each team member has served Barbara well. "One of our rules," Barbara says, "is that everybody should be doing the activity that puts them at their highest productivity level. I'm one of the best typists in our office, but that doesn't mean that it's my most productive activity. It's also critically important that every employee is working with his or her greatest strength(s). There's a great book, *Now, Discover Your Strengths* (Free Press, 2001), by Marcus Buckingham and Donald O. Clifton, that discusses in depth the importance of finding out what your strengths are and then finding ways of using those strengths."

This so-called highest productivity level principle first became clear for Barbara when she took a strategic coaching seminar in the mid-nineties. One of the seminar's core principles, Barbara says, "was to find out what your unique ability is, and then delegate everything else. As part of the program we had to write a letter to ten people and ask them what our greatest strength was. This was uncomfortable for me, but I'll tell you now that those letters are ten of my most precious possessions. The letters consistently said that I cared about people, that I did what I said I was going to do, and that people could trust me. So, with my clients, and even with my team members, my strength really is in the relationship. If the world were perfect, 100 percent of my time would be spent with people—with my clients or with my team members—in the relationship. Not preparing for appointments, but meeting with people in appointments."

Barbara's talent for building relationships has strongly influenced everyone on the team. "The values and beliefs of Hudock Moyer come from every single employee," Michael says, "whether we're on the phone or meeting in person. Every time I pick up the phone, I want the caller to know that it's going to be a good call, that they'll find out about what's going on, have at least one laugh, and feel good about their day. This way, from the center of my core, when I go home at night I know I'm making a difference in the world. Making people's lives better is what it's all about."

"There are times," Barbara adds, "especially with our older clients, when talking with one of us is the highlight of their day. Or when they receive a letter from us, or birthday candy or flowers, it's truly meaningful and uplifting for them. We all get so involved in how busy we are—we've got people waiting in line to talk to us— that I think sometimes we forget that there a lot of people out there who spend their whole day by themselves. When one of these folks gets a call from our office, it becomes a good day."

As Michael sums it up, "There's going to be up markets, there's going to be down markets, but when all of that is out of the way, what you have is the relationship."

MANAGING THEIR CLIENTS' WEALTH

Barbara and her team pour their hearts and souls into every single client—as the front of their new brochure states, "Realizing Financial Goals, One Client at a Time." The team's mission statement is even clearer about this: "It is the Mission of Hudock Moyer Wealth Management to define and achieve the financial goals of each individual client." Or as Michael puts it, "The reason we're here is our clients—and that's it. They are number one. If they come in, if they're on the phone, we want to make them feel special. The enthusiasm and the energy that people see when they walk through the door separates us from every other firm out there."

The process begins with deciding which clients to take. "One rule here is to not take clients if we're not going to keep them," Barbara says. "If you don't feel that they're the type of people whose company you would enjoy at dinner, then you don't want to start a relationship with them. It's hard to say 'no' to new clients in the first place, but if we know it's not a good fit, it keeps everyone from being disappointed later."

Put more positively, Barbara says that another principle she learned from an industry seminar was "Don't work with people when you get that knot in the pit of your stomach. Life's too short. Wouldn't it be wonderful if every day you come into the office and you knew that you were only going to talk to wonderful people, and work with wonderful people? I look back on my life and that's the way we have it today. It's almost like a definition of qualifying to do business with us: You have to be wonderful."

Given how they feel about their clients, it's not surprising that the first step in any given client meeting is listening to the client with the goal of really understanding them. "They say the greatest need we have as human beings is to be understood," Barbara says. "To be heard. To really be heard. I truly think that's one of the things we give our clients. We really listen to them. So even though I'll have a review file with me, I'll say to a client, 'We are going to go through this, but before I do, what's important to you right now? What questions or thoughts or concerns do you have? I want to make sure I address what's most important to you before going to my agenda.'

Sometimes there is something major going on and sometimes there isn't. But I think giving them the opportunity to speak first is a whole lot more important than me getting through my agenda. It's just so rare that people really feel heard and responded to. For example, when somebody is in mourning, they need to be heard. It can't just be, 'So how are you doing?' and then moving on. It has to be, 'How are you ... really?' It makes a difference."

Understanding the emotional and financial situation of each client allows Barbara and her team to proceed effectively with managing their clients' wealth. "Financial management," Jason says, "has to grow out of client service, and by that I am including the kind of listening that we do, because if you don't know what the goals are, then what you're doing is irrelevant. It's different things to different people: what we may think is a good return on an account might look bad to one person and phenomenal to another. So, we begin with what's in the client's account and what they are going to do with it. What are the client's expectations? It's critically important to understand that."

Jason continues with a story about a client who had a child going to private school. "She was a brilliant, gifted child," Jason says, "and although her parents couldn't really afford it, they managed to pay the tuition. They didn't have a lot of money by a lot of people's standards, but they were very comfortable in their lifestyle. It meant everything in the world to the mother that she could find a way to pay the tuition. She said to me, 'Barbara told me fifteen years ago, when I became a client, that her definition of being rich was to be able to do what I wanted to do with my money and thereby accomplish my goals. I know what she means now because I feel rich because I can pay this bill.' That's what really mattered to her."

Barbara tells a similar story of a physician client. "There was a great pediatrician who loved his work and worked very hard. His wife had come to us for a seminar on putting your money where your values are. It had resonated with her, so they scheduled an appointment to meet with me and he started talking to me about how his wife loved her horse. He was working full-time, and said what he really wanted to do was to get a horse, work part-time, and spend more time with his wife and their horses. So we ran the numbers and I said, 'You are going to have to compromise and cut back. But if it's worth it to you, and these really are your priorities, then you can do it.' He said, 'You know what? My friends travel, go on cruises, go to Europe. I don't want to do that. I love being here.' So he did it, and now they are so happy and have several horses."

"Later," Barbara adds, "they rescued a mustang. Eventually they got it to the point where the mustang would come over and eat out of my hand. It was just such an amazing experience to be there and see them living their dreams. Working with these kinds of clients, with real people in real-life situations with real-life dreams, is what we do. We start with their life, and then plan their money around it."

Of course, such planning is done according to a set of well crafted principles and procedures, beginning with their assessment of a client's risk/reward tradeoff. As Jason says, "Barbara's great premise has always been that we don't want to take any more risk than we need to take, which is why when we structure portfolios we limit volatility and avoid unnecessary risk. You do want to strive to beat the market with the portion of your assets that need to be in equities, but what portion needs to be in equities? You just can't take the old formula of one hundred minus your age and say that's your optimal equity percentage. That's not the way it really works. One client who is seventy might want to be very aggressive with a percentage of his assets, because he has a big estate goal or something he wants to accomplish. Another client who is seventy might feel like she has all the money she needs, and she can live comfortably on it. So her goals are met, and she doesn't want to risk that nest egg because she can't go out and make it again."

After deeply listening to their clients, assessing their true goals and risk tolerance, and throwing in a heavy dose of investment planning, Barbara and her team use a combination of outside money managers and fee-based investment strategies to invest their clients' funds. They choose money managers based on peer group performance for one-year, three-year, five-year, and ten-year time frames. "We like to have three out of four of those be in the 25th percentile or better," Barbara says. "We do fire managers. First we will put them on probation. When we do this, we are basically trying to determine if it's a great manager who's having a bad year, or if it's a manager who is no longer great. Once we make the decision, we terminate them, but we usually do it gradually. We'll stop adding new money first, and then continue to watch them. If the trend continues, we'll pull the plug."

Significantly, following the motto of her birth state, North Carolina—*Esse Quam Videri*, "To Be, Rather Than to Seem"—Barbara and her team personally invest in the same managers and funds their clients invest in. "I really do want to put my money where my mouth is in all senses of the word," Barbara says. "We don't have any type of investment that we do for clients that I haven't done for myself. Everything they have, I either have or have had in some form, because I think it's really important for me to know what it feels like to have that investment. A lot of team members also have these same investments, based upon what they can do. Then we can truly empathize with clients because we know what it really feels like when something we recommended loses money. So I'm not just telling my clients to do something, I'm doing it for them and for myself—with their interests first."

Once a client's life plan is in place, the team meets with the client on a regular basis, usually two or three times a year, to discuss any major changes in goals or life circumstances and the need for rebalancing, if any. Framing these regular meetings is the team's overall service orientation, which consistently shines through in many ways. For example, Jason says, "We want to be part of the big picture. You wouldn't believe what people sometimes ask us to do, like booking airlines reservations on occasion. That's fine. We want them to know that if they have a question or a challenge, all they have to do is call us. As Dee likes to say, you might not even know the scope of your problem or how to solve it, but all you have to do is call. That's why our clients see us not just as financial advisors, but as life advisors and life supporters. Having gone through so many major life events with our clients—births, deaths, 9/11, clients finding out they have cancer or are in remission—we're sometimes the first phone call they make. We have shared so many tears and so much joy with all of our clients. How much of an honor is that, that they want to share on that level with us?"

One of the better decisions Barbara and Jason made was the creation of a Board of Advisors (BOA). This is a small group of current clients who share the HMWM vision and understand the value they add. Barbara reflects, "We've learned so much from them and have implemented many, many changes and improvements because of the advice they gave us. One of these changes was adding an Executive Summary page to our appointment file that includes a summary of the recommendations we're making at that appointment. This gives the client something to take with them so they can look back and know exactly what changes were made, when, and why. We've found that the clients greatly appreciate this addition."

"The Board of Advisors," Barbara continues, "was also critically important in giving us feedback on our team brochure, which is now getting rave reviews. Although it took us four years to complete, the final result was worth it. If the BOA hadn't been so judicious, we'd have a team brochure that looks like every other firm's. The recommendations from the BOA have ranged from advice and guidance on buying a building to giving us feedback about mailings we've sent out. It's really terrific to be able to run things by a group of caring yet opinionated and discriminating clients before we 'take it live.' They are a tremendous source of information and counsel for us."

THE WISDOM OF WEALTH TRANSFER

One of Barbara's favorite topics is the wisdom of wealth transfer. "It's from shirtsleeves to shirtsleeves in three generations," Barbara says. "The idea that wealth never survives three generations is heard all around the world. The Chinese say 'From rice bowl to rice bowl in three generations.' In Holland it's 'From clogs to clogs in three generations.' Multiple studies have shown that 70 percent of all wealth transitions have failed. 70 percent! It doesn't matter if a country has estate taxes or not. It doesn't matter if it's new world economy or old world economy—70 percent fail. Well, if the weatherman says there's a 70 percent chance of rain, we're going to carry umbrellas, so let's find a way to help protect our families and children from having this happen."

"The first generation," Barbara continues, "is the generation of creation, where the parents create the wealth. The second generation is the generation of observation, where the children observe the creation of the wealth. They don't have quite the same understanding of it, but they respect it because they saw how hard their parents worked to create it. The third generation, if we're not careful and proactive, is the generation of gratification and entitlement. Here the children have no respect for wealth creation and blow the money. The fourth generation is the generation of lamentation. *Webster's* definition of lamentation is 'To mourn aloud.' This mourning and the generations of lamentation will continue until another creator comes along. What's extremely interesting to me is a conversation I had with Jason recently. He took this concept to a much higher level and overlaid it onto our economic cycles. The possibility exists that we're now in the 'gratification' cycle. The 1930s could have been the 'lamentation' period of the last cycle."

"Unfortunately," Barbara continues, "when we are creating wealth, we usually don't know that's what we are doing. We're often just putting one foot in front of the other. We gain the wisdom of wealth, but we don't know that it's important to pass the wisdom of wealth on to our kids. We think that doing estate planning will take care of it. But too often parents try to make things easy on their kids.

I'm giving a series of educational events on how to raise financially responsible heirs, and one of the things I talk about is adversity, and how many of us strengthened and developed our characters because of the adversity we had to face. But how many of us try to take that adversity away from our children? We try to make things easy for them. As Paul Harvey says, 'We tried so hard to make things better for our children that we made them worse.' Or, as Shakespeare says, 'Sweet are the uses of adversity, Which like the toad, ugly and venomous, Wears yet a precious jewel in his head.'"

"The greatest gifts you can give your children," Barbara adds, "are the roots of responsibility and the wings of freedom, and that's why we believe it's as important to pass the wisdom of wealth as it is to pass the wealth itself. So why can't we structure adversity into our children's lives and make it part of their education? We should make it so they don't get everything they want immediately, without having to work for it. If we don't teach them the lessons, they are going to go out in the world and they are going to find that it's not as gentle a place as Mom and Dad made it."

Barbara also feels it's very important to teach children what she calls the one-third rule, which was established by a wealthy American family prior to the advent of income taxes, the public relations profession, or the widespread notion of philanthropy. "According to the one-third rule," Barbara says, "a child didn't get an allowance for doing chores, because doing chores was the child's admission ticket to being part of the household. An allowance was given to the child with the understanding that one-third was to be saved, one-third was to be given to a charity of the child's choice, and one-third was a discretionary third that could be spent on anything the child wanted."

"Well," Barbara continues, "I told a client about this, and she decided to implement it with her granddaughter. Her granddaughter came up to me at our holiday event, and I asked her how her allowance was coming. She said, 'Very well. I'm saving one-third of my allowance, and I'm giving one-third to the food pantry, which helps people who are hungry and homeless. I get to do anything I want with the other third, and I've saved it too.' I told her that one day she was going look back on that decision as being one of the best of her life and she was going to be my best client. We both giggled. She subsequently sent me a note saying that she and her brother had received the Citizenship Award at her school because of her charitable gifts and the influence she had on her classmates. What it teaches children is immensely important, including: (1) to live within their means, (2) to save part of everything they earn, and (3) to view the world asking the question, 'How can I make the world better?' There are innumerable other lessons intricately woven into the one-third rule as well."

GIVING NOW AND LOOKING TOWARD THE FUTURE

Following her motto of "To Be, Rather Than to Seem," Barbara has struck a fairly unusual deal with her two partners, her son Michael and Jason—who she says "is like a son to me." Over the next ten years, Barbara plans on transitioning 90 percent of the ownership of Hudock Moyer over to Michael and Jason. "What I'm trying to do," she says, "is to make sure that the culture of the firm continues, that it doesn't become just a way of making a living, which I know it won't as long as the two of them are involved. So the transfer starts out at a low level, but over the years their portion becomes larger and my portion becomes smaller so that at the end of that time, I'll have 10 percent and they will jointly have 90 percent. Then I'll keep my 10 percent until they either fire me or I die."

When the unusual nature and generosity of this arrangement is pointed out, Barbara responds, "I recognize that I'm getting older, and they are young and just really in the prime of their lives. I want them to feel ownership in it. Even now, for the most part, I bring them in on every decision, and I give them the opportunity to out-vote me. For example, I believe that spending money on our clients is an investment, but that means we have to write checks. Now that Jason and Michael have ownership, money spent on our clients means money not going into their pockets as well. What I want them to understand is that it makes us all better. It makes our clients happier, and in the long run, it's a good business decision. As always, you have to give to receive."

"Also," Barbara adds, "I didn't want to feel guilty when I want to take a vacation or be out of the office. I'm pretty open with my clients about this; they know I'm not going to live forever. As much as I love working—and I really do love working—I also love doing other things."

These other things include yoga, skiing, and scuba diving, spending time with her parents and her family, as well as involvements in a variety of different charities. As with so many things, Barbara's approach to charitable giving is practical and straightforward, and derives from an early life lesson. "I loved going to church as a child. One day I was sitting in church with my allowance, which was 50 cents. Tithing was not something that we discussed at home, but somehow I picked up the idea. Well, I knew that a tithe for me was a nickel, and I knew that that nickel could buy me a Cherry Hump Candy Bar, which was my favorite. That nickel was the hardest nickel I ever gave up, because all I could think about was the candy bar I could buy with it. I put that nickel in the plate and somehow that planted a really positive seed of giving that's lasted my whole life."

One flower from this seed bloomed during the early years of Barbara's practice. "Even in the beginning of my practice, I would cull my book and give away a hundred clients a year that I felt weren't completely aligned with my philosophy. I didn't feel that I was adding value to them. At first it felt like I was giving up a lot, all these assets and commissions. In reality, it freed up my time and energy to focus on the clients for whom I was adding value. Giving away those clients was kind of like tithing that nickel instead of buying the candy bar."

Recently, the seed has blossomed into an important change in firm policy. "We made a decision a few years ago," Barbara says, "to spend no more money on advertising, except a small amount for the billboard at the airport—when you go inside the front door, you can't miss it, because we've got a one-gate airport. We decided instead to take that money and give it to the Symphony, the Community Arts Center, the Community Theater League, and many non-arts charities. It's really important for us, and actually part of our mission, to make a difference in our communities. I recently calculated that over the last five or six years, either personally or as a business, we have collectively given hundreds of thousands of dollars. Our core purpose, our passion, is to make a profound difference in the lives of the clients we serve, in the lives of our teammates, and in our communities."

DOWN HOME WITH ADVERSITY—
AND BACK AGAIN

In 2000, for a variety of reasons, Barbara and her core staff left Williamsport for a new location in Pittsburgh, which Barbara affectionately calls their "six month summer vacation in Pittsburgh." The move did not work out as planned, and Barbara and her team returned to Williamsport a few months later. A year after that they left to form their own independent firm.

Despite having to change their clients' account numbers three times (once moving to Pittsburgh, once moving back to Williamsport, and once more when they formed their own firm), the team managed to keep 90 percent of them and was soon thriving again. This remarkable retention rate and the overall success of the new firm is a testament both to the team's ability to face adversity— individual team members had to find places to live in Pittsburgh, some sold their houses, and some spouses quit their jobs—as well as to Barbara as an individual. "It was tough, but something that the adversity in my life has given me is the knowledge that you really can't count on other people to come and save you. You've got to do it yourself. So the team pulled together and accomplished remarkable things."

Jason's perspective on their return is very informative. "I'll never forget the day we had a meeting with our clients to announce that we were coming back to Williamsport. Barbara had prepared a speech about what we were doing and why. She was very, very afraid, I think, of what the clients were going to say since we had made the move and were returning four months later. She began, 'This was a total mistake. We are sorry that it happened to you, but it happened to us as well. But we are trying to come back and make it all right and return to our roots and grow again.' Well, she got through the first sentence, and the room burst out into applause because we were coming back. It was what the clients most wanted. Barbara started to cry."

"I was so happy to hear the applause," Barbara says. "I didn't have to finish my speech." Jason adds, "They were so supportive of what we were going through. They were mainly worried about us."

Was the move to Pittsburgh really a mistake? Perhaps so, but the entire team has grown stronger because of it. As Barbara says, "If we make a mistake, I want to admit it and face it head on." That's just what you'd expect to hear from a woman who started out shy, who gladly accepts the label "down home," and who places more emphasis on relationships and trust than on anything else.

"I am awed by my team," Barbara says. "I am so grateful, so thankful, and so blessed. I don't know how it happened. In the beginning, I felt that I had to fit into a certain role, to be a certain way, and so I kind of buried myself and put on the 'expected' face. But over the years, as our clients have gotten to know us, and as we've gotten to know them, as real human beings, I realized that I could actually express how I really feel. I can be authentic, be who I really am, and know that that's okay." Barbara notes that Warren

Buffett, one of the world's wealthiest individuals, once said that success in life could be defined in these terms: "When you reach the end of your life and you find that the people who should love you, actually do love you." Clearly, in these terms Barbara Hudock has already had an extremely successful life and career, and is very likely to grow even more successful in the years ahead.

CHAPTER 11: CHRIS BALDWIN AND TEAM

CREDIT SUISSE SECURITIES (USA), LLC
CHICAGO, ILLINOIS

(Left to Right) Chris Prassas, Chris Baldwin, and Tom Tyndorf

Chris Baldwin, with the help of his two partners and just three staff members, has consistently earned a place in The Winner's Circle Top 100 Advisors. When asked about his success, he quickly states that "there's no magic ingredient or special sauce. If you're passionate about the business, as well as practical and disciplined, and if you're in it for a long period of time and—most of all—truly care about each and every client, you can be successful."

"I'm not a superstar," Chris continues. "Some really talented advisors who've been in the right place at the right time have prospered very quickly. But honestly, most of success is discipline. It's blocking and tackling your way every day. Many people are too wild with their schemes and abandon their thoughts and ideas too quickly. On the other hand, most of the very successful people I know have confidence in their strategy, and they stick with it. We built a business brick by brick. We've gone a long way to do it, but you know what? I'm enjoying the long way to being successful."

Chris's "long way" to success has indeed been challenging, and more than once he's had to completely reinvent himself and his business model. What has sustained him through all this, and has enabled both Chris and his team to be ranked so highly in The Winner's Circle? Ultimately, it's a combination of Chris's passion, his straightforwardness, and his great drive for personal and professional improvement.

"I have a passion for this business and the investment markets," Chris affirms. "I've had experience with them under some difficult conditions, I enjoy reading about them, and I've developed a very wide, broad-based, and diverse set of skills. At Credit Suisse we try to put our reading and research on investment strategies to use by thinking creatively and staying ahead of the curve."

As for his straightforwardness, Chris, who played high school and college football, is fond of another sports metaphor, this time from golf. "We're pretty much straight down the fairway in everything we do," he says. "We develop in-depth relationships with people; we bring in assets; and we diversify those assets in ways that fit our clients' risk profiles. And in order to diversify our risk and the firm's risk, we make sure that we have a diversified client base. Everybody is best served in this way."

Finally, there is Chris's constant drive for self-improvement, both personal and professional. "I strive to be a better man every day," he says. "I think that's really important. What does that mean? It's doing the things that are hard for me. It's coming home at night and taking the time to pay quality attention to my two kids. I'm striving to become a better husband and a better dad, and I take the same approach to the rest of my life, to my friends, and to the people around me whom I influence. That's what it's really about. And that's also how I view my business and the professionalism I bring to it. I try my best to make money for my clients and always do the right thing. Following this approach in my personal life and my professional life—you have to do it in both—is really what my life is all about."

BECOMING A SALESMAN

As a child and as a teenager, Chris took no interest in the stock market or related subjects. "My father, who was in the advertising business, wasn't involved in the financial markets in any way. I didn't really show any interest until I was going to college and realized that I was going to have to enter a profession and make a living. That's when I became intrigued by the financial markets."

Chris's family was not wealthy by any means. "I worked and paid my way through college," Chris says, "attending Marquette University in Milwaukee, which isn't known to be a really expensive school. I had nothing. In fact, Renee, who is now my wife, would visit me at school and buy me groceries with her mother's Visa card."

Chris hoped to become a securities analyst after finishing school. "I was more mature and practical than most of the kids coming out of school, and I had already determined my career path. I had majored in finance because I liked the financial services industry and the analytical processes behind it. I thought I saw a good opportunity in financial services. It was an industry where other people were doing well, so I thought I could probably do well there too, and that I would enjoy being a securities analyst."

For reasons of economic necessity, however, Chris had to give up the dream of becoming a securities analyst and go in a different direction. "I found that I needed to go back to business school to become an analyst. I had already worked long and hard and was financially in need. I knew someone in the industry, a family friend in Lake Forest where I had grown up, and they suggested that I go into the sales side of the industry. So that's how I started. I didn't want to go into sales. I thought I would be more suited to the analytical side, but this was my only entry opportunity."

"At that time," Chris notes, "when you went into our industry, you were a salesman. You weren't an advisor. You weren't any other name they give it today. You were a salesman. If they recruited you, you went into sales and you made cold calls. I didn't really like it very much. But the promise of making money was enough of a lure. That's how I started in the business."

EARLY SUCCESSES

"Although I didn't like it," Chris says, "I did a lot of cold calling. I didn't think it was particularly successful, and I still don't think it's a very successful method, although now we do occasionally make focus calls to people we don't know." Chris notes that as far as his own personality goes, "I've noticed that a lot of the really successful people in this industry have a tendency to be quite extroverted, but I've never been very extroverted myself. So, unfortunately, I wasn't able to build a business around that—that was the hard part of the business for me early on. Instead, I've tended to focus more on a combination of the practical and the analytical. Today, at forty-nine and with twenty-five years in the industry, I've earned my stripes and have developed a significant business by meeting people and gaining references from them."

In addition to his analytical and practical nature, Chris attributes his success to his intuitiveness. "A large part of success in this business has to do with how intuitive a person is. If I were to hire somebody from one of the business schools today, I'd probably be in awe of his or her resume. But it's very difficult to predict from a resume how well somebody is going to do, because an intuitiveness about markets, and about your business, is really the key to long-term success. It has been for me, anyway."

And while he didn't like cold calling, Chris's intuitiveness did enable him to achieve some initial successes through those early phone calls. "I wasn't calling people from a marketing perspective," he says. "When I had an opportunity to get through to those folks who were legitimate business prospects, I felt I could do business with them and help them. I do think I'm very effective with people in that way. So I think my early cold calling was helpful and did teach me a lot. It taught me a lot about people, and about how they respond to being approached. In the end, you need different approaches to develop relationships with different people."

"One of my first clients was a gentleman who bought a utility offering from us. It must have been the seventh or eighth time I called, and he finally said, 'If I buy a hundred shares from you, will you promise not to call me again?' He bought a hundred shares, and I never called him again. That's the way we built the business back then: You did a lot of business with a lot of small clients, and none of them was very memorable."

Chris's first truly memorable client experience exemplifies the steady, hard-working, and relationship-oriented approach that has come to characterize his career. "In 1993 I was working for Donaldson, Lufkin & Jenrette [DLJ] and I was assigned to cover the IPO for a client whom the firm took public. When I started doing business with this client, the account would not have made headlines. We did a lot of visiting and keeping them abreast of the markets, and I developed a very serious relationship with them over the course of many years. I think I got lucky with these folks, in part because they shared my values and thought about the world the same way I did. In our part of the world and for what we do, I probably came off as a pretty aggressive guy, real New York or very Chicago, and despite that they've stuck with me and it's worked well for a long time. It's a relationship that I don't think will ever change, and it's been the single most important one in my career."

REINVENTING HIS CAREER

Like many advisors with long careers, Chris has worked for a number of different firms. Sometimes the change was mainly in name, when one firm bought or merged with another. But about one-third of the way through, he took a distinct step that enabled him to completely redesign and reinvent his career, and to move from being a retail advisor to working with the ultra-high-net-worth clients that today constitute almost his entire client base. "I've been in the business since 1984," Chris says, "and my career has seen a tremendous evolution from when I started as a retail guy who would have considered a million-dollar account enormous."

The major sea change in Chris's career occurred in 1992. "I was working at a major securities firm and had found my mentor, Peter Skoglund, the single most influential person in my business life. He and I had an opportunity to open a Chicago office for the firm Donaldson, Lufkin & Jenrette, and making that move was what really changed my career. We wanted a more boutique, upscale environment, a smaller firm that had a different culture and that was a leader in the middle market. So I made a clean break from the stock brokerage model and was able to start a new business with a new platform at a new firm. Although it didn't have the muscle, cachet, product, and wealthier clients that I wanted, I still thought the firm was one step ahead of the wirehouses in terms of the people they called on and the way they thought about the markets. What they tried to deliver was leagues ahead as well."

"I had spent from 1984 until 1992 in the retail business," Chris notes, "and I just didn't like the way the retail industry was going in terms of how brokers were pushed out into the public, how they had to market, and what they had to do with their clients. I thought the industry would survive, but I just didn't see this as the way I wanted to build a life for myself. I had accounts, not clients, with individuals who bought a thousand shares of stock or had something in mutual funds. These weren't the mandates I wanted. I thought there was a better way to do it, and the only way to find out was to get into a different firm."

"It's hard to shift gears and just start doing something differently when you're already at a firm. Yet Peter Skoglund and I were talking about risk management and diversification long before other firms considered these subjects important. I don't think the industry really got focused on wealth management or risk management until the bear market event we had in the early 2000s. And the industry knows it. I could tell from the people we called on, and the people whose accounts we won afterward, based on what had happened to their portfolios during the decline."

PERFECTING THE BUSINESS MODEL

Finally, in 2000, Credit Suisse—a leading global bank focused on investment banking, private banking, and asset management, and headquartered in Zurich, Switzerland—acquired DLJ. In terms of the business model Chris was determined to follow, all was not smooth sailing at first. "When we started at Credit Suisse," he says, "they had huge aspirations for our DLJ business, which was mostly general brokerage business with some wealth management infused in it. Although we did have some bigger accounts and big orders, I spent about three years chasing big mandates when I should have been attacking the business in a different way. The big mandates are always going to be there. You can always read the tape, and there's always somebody in the office who can say, 'XYZ was acquired by XYA. Here's the guy you should call.' Those calls are easy to make and take just ten minutes out of your day; you can hire somebody to make them."

"So," Chris continues, "I spent three years of my career chasing unreasonable goals unsuccessfully, and at a time when we didn't have as much brand recognition as we would have liked. Then one day I woke up and realized that *this was a relationship business, and the only way I was going to consistently develop large clients was to consistently be in front of wealthy people.* It was simple. And how was I going to do that? I had to start asking the right questions, and I had to start making personal time commitments to being involved in charities and sitting on boards. I had to do a lot of things that involved stepping outside of the box, things that made more demands on my personal time than I'd ever had before. So that's what I did, and it started to really pay off for me."

"When we were at DLJ we built a fledgling wealth management practice from scratch. Then we took it another step forward at Credit Suisse, based on what we thought the market needed. We've always known that we wanted to have a business built on integrity and diversity. As a result, today we have, in my mind, the purest wealth management model in the system."

What does the business model look like today? "I'm not the kind of person who's going to focus exclusively on the largest accounts," Chris says. "That's a great market and we have plenty of clients in that space, but it's a high risk as a business model. There are plenty of really wealthy people below that threshold who want to do business with us. You also have to keep in mind that you can't be too idealistic about whom you do business with. Every client is unique. And that's a challenge. Not so much from a resources standpoint but from a risk management standpoint. Occasionally we have clients who want to take too much risk, and there are people who will naturally take more risk than we think wise. We don't shun that business; we're not that idealistic. But in the main, we have a core part of our business that we can count on and that we know will be there, and we know those clients won't suffer dramatically when the markets go down."

"In that way," Chris continues, "it's a somewhat boring business. It's not the type of business where we have a great month, then do nothing for the next three. But we're happy with it. It's the type of business we want for our clients, for ourselves, and for our families." Chris notes, as well, that he and his partners "don't really run a distribution business. Our business isn't about how we are going to go from three partners to fifteen and run a business that generates huge revenues. We're not interested in the megateam concept. First and foremost, we're in this for our clients."

"Lastly but very importantly," Chris adds, "I believe our business is very diverse in contrast to many large producers. The large producers I've been around during my career tend to get lucky either by timing or coincidence, or they are talented people who have one or two very large accounts that dominate 50 or 60 percent of their business. If you cut through most of the nonsense that you hear on the Street, one or two very large clients drive many of these larger practices. Our business is the furthest thing from that. Last year, when we had a record year, we had one client who represented around 9 percent of our business. That's a very big number for us. This year our team's business will be up significantly, and I can't think of a single client who will be responsible for more than 5 percent of it."

WORKING WITH HIS PARTNERS AND TEAM

Chris has two partners, Thomas M. Tyndorf, with 18 years in the industry, and Christopher J. Prassas (Chris P.), with 17 years in the industry. "When I was at a prior securities firm," Chris says, "I hired Tom, believe it or not, to market for me, to cold call. When we moved to DLJ, I brought Tom with me and his initial role was to market. As we gained clients, in addition to continuing his marketing, Tom began to help service them. Over the years Tom has become a full-fledged business partner who does some selling but probably not any more than Chris P. or I. I would say that today Tom is probably about 60 percent coverage, 30 percent marketing, and 10 percent everything else."

"Chris P. came to us in ninety-six or so, having been involved in the fixed income business. He started here at DLJ in a partnership with another gentleman who, ironically, left DLJ for what was then Credit Suisse First Boston. Chris was looking to partner up with somebody and we liked him, liked his attitude, and thought he had a lot of upside. I thought he was a good marketer, and he knew wealthy people. We like to use the term that Chris just 'gets it.' We knew that he understood 'it,' and that he would be a success with us. So he came in as a partner, with a book of business, and it's been the three of us ever since. That was over ten years ago, and it's worked out very well."

Importantly, Chris, Chris P., and Tom have a true horizontal partnership, which benefits their clients in a number of ways. "Everybody covers all the accounts," Chris says. "I've seen a lot of partnerships that are not really partnerships. They look at who covers an account, and they split the revenues that way. We don't do that. We run a pure partnership, and the revenues are split on a formula, that is, the revenues are mandated so that I get X percent, Tom gets Y percent, and Chris P. gets Z percent. So we are each compensated out of the total revenues that are generated here according to a fixed percentage. We've done it that way because we don't want to have conflicts of interest in our partnership. We want to make sure that everybody lends a hand in covering all the same relationships."

While Chris's group doesn't use titles, it's fair to say that Chris is the senior partner and receives the largest single share of the pie. "I've always felt that the people I've worked with needed to be compensated well—it's a necessary component to long-term success—and I think I'm a very generous person. In fact, I'm astounded that most people aren't more generous. I'm that way in my life with my money and the things I do for charities, friends, family and other people in need, both in terms of time and money, and my wife is the same way. I've been together with my two partners such a long time in part because we have a very generous arrangement here and we've tried to build a business that works for the long term."

"Still," Chris notes, "the challenge is to say, 'Okay, at what point do I want to start taking a pay cut, because the more of the business I give up to my two partners, the less money I make. But ideally, in order for them to accelerate their growth, there will come a point in the future where we're all close to being compensated at the same level. But they are both relatively young men—both in their early forties. So there's a lot of room for growth, not only in terms of total revenue, but in terms of the percentages they receive."

While the three partners provide coverage on almost all of the accounts, "that doesn't mean," Chris notes, "that there aren't a few relationships where Chris P. or Tom won't talk to the clients. But that's unusual, and most often occurs with legacy clients who were mine before we got together as a partnership. Even in those cases, I try to select one of my two partners to give me backup coverage. Likewise, there are a handful of clients who I don't interface with on investment decisions, but still, they know me."

At least part of the partnership's success can be attributed to the easy, free flow of information that characterizes their working conditions and decision-making process. "We sit here together in a single corner office," Chris says, "and all three of us can see each other. Our staff sits right outside our office and we look through our glass windows at them. It's a constant give and take here during the day about 'What do we do with this client?' 'What do we do with the markets?' 'What's going on with the bond market today?' 'Chris, what do you think about our decision to move $9 million of this client's money into the municipal bond market since the cash markets have been a disaster ... is this the right thing to do?' 'Well, let's talk to the trader and find out how he feels about it.'"

"So there's a constant interplay between us," Chris continues, "and most of the decisions we make here are done by consensus. It's almost like a trading desk in a lot of ways. The toughest part for me about working in an office with three people—and it's been ten years now—is that I tend to get really focused. Interruptions make me somewhat less productive, especially from the marketing standpoint, but overall our constant communication is definitely worth it."

The kind of constant interplay among the three partners and their team, and the free flow of information facilitated by working in the same room, makes sense in terms of how Chris likes to run his days. "You may think this is crazy, but I've always felt that I was less productive when I tried to structure my day. The things I have to do on a daily basis change from day to day. When I come into the office in the morning I know what I have to get to from a client standpoint and a market standpoint. But outside of the obvious—getting to my newspapers, understanding the general direction of the markets before they open, what client issues I have to deal with—I'm coming into the office every day pretty much creating as I go."

"That's the kind of environment I've tried to engender around here: being creative, staying on your toes, and being dynamically in tune with the ebb and flow of the markets. While we do have some structure as a group, and while Chris P. and Tom are probably more structured than I am, we aren't the kind of group that says, 'We're going to call clients for an hour today from ten to eleven o'clock.' We're just not that way, and really never have been. I always figure that if somebody has a clean desk, he must not have a lot to do."

Three staff members support the partnership. Amber Dag, who joined Credit Suisse in 2001, manages daily operations including order execution, client reporting, and administrative support for clients. Lyndsey Handschiegel, who joined Credit Suisse in June 2007, handles daily business actions, and provides administrative support for clients. And Ryan Miller, who provides analytical support, is the team's most recent addition, having joined in early 2008. "At this point our support is kind of lean," Chris says, "so we're now discussing beginning interviews to bring on a fourth person."

BUILDING THEIR CLIENT BASE

Overall, Chris and his partners have roughly 100 client relationships. "We get about 80 percent of our business from probably fifty key relationships. But remember," Chris adds, "when I say 'relationship,' I may mean a wealthy family and all of its extensions. A family that has $350 million with me may have a total of twenty-five accounts." The vast majority of these clients, then, fit into the ultra-high-net-worth category, although Tom also has a small institutional business that he brought to the firm. On occasion, Chris will also handle smaller accounts. For example, the executive director of a charitable board recently approached him, and Chris agreed to run his $3 million portfolio, although his typical account is more on the order of $15 to $35 million.

Chris and his partners are very pleased with their current client base and how they're able to service them. "I'm happy that we have clients we can focus on and we don't need to be marketing oriented per se. I like this model of having fifty to a hundred core accounts that we service and provide with a wide range of products and services. I think it works because our clients are a little wealthier than most. We simply don't aspire to having four hundred relationships."

Still, the team does look for new, appropriate business, and at this point most of that business comes from referrals. Ultimately, Chris feels that referrals "are easier to get than you think. It's just that asking for referrals is sometimes uncomfortable. What a lot of people don't realize about the high end of the market is that even though these folks may socialize with each other, they may not be excited about your doing business with their friends—particularly in smaller towns. Some people are just naturally good at referring people, and other wealthy clients would love to send us business, but they just don't have the network. Some people are a wonderful referral source, and others aren't. It is what it is. I don't take it personally."

In short, Chris feels that "the referral thing is nice. It's really nice." But in addition to referrals, Chris and his partners occasionally directly solicit business. "Frankly, I'm landing a few accounts right now. But these weren't exactly cold calls. These were people I either knew through an organization, or they knew somebody else I knew. The name we've developed for ourselves inside the firm—the social equity we've built here as well as with The Winner's Circle— really helps us when we contact people. Early in my career it was hard to bring in new people, but every day I'm in the business, it gets easier. And the firm has helped quite a bit, just because of the name. What's really important is that we keep our pipeline full, stay in front of those people who are eligible for our services, and get that first in-person meeting."

What about soliciting business from wealthy personal friends, or joining organizations and social circles to meet people in order to get their business? Chris is very clear about this: "I don't think it's fair to the people I know—or to me—to associate with somebody purely because he or she has a lot of money. I've been really careful with that, because although there are a lot of things I can accomplish in this business and in my life, the one thing I'm not going to do is sell myself out to do it. The people that I spend time with are very diverse, and most of my closest friends don't happen to be very wealthy. They're people I've known for a long time, whom I trust and respect, and who share my values, such as being charitable and caring about others. Now, none of this is meant to discredit wealthy people. I've done pretty well, and I like and am happy with myself. And my friends who are very wealthy are great people. But I wouldn't pick my social circle based on wealth. I know people who've done that, and I can't tell you what the stress has done to them."

The other side of this is how close Chris allows himself to become with his clients. "Some people like to be really chummy with their clients. But that doesn't really feel too good to me. I have clients I like, and new clients that I have brought on that I spend time with personally. One of my closest personal friends happens to be a very good client. But he's the only one. I've learned my lesson the hard way here too, and there's a fine line you need to respect. You have to be mature enough to know how to grow and facilitate relationships while keeping them in perspective. And while we do develop some pretty strong relationships with our clients, we're a business, and we focus on business. I don't have any serious client relationships where business doesn't come first."

"My biggest single worry from a business standpoint," Chris continues, "is losing clients. Every day I think about how to keep my clients informed and happy, and whether I'm doing what I'm supposed to be doing for them. That's probably the single most important issue I face on a daily basis. Anybody can get accounts; what's critical is retaining accounts, and in many ways, that's much harder than winning the business in the first place. So I work very hard at communicating with our clients and making sure that they understand what they're investing in. You make your best effort with a product—give it an opportunity to work—and if it does, it does, and if it doesn't, it doesn't, and then you move on and do something different for the client."

"The real key," Chris adds, "is to make sure that your clients understand that you're looking out for their welfare. What's difficult is being pulled in fifty different directions—with two partners and three support people, with things happening inside and outside the office, plus your personal life—and then a client calls on the phone. You have to learn to set everything else aside and focus on communicating with the client. We are driven towards 100 percent client satisfaction, and as a result we rarely lose clients. In fact, we have a very, very high retention rate, with almost zero attrition among our larger clients. Given the care I take, I've always felt that if I lose a client, they're probably not going to be somebody else's client for very long either."

SERVICING CLIENTS AND BEING STEWARDS OF THEIR WEALTH

Chris and his partners keep their clients satisfied—and therefore keep their clients—both by providing a high level of service and by being stewards of their wealth. On the service side, Chris says, "I'm always going out of my way to service our clients, getting on airplanes and going across the country. Recently, a client who was the patriarch of his business and his family passed away, and I needed to be there. We also go to many weddings and similar events. What we strive for, to boil it down, is to provide an institutional-quality experience for our clients, from service through product. The heart of our mission is to find product that we think is a cut above what our clients could find elsewhere, and superior service comes along with it. I don't talk a lot about service, because it's just naturally part of what we do."

In addition to the institutional-quality experience and service that they provide, Chris and his partners really shine in the way they serve as stewards of their clients' wealth. "We've never veered from our concepts of wealth management and risk management," Chris says. "Wealth management really is risk management, and when the markets were really down, we didn't talk about anything else.

"Basically," Chris continues, "I am a steward of my clients' wealth. I don't think taking less risk necessarily means you have to take less returns. I just think you have to be a lot smarter about it, and that's what people pay for. The trick to keeping large accounts today is providing some value above what would generally be expected elsewhere. You really have to do that today. The time has passed when you could deal with $30- or $50-million-dollar accounts, or more, and just provide market-level returns. That just doesn't work any more."

"When I look at an investment product," Chris continues, "I try to analyze what's in front of me. Nothing more, nothing less, and I try to understand the worst case possible scenario that could develop out of it. Fortunately, we have many different alternatives and high-quality institutional-level products to choose from, coupled with strong due diligence. We can offer a unique package to anybody who's got serious wealth and needs help in managing it."

"For example," Chris says, "globally, Credit Suisse has one of the largest private equity distribution businesses in the world. We are a sponsor or an agent for the big LBO firms when they raise their deals. So as part of Credit Suisse, our little group—along with just 250 or so other advisors in this country—has a structural advantage in terms of all the resources we have behind us. I think this gives us a really interesting and unique advantage."

UNDERSTANDING CLIENTS ... AND HOW CLIENTS CHANGE

When starting with a new client, the first step for Chris and his team is to understand everything that's relevant about that client. "We don't recommend investments to people unless we know a lot about them," Chris says. "Once in a while I'll get a referral from a friend in our banking department who says I should talk to a certain very wealthy individual who's interested in a private equity deal we're doing. Even if he has $50 million of net worth and is quite sophisticated, I wouldn't recommend a specific transaction to him until I met with him and was convinced that he was qualified from a risk tolerance standpoint."

Chris continues, "All of our business is based on knowing as much as we possibly can about our clients. We develop our own new client questionnaires, and ask a lot of questions that I think are important. To begin with, our clients and potential clients must understand the kind of business we run. They need to know that it's a wealth management business predicated on risk management, and that I can't make a recommendation to them unless I know what they own, how they own it, what their income is like, and what they think about risk. One thing leads to another, and it's just a very natural conversation. This could be a very awkward conversation if we didn't position our business right. But since we do position it right, these conversations are very natural, and I've had very little pushback from clients saying 'No, I'm not going to tell you this or that.' They tend to tell me everything."

In addition to learning everything he can about his new clients, Chris also shares some hard-won advice with them. "I tell them they have to have the courage of their convictions, and to stick by their thoughts and ideas for a reasonable amount of time. During our initial meetings, I can get a new client 95 percent of the way there—I can help them understand why they should own one thing over another, and help them see how the pieces fit together instead of just looking at each thing under a microscope. This makes them more apt to stay with their investments long enough for them to be fruitful. I also tell them not to accept anything but the best, because I really think there are superior products and services out there. I encourage them to look at the numbers, to look at what's behind a product, and to look at the experience they're getting. I also tell them to expect to get what they're paying for, or, put differently, to expect to pay for good results."

"With our bigger mandates," Chris continues, "generally for individuals who've sold a business, we start from scratch. Maybe it's $50 million, or $60 million, or higher. Fulfilling those aspirations can take longer, up to six months to two years. A lot of that has to do with the fact that the markets are dynamic. You never really know, once you've proposed your asset allocation, how the markets will react. We tell our clients that we prefer to let the markets come to us and tell us when we should implement the asset allocation. A little common sense, patience, and pragmatism goes a long way in this business. I learned the hard way that if something doesn't feel right, you should just wait. You'll find your answer—whether it takes a week or a day or a month. Sooner or later the market will come to you. So when I don't feel right about something, I work hard on being patient. Fighting the urge to 'just get the money invested' can be difficult."

"Also," Chris adds, "the client changes. The client is never the same, particularly a client who has a lot of money but who has never been through this process before. Clients never, or rarely, have the same intentions and objectives, or see things exactly the same way, after you've been in dialogue with them for six months. I like to tell my clients that 'the theory is great, but it's my job to take the theory and apply it in a practical way. And while we may have a wonderful template that tells us what your portfolio should look like, let's be practical in the way we apply it.' People really do change."

CONCENTRATED DIVERSIFICATION: PORTFOLIOS, MANAGERS, INVESTMENTS

On the one hand, each client has his or her own specific needs, which are carefully and individually addressed with a specifically asset allocated portfolio. "Everybody's portfolio looks different," Chris says. "It depends on the client's risk profile and need for income, as well as his or her particular trust and estate situation. Once you factor in all of the non-investment-related issues, we create a strategic profile for the client in terms of equity, fixed income, and their sophistication level regarding risk."

On the other hand, there are also many commonalities in the portfolios the team constructs for its clients. "Generally speaking," Chris says, "at least where it's suitable for a client, we are working in the same product categories, with the same managers across all of our clients. Having done this for as long as I've done it, and having been professionally involved in helping my clients select money managers, and having placed a lot of money with long-only managers and hedge fund managers, I really believe that there aren't a lot of truly talented people or original thinkers in this business. At the same time, I don't think your average client can follow the Warren Buffett model, where his concentrated exposure and what he really knows is what has made him a lot of money."

"There's an irony in all of this," Chris notes. "The Street today pedals this idea that your clients have to be diversified. So what do you see? You'll see a client with thirty different products and fifteen different managers, and with all this product he has no prayer of adding any value in his account over and above the indices. He really doesn't. Because the closer to the markets you get, the more diverse you get, and the more diverse you get, the more you are the market. So why doesn't that client start thinking more about trading some of that market risk for fundamental risk, and pull it back in a little bit, finding some middle ground between having too many investments and having too few? I prefer what I would call a 'concentrated diversification' so that our clients have some things that work, things they can follow and understand."

"It's nice to talk about asset allocation," Chris continues, "and you may very well want mid-cap, small cap, and large cap. But you've got to apply some common sense to all of this and narrow your focus down to the managers who you know, who you intuitively believe have a formula that can work day in and day out, and who can replicate their performance long term. Along with the firm's due diligence group, we've developed a strong intuitive sense from having looked at so many managers. So we work within that model, and are probably only using ten different long-only managers out of a much larger list."

"Most of our recommendations are based on macro themes. As much as we can, we heed what our analysts are saying about the relative attractiveness of global markets. And we like to stay focused. If we have fifteen or twenty things we are really concerned about at any one point in time, that's a lot for us. That way we can always stay on top of how the categories we're interested in are performing."

"What I worry about every day is what I don't know," Chris continues. "We look for the warning signs and for the coming of bear markets. If you can convince yourself that it *could* happen, you will be better prepared when it does happen. Bull markets have a way of pulling you in with their momentum, and you have to fight that urge. There's nothing wrong with overweighting specific themes or managers, but you have to be able to pare and trim and do the smart things for your clients so that you are part of the momentum but not engulfed by it. In that way, when the bull market ends, you've got the portfolio better positioned to buffer a major shock, and won't likely lose a lot of money. That's really the best you can do—have the intestinal fortitude to step back once in a while and try to figure these things out—because you can never see the top."

"As for particular investments," Chris says, "before I take anything to the next level, the most important question is always, 'What is the worst possible scenario here? Does this investment have attributes that could cause my clients to lose a substantial amount of money in this?' That's the way I look at investments. In my job, I'm conditioned not to lose my clients' money. I've been around this industry long enough to see the guys who drink the Kool-Aid and keep marching in the wrong direction and never see the forest for the trees. Their mantra is always, 'We're going to do the most business. Sell, sell, sell, sell.' Instead, I think you can use your brains in this business to help your clients keep their money and to make them money."

How does Chris do this for his clients? "You have to be very cynical about what you do," he says. "If you are not cynical about what you do, you'll get caught up in things. And I have made mistakes, believe me. But now it's very rare for us to get onto something we like so much that we'll over-concentrate it with our clients. With over $1.5 billion in assets that we hold here, not including clients' assets that are custodied elsewhere, I think the highest concentration we have in any one investment is probably around $70 million with a very successful long-only equity manager that we have in New York. If we recommend a new product because we really like it, we probably won't do more than $30 or $40 million at a time."

Finally, it's worth noting that while Chris and his team, through Credit Suisse, have access to some unique and interesting private equity products, that's not at all where they place their focus. "I really think," Chris says, "that you have to build your business around the core parts of a client's portfolio, where it tends to be the most competitive. That's a tough place to be—it's ultracompetitive, because everybody wants the fee-based business that's at the core of the portfolio—but it's where you want to build your business. That's what drives our business, and that's where we want to roll up our sleeves and compete. So we don't do a lot of high margin product here. We do some—we do have great products—but we tend to be very, very discreet about the alternative and private equity products that we use."

LOOKING TOWARD A PROSPEROUS FUTURE

When reflecting on his overall life and career, Chris says that he "doesn't have many regrets at all. I took an opportunity that was given to me when I was in the retail business, when nobody was doing asset allocation and wealth management. So much has changed, and the business climate has changed. The painful thing is that because the business has been so tumultuous as a result of the markets, we've had to recreate ourselves three, four, or five times over the course of my career. That's been tough, but I think we're finally now in a space where all systems are go. I don't think you get much better in terms of product, support people, and company. I think it's pretty much smooth sailing from here on. At least, I hope it is."

"You see," Chris continues, "I'm a very superstitious person. I've struggled a lot. My background has not been easy, and I tend not to extrapolate from my success. I don't like to talk about it too much. That's just the way I am: I don't like to tempt fate. I don't like to look too far forward, and I'm not drawing any conclusions about where I'll be a year from now. I recently told my older son, who is fourteen now, that I would much rather have him be pleasantly surprised if he gets on a specific hockey team than dejected if he doesn't. That's kind of the way I like to look at things. I like to be surprised by my success, rather than be caught unprepared."

Still, Chris is optimistic about the future of his business. "We have a business that is consistently growing at a healthy rate, and I think the future looks very good. If I think in terms of revenue, I know I can back into how many clients we'll need, and I like to think that in five years we'll be 50 percent higher, and in ten years, we'll be double. At that point, we'll probably add a partner and maybe another two support people."

"Bringing in new clients," Chris emphasizes, "is not the hard part. To grow a business, you have to service the existing accounts, monitor the relationships, and develop new relationships, and frankly, that just requires more bodies. The challenging part is finding people who are qualified enough, but aren't yet in a partnership. The tough part is finding people who will have some permanence, who can stay with you, who are not just people in transition. These people have to build themselves."

As to the medium- and long-term future, Chris says, "I'm not a kid in the business any more. When you're thirty-eight or thirty-nine, you still absolutely have your best years ahead of you. I'm not saying that I don't, but I am saying that the curve is a little different for somebody who is thirty-eight or thirty-nine than for someone who is forty-nine or fifty. Once in a while I think about whether I'll have as much impact as I get older in terms of bringing in new accounts, managing the business, and helping my clients. Ultimately, we'll keep growing the business, and ideally I'd retire and leave the business to my partners. So far I am not financially well off enough to do that. And I'll tell you this: I know people who have become busier in their retirement. I'd be happy to be put in that position right now; it's a decision that I look forward to having to make."

A BUSY LIFE

However impactful Chris may be at some point in the future, there's no question about how much impact he has right now in the many areas of his life. "I think your life needs to be really full, and the only way it can be really full is if you are involved in a lot of different ways, or as many ways as you can handle. The most successful people I've met are incredibly busy. It's because they're involved not just in their businesses, but in their communities and with charities, and then the time they do have to themselves is spent with their families."

This description pretty much sums up Chris's life as well. In addition to his very busy and often stressful life as a financial advisor—"there's no doubt that there's constant pressure for performance," Chris says—he has deep and ongoing charitable involvements, firm involvements (Chris serves on Credit Suisse's Advisory Committee for Excellence), sits on the board of a technology company, has a very active family life, and also makes sure he takes care of himself physically and has some fun (the family owns a vacation home in northern Wisconsin where Chris fishes and his sons go bow hunting).

Of all his outside commitments, the most significant for Chris in terms of his time, money, and passion is UNICEF, where he is on the Board of Directors for the Midwest Regional Office in Chicago. "UNICEF is an international organization that provides funds primarily for children and women and saves more lives than any other organization in the world," Chris proudly says. "It's primarily about low-technology field solutions that actually save lives. We're not developing technology or trying to find a cure for cancer; we're feeding people, getting them medical supplies, teaching them about AIDS, providing potable water, finding parents for orphans and getting kids into school. I spend a lot of time on this, and contribute a significant amount of my income to UNICEF. My wife, Renee, is also very giving of her time, and serves as the President of the Board for the local Montessori School."

Not surprisingly, both of Chris's sons attend the Montessori school. They are also both very involved with sports. "I think sports are important. Sports provide kids with discipline and camaraderie. When I played football on a high school and college level, I learned a lot about myself, about discipline and how to apply that to business. And I've always been very physically active, exercising four, five, and sometimes seven times a week. So we are a very busy family right now, and not a day goes by when I don't have to call Renee in the morning and ask what my schedule is after work."

Importantly, Chris is determined to provide his kids with a better start to life than he had. "Ideally," he says, "I don't want my children to have to face the stress of not having any money. Who needs that in life? It didn't make me a better person. Maybe it made me a bit more successful, but probably not by a whole lot. I wouldn't wish that on anybody, to have to go through what I went through—work my way through school, then start out with literally no financial resources. If I've got an ambition for my kids, it's that they're provided with some of the basics, so they don't have to fight such an uphill battle. I do think a good work ethic is important, but if I can, I'm going to enable my kids to start life comfortably, such as by helping them to get their first homes."

Chris's deep and successful involvement in so many things—his business, his family, UNICEF—is only possible, somewhat ironically, because of the cautious approach he has taken to his business and personal life. "I've put a lot of limits on myself and on the way I've conducted my business," he says. "That includes the way I've spread my income around in this partnership, the way I've diversified the business, and the way I've conducted myself away from the office. I have confidence that the things I say, the things I do, and the way I act will continue to work for my clients, my family, and myself over the long run. That's what I'm comfortable with, and that's what's worked for me." Notwithstanding the limits he's placed on himself, it seems that success is what's likely to continue characterizing Chris's business, partnership, and life as time goes forward.

CHAPTER 12: THE LOCNISKAR GROUP

MERRILL LYNCH & CO., INC.
DETROIT, MICHIGAN

(Left to Right) Denise Boisvert, Matt Biddinger, Sandra Kinsler, Dana Locniskar, Angeline Miruzzi-Cooney, Lila Wetzel, and Daniel Angelucci

One of the primary factors behind Dana Locniskar's extraordinary longevity—he began his investment career in 1968—and success has been his ability to recognize and pioneer underserved markets long before most advisors knew they existed. Today, Dana—who works for Merrill Lynch in the Detroit, Michigan area—advises about 53 households with $2.4 billion and, taken as a whole, his team advises about 160 households with $3.4 billion.

"The best way to describe what we do," Dana says, "is to say that we're the principal financial advisor to families who possess significant wealth. We look at the entirety of their wealth and how to deal with all of its different aspects, including everything from insurance to personal business loans. I placed my first insurance policy with an estate planning goal in 1976, and it's been intuitively obvious to me ever since that the best service we can provide is to take care of all of the client's financial needs. For example, if a client has multiple advisors, issues tend to fall through the cracks because no one is looking at the big picture. Our strategy is always to look at the big picture, and make sure all of the pieces of the client's puzzle are in place and attended to."

"Keep in mind," Dana continues, "that as an advisor you're playing both offense and defense. Our comprehensive approach is defensive, because if I'm addressing the larger financial picture my competitors have less chance to get their noses under the tent and get the client's attention. If we're taking care of a client's insurance and estate planning needs, then when a competitor calls and says, 'Gee, we can help you in these areas,' the client responds, 'Well, I've got that covered, Merrill Lynch is already doing that for me.' And it's offense as well, because we're actively involved in doing more work for the client. We pride ourselves on doing the very best job we can for our clients, both to help them and satisfy their needs and to eliminate the competitor's threat before it takes root."

This way of working with clients has become part and parcel of Dana's way of doing business. "It evolved over time," he says, "alongside my understanding of how important it is to approach clients this way. Today every review session we do touches on several financial areas that concern the client, including inter-generational wealth transfer and philanthropic intent. These are core issues because it's what people are interested in. Are they okay personally? How are they going to take care of their family? What legacy do they want to leave? To me this is all one subject, a seamless whole, and it's our job to touch on all of it."

"What I've found," Dana notes, "is that the more time I spend with my clients and their family members—we regularly try to involve the next generation in family meetings—the deeper our relationships become. It takes time to find out how people feel about charity, what they want their legacy to be, and how much money they want to move to their children. It's also important to recognize that a client and his or her business are usually inseparable. For the most part, new clients come to us as the result of liquidity events (e.g., sales of their businesses). So either they're new clients who have had a liquidity event that's forced them to look at how they manage their personal finances, or they're existing clients whom we have advised on the sale of their businesses."

"If I know a client well enough," Dana continues, "and we're deeply involved with him, we'll ultimately be advising him on the sale of his business. The very last thing I want is to open up the newspaper and find an announcement that my client's business has just been sold. I've failed in the relationship if that happens, and whoever has facilitated that sale now has a front row seat at the liquidity event, not me."

"Ultimately," Dana points out, "people with significant wealth are living their lives, not watching their money and worrying about it. They want to do other things. A lot of high-net-worth clients would consider consolidating all their activities with one advisor if they could find one whom they really trusted. What wealthy clients want to know is that someone who's competent, and who cares about them, is helping to take care of all the pieces of the puzzle for them."

And being competent and taking care of his clients is something that Dana has excelled at. For example, amid the sharp decline in stock prices that took place from 2000 through the spring of 2003, Dana, unlike many advisors in the industry, didn't have to wonder how his clients and his business would survive. Instead he and his team executed the plan that Dana had carefully crafted in anticipation of the inevitable downward turn, a plan that cleared the way for Dana to scale yet another mountain in becoming one of the industry's most prominent investment advisors. None of this comes as a surprise to anyone who has ever known Dana or been aware of the success he's enjoyed throughout his career, which spans five decades.

THE EARLY YEARS

Dana was born in Detroit, about three miles from where he works today. His childhood years were far more uncertain than the life he now enjoys. "My parents divorced when I was an infant, which created a lot of financial instability for my family," he recalls. "I remember living in many different places."

At the age of 19, Dana returned to Detroit to attend Wayne State University. During his college years he signed up for a marketing class where he was given an opportunity to subscribe to the *Wall Street Journal* and *Fortune Magazine* for only $10 annually. He took advantage of the offer and began reading about Wall Street—and how it worked—with considerable interest. At first his interest was casual, but the more he learned, the more he wanted to know. "At the time, I wasn't thinking about pursuing a career in financial services," he says, "but there's no doubt that this marketing class was the spark that ignited my interest in investing."

As Dana approached the end of his college days, he wasn't sure what he wanted to do professionally. Encouraged by the good living his father made as a funeral director, he decided to become one himself. He worked with his father for about six years, and did well, but could not ignore a nagging feeling that he was unfulfilled. Then one day in 1968 Dana came across an ad in *The Detroit News* for a part-time mutual fund salesman. His interest in the stock market was reawakened. "The time was right," he recalls. "I was looking for a change, the stock market was strong—a bull market had started in the early fifties—and individuals were increasingly interested in it."

Dana applied for the job and landed it. Every Monday evening he would show up at a small office that had, as he recalls, "little desks lined up in rows." He made cold calls in an effort to secure appointments for Tuesday and Thursday nights. "My approach was this: I would inform prospects—mostly first-time investors—that I was planning to be in their neighborhood on Tuesday at six-thirty or Thursday at eight-thirty in the evening, and I would ask 'What would be a better day for you? Tuesday or Thursday?' This question had better results than, 'Do you want to meet with me?'"

Dana enjoyed the job. "Back then, it seemed that everybody was selling mutual funds part-time—garage mechanics, shoe salesmen, you name it," he laughs. "And we were all selling pretty much the same thing: contractual plans. They were very popular. The purchaser would agree to invest a fixed amount of money each month. Half of the first year's investment would go toward commissions. You would never see an investment like that on Wall Street today. But a lot of things were different then. For example, the stock market was closed on Wednesdays because the exchange could not keep up with the paperwork."

Success at selling mutual funds encouraged Dana to think about making a career on Wall Street. He decided to apply for a job as a full-time investment professional at Merrill Lynch, because of its name recognition. After several interviews, Dana received an offer to become a registered representative with the firm and began his career at one of the nation's leading brokerage firms on May 25, 1970.

"I recall the day vividly," he says. "The Dow Jones Industrial Average dropped 30 points to 630, which by today's measures doesn't sound like much, but back then, it represented a decline of nearly 5 percent. It was a dramatic fall. Penn Central had filed for bankruptcy that morning. Chrysler was in a very weakened condition and rumored to be heading for bankruptcy. Television cameras were in our office. That day marked the low of the late 1960s and early 1970s bear market."

"The market would rebound in the coming weeks and months," he continued, "but the decline was a harbinger of things to come. This was a period when Wall Street was approaching the end of a bull market that, some might say, had begun soon after the end of World War II. Looking back, the late 1960s were similar to the late 1990s. The Dow would fall from 1,000 to the 500 level in 1975. That market is still regarded as one of the most grueling bear markets in Wall Street history."

Although the stock market was destined for tough times in the 1970s, Dana was not—at least not initially. At Merrill Lynch, he was able to focus on building a business, instead of working as a funeral director by day and prospecting for mutual fund sales at night. In addition, because the Merrill Lynch brand was already widely known and respected among the investing and noninvesting public, he didn't have to go through a long-winded explanation about the company with every cold call that he made. "When you work for a small, relatively unknown business, you have to devote a few minutes of every call to describing the company before people will even give you the opportunity to discuss investments with them," he offers. "It can become very taxing over time."

Dana discovered early on that because of the Merrill Lynch name he could convince many more prospects to meet with him than when he represented the small investment company. As a result, Dana was highly motivated to call on as many prospective investors as he could. And call he did.

"Back then, a new financial advisor's ability to succeed was no different than it is today. I would contact a hundred people, turn at least ten into prospects, and strive to land at least one account for my effort." Unfortunately for Dana, though, as the long bull market started to fade, landing new clients became increasingly difficult. And things would get worse before they got better. The Dow Jones Industrial Average hit 1,000 in 1973, and the valuations of many companies fell by as much as 90 percent over the next two years, just as happened during the two-and-a-half-year period after the NAS-DAQ Composite eclipsed the 5,000 plateau in March 2000. "Every stock I recommended seemed to be going down. At one point, albeit briefly, I gave serious consideration to leaving the business, and many of my colleagues did leave. But I stuck it out, and found a way to build client relationships that grew into friendship."

Until this point, Dana had been so busy recommending stocks that he hadn't given much consideration to other investments. He began to think differently about his business in the new environment, however, and instead of spending his days wondering which stocks to propose to clients and prospects, he began asking himself, "What do my clients really need now? What would help them the most?" After some research, he concluded that municipal bonds were the most logical choice. "Municipal bonds offered attractive tax-free yields, and it seemed that most of my clients were interested in keeping more of what they earned—especially since the highest tax bracket back then was 70 percent. So I began introducing people to these investments."

The strategy paid off. But it wasn't just municipal bonds that helped Dana improve his business and ride out the grueling bear market. Dana's clients were gravitating toward him because he was systematically thinking about *their needs* before deciding which investments to recommend. Once he realized this, he felt confident that he could overcome any obstacle to success—for his clients as well as for himself.

A WINNING BUSINESS MODEL

Despite the many changes on Wall Street over the past five decades, Dana has remained true to this simple and highly effective principle: "Make your investors your priority every day, and they will stick with you through good times and bad."

This instinct, Dana says, has been the secret of his success, and that is supported by his clients' loyalty. Many of the people with whom Dana did business 30 or more years ago are still with him today. Some are even children and grandchildren of those clients.

This "client-first" approach has also helped Dana attract an ever-growing number of high-net-worth investors, including successful businesspeople across most major industries—from entrepreneurs of small- and medium-sized corporations to senior-level executives at Fortune 500 companies. Dana enjoys working with high-net-worth clients because of their accomplishments. "Some have built great companies, provided employment for hundreds, and, in some cases, thousands of people," he says. "What's more, they have interesting, broadly diverse lives."

Dana's passion for building relationships with successful individuals comes through during his presentations. "I tell them, 'You're good at what you do, perhaps as good as anyone who does what you do.'" He follows that compliment with a compelling analogy: he is their equivalent in the financial services industry. "I not only bring the knowledge that you need, I offer you substantial experience. Only a very small percentage of all financial professionals today have been in this business for several decades."

This presentation resonates with successful individuals. Not only do they want to work with someone who knows what they should be doing with their assets, but they are attracted to a professional who can draw on a wealth of experience in making important financial decisions, particularly when market conditions are highly uncertain.

"During difficult periods in the market," Dana points out, "many investors want to sell stocks and ask questions later. I remember one person in particular who called me after the 9/11 terrorist attacks and was so nervous, he wanted to sell everything. I helped him create a different perspective with the following commonsense approach."

"First, I explained that as horrific as those events of September 11 were, they didn't change the national and world economic outlook. Next, I told him that, while past performance is no guarantee of future results, historically the market has experienced difficulty following major tragedies but has shown resiliency over the long term. I concluded our discussion by telling him that he was not alone in his fear for the market. I explained that most investors want to sell during uncertain periods, but they never know when to get back into the market. As a result, they wind up missing major market moves. After a lengthy discussion, this client decided not sell, and is grateful today that he didn't."

Dana paused, reflected on the story and offered the following philosophical perspective about the importance of a financial advisor: "Investors need us to help them establish and execute a financial strategy for their futures. They may not need us quite as much when market and economic conditions are favorable, but they really rely on our advice when the stock market starts to sputter and their desire to run for the safe haven of cash becomes intense."

A PERSONALIZED INVESTMENT STYLE

Dana's thoroughness in helping investors create and execute a plan is a key component of his successful business model. When you first hear him talk about his investment style, it doesn't seem very different from that of thousands of advisors. He emphasizes the importance of identifying a client's unique goals, developing an investment strategy designed to achieve them, and creating the discipline to adhere to it, while making modifications as needed along the way.

What separates Dana from other investment professionals is the way he executes his strategy. Unlike many financial advisors today who rely heavily on computer models to build client portfolios, Dana takes a personal approach to analyzing and recommending a course for each client. "Everything I recommend is custom-tailored to the client's needs," he says. "And every member of my team follows the same model. We recommend only investments that are designed to help clients achieve their unique investment goals."

Another way Dana stands out among financial advisors is that he consistently emphasizes what he calls broad diversification. "Broad diversification," Dana says, "is diversification across global financial markets, stocks, bonds, and commodities; no one, regardless of his or her reputation and knowledge base, is smart enough to know which asset class is going to be the best performer from one year to the next." It's not uncommon, then, for Dana's clients to be invested in most asset classes, including domestic and international equities, fixed income, and money market instruments, as well as a wide range of esoteric products, from private equity to the occasional hedge fund.

"Starting several years ago," Dana notes, "we added exposure to the broad commodity indexes and the global raw materials business. We always tell clients that what they really want is the return of a broadly diversified asset allocation. Can I figure out what the single best asset allocation will be this year? No. But I can give you access to managers with markedly different disciplines, and that may take some of the bumps out of the road. Along with diversifying risk, investing in many different areas affords a client the opportunity to capture investment results that best reflect the total return of the global economy."

For some clients, Dana provides the general framework of how money should be invested, and then works with them to select independent, third-party money management organizations with specific investment expertise. Dana only recommends professional managers who have met his own strict criteria as well as Merrill Lynch's high standards, but he allows the client to make the final decision.

"Our bias is to select investment firms that have a single focus, as opposed to large firms that offer a product in every investment segment," he says. "For example, if I want a value-oriented equity manager, I will typically select a manager who does nothing but value investing. In effect, I try to recommend specialty firms that do one thing best."

Dana says that investing with these so-called "single-focused firms" also provides the client with some downside protection. "Unlike firms that have many lines of business, a single-focus firm succeeds or flounders based on its one specialty. As a result, the company has an added incentive to make sure that it exceeds our expectations."

GROWING HIS TEAM

Dana's ability to serve his clients is due in part to the team he has put together over time. For example, in 1979, long before the use of word processors became common, Dana hired a part-time word processing person to assist his full-time secretary. She worked on a mainframe computer about ten times the size of today's laptop computer. "It was literally half the size of a desk, and it rolled around on wheels," Dana recalls with a laugh. "And it wasn't cheap. I bought it used for $15,000 in 1979."

As the years went on, Dana expanded his operation. In 1987, Lila Wetzel, registered client associate, joined the staff as his personal assistant. "We're very fortunate to have Lila as part of our team," Dana says. Another longtimer is Sandy Kinsler, registered client associate, who joined Merrill Lynch in 1983 and has been part of Dana's team since 1991. Similarly, Angie Cooney, registered client associate, has been with Merrill Lynch since 1987 and with Dana since 1997, and Denise Boisvert, client associate, has also been with Dana since 1997. Other team members include financial advisors Maral Thomas and Mike Muirhead, and Matt Biddinger, investment analyst.

In recent years, Dana has hired and trained members of his team for highly specialized roles. One such role is handling what Dana calls liability management for higher-net-worth families. "As strange as it sounds," Dana points out, "for any number of reasons, many wealthy families happen to be very large borrowers."

Dana also has two partners, Marie Vanerian, financial advisor, and Dan Angelucci, financial advisor. Marie, who heads up the investment consulting for high-net-worth investors and small institutions, has been with Merrill Lynch since 1976. Dan Angelucci is responsible for smaller accounts with $10 million or less in assets. Dana takes care of accounts with more than $10 million. As for the smaller accounts, those below his $10 million minimum, Dana says, "We continue to service these accounts because these clients grew up with me and are my friends."

Every member of Dana's team is committed to delivering a high level of proactive, quality service. For example, each week Lila calls certain clients just to see how they are doing. She might ask if they have any questions about their accounts, or if they have any problems regarding their statements. "The clients may not need any help," Dana says, "but they appreciate the fact that Lila is taking the time out of her busy schedule to call."

REGULARLY EXCEEDING EXPECTATIONS

Dana adds that he and his team don't just do what their clients expect of them. They provide a level of service that far exceeds even the loftiest expectations an investor might have. For example, if a client has a particular need that falls outside the normal services that Dana provides, he will try to help in any way he can.

Helping clients on the credit side of things is not unusual for him and his team. "As they get older, most of our clients have less appetite for debt in their balance sheet," Dana says. "However, clients with substantial wealth often have reasons for borrowing. It can be for reasons of timing, business requirements, convenience, or private equity capital calls.

"Since there's a whole raft of reasons why people with substantial wealth will borrow," Dana continues, "we typically provide clients a credit facility linked to their accounts so that it's available if there's a need for short-term borrowing. This way, if they want to borrow they can do it immediately without upsetting their portfolio holdings or incurring unnecessary tax consequences. Often the credit facility goes unused, but since we've already put it together, it's there for their use if they need it. Since these are wealthy people, there are no credit issues, and since we already have access to their assets, putting the credit facility in place is routine."

"For instance, today we're putting a credit facility in place for a client who wants to buy a boat. We're able to do better for him than an offer from another lender because we're not lending against the value of the boat, we are lending against the client's collateral base, which is liquid. Another client is buying a new home and hasn't sold his existing home because he doesn't like the housing market right now. Eventually he will use cash from the sale of his house, but for now we are providing him with a convenient short-term financing vehicle."

"Another example," Dana continues, "is a client who has multiple commitments to private equity funds. He doesn't necessarily want to keep enough liquidity on hand to meet his capital calls, because that would hurt his portfolio performance. So instead, he draws down on the credit line we provide him, and as sales happen in his private equity portfolio, those monies are returned to reduce the credit line. Rather than maintaining a large cash cushion to meet his capital calls, we meet those calls by utilizing his credit line."

"On occasion," Dana notes, "we'll help provide a client with working capital for his or her business. I have one second-generation client who started a business a dozen years ago. Along the way, we've provided working capital financing, and then advised on the partial sale of the business. Now we are expanding the working capital line to help grow the business. We've been instrumental in advising this client on financing the business, the partial sale of the business to a financial partner, and providing credit lines for growth capital."

"We do a lot of things for clients that never translate into revenue for us," Dana explains. "We do it because it's the right thing to do for the client. And when you do what you believe is in the client's best interest, you're not only helping him, you're effectively earning goodwill and making an investment in your own good name as well."

"Let me give you another example," Dana continues. "Recently, I called a client to remind him that he might lose a tax benefit in an account that was not held at Merrill Lynch, and that he needed to take a particular action within a specific time frame. Reminding him had no material benefit for me, but it was the right thing to do because it was in his best interest. That client will remember what we did, and our thoughtfulness will come back to us in some way. I

believe that. We're always working toward each client's best interests, whether it directly benefits us or not."

Dana's commitment to exceeding expectations has not only
helped his ongoing effort to maintain a loyal following among his
clientele, it has enabled him to turn some investors into lifelong
clients and friends. Simply put, they know what they can expect
when doing business with Dana and his team.

"We have been focused on providing such a high level of service
for so long that our clients have come to expect extraordinary
service in everything that we do," Dana says. "Sure, that raises the
bar for us, but that's not a problem. This expectation has made it
increasingly difficult for other advisors to attract our clients. Many
advisors would feel they were giving up too much to provide all the
service our clients expect. We feel differently. Exceeding expectations
is an integral and fundamental part of our business model. It always
has been—and always will be—this way. When we establish a relationship with a client, we're not looking at that individual as someone we'll know for a few years. Our hope is that we'll serve them
and their families for decades."

"In fact," Dana continues, "if we're an advisor for a high-net-
worth family, and the family dynamic supports it, then for continu-
ity purposes we'll often include the adult children in certain family
meetings. Not every family is going to want to do this, but it's a best
practice not only from our perspective, but from the family's
perspective too; it allows the parents to explicitly communicate their
values and financial understanding to the next generation."

"The other side of this," Dana notes, "is that, as a team, you also
have to have a good succession plan and younger team members in
place. If a potential client is considering our team and is looking at
me, he or she might rightly ask, 'Dana says he's going to work a long
time, but will he be here long enough to take care of me?' The value
of my age and experience is tempered by the client's concern that I
might not be around as long as he needs me."

Dana continues, "If you're sixty, you want to hire a physician
who's forty-five, not one who's seventy. So, ideally, on a team like
ours, you've got to have both younger and older team members.
Moreover, the era when you saw a physician, lawyer, or accountant
who was a sole practitioner, in an office by himself or herself, is
pretty much over. Sophisticated high-net-worth individuals are used
to working with providers who have depth, which is why we continue to build our team."

BULLISH ON MERRILL

When Dana talks about the many factors behind his success, he never forgets to give credit to Merrill Lynch. "The company has always had a reputation for product innovation and quality execution of its ideas," he says. "These attributes have given me both the opportunity to serve my clients better and an important edge over my competition at other brokerage firms."

In 1977, before anyone else had money market checking, for example, Merrill Lynch introduced the Cash Management Account (CMA), which increased Dana's ability to help clients better manage their cash and, in some cases, earn higher yields than they could at other financial institutions. "CMA is an investment and cash management tool that enables clients to consolidate all of their cash, securities, and other investments under one roof and keep it all working virtually all the time," Dana explains. "It effectively gives clients the same control over their assets that large corporations and sophisticated investors had had for years."

Merrill Lynch's introduction of the priority client statement in 1979 also helped Dana solidify his client relationships. "This statement was comprehensive and revolutionary because of the specific information it provided—such as the date an investment was purchased, cost basis, unrealized profit and loss, and more. Investors loved it."

Dana says that the creation of both the CMA and the priority client statement gave him an edge over financial advisors outside Merrill Lynch. He was able to capitalize on that edge for several years, because that is how long it took most competing brokerage firms to create a central asset account and a client statement equal to Merrill Lynch's. "These two developments helped me accumulate assets during a difficult equity market and to position my business for the bull market of the 1980s," he says.

Dana believes that by pursuing growth markets once dominated by other financial services companies, Merrill Lynch will continue to serve his business well in the years ahead. "In recent years," he says, "Merrill Lynch has become a leading wealth management firm offering private banking capabilities. Many people may be unaware of this fact. For example, they may not see Merrill as the top-of-mind firm to go to with the proceeds from the sale of their company, but we are gradually changing that perception.

"This has already helped me expand my business. For instance, I have been involved with helping entrepreneurs find buyers for their companies and helping other high-net-worth investors and their families achieve highly specific financial goals." Dana says that although he usually comes in contact with these individuals through referrals, sometimes he meets them in unusual ways.

"About seven or eight years ago, I was on a hiking and rafting trip in the Grand Canyon with about sixteen other people. We were together for about a week, so we got to know each other pretty well. One of our companions told me that she was anticipating a liquidity event—a payout from a family trust—in the future. During a ride down the river, she and her husband and two children, along with their boatmen, got their rubber raft caught up on a large rock in the middle of the river. They were trapped and the current was too fast to swim. After several anxious hours, they were rescued. That experience brought everyone in the group closer together. After the trip, we stayed in contact, and eventually they contacted me to manage their substantial assets."

SERVING SOPHISTICATED HIGH-NET-WORTH FAMILIES

Merrill Lynch has also provided Dana and his team with up-to-date information and technology processing systems. Such systems have changed certain aspects of how top-notch financial advisors do business. "Twenty years ago," Dana says, "the financial advisor had access to much better information than his or her clients, and so of course we acted as a conduit of information. Well, today, anybody with a desktop or a laptop can have access to the best financial information available. The question, then, is how do you use that information, so our role has changed somewhat from being deliverers of information to interpreters of information."

"Fortunately," Dana continues, "high-net-worth families are used to delegating management responsibility. Often, they got that way by owning businesses that they've now sold. Well, in running a business you have to delegate authority to your various managers, so the transition to having us oversee their money managers isn't such a big stretch. Most wealthy people want to know that their affairs are being handled properly so they can go play golf or go skiing or do whatever they want to do without worrying about the day-to-day oversight of their portfolio. People want to know that they have a proper asset allocation, one that fits their risk tolerance, and that they can live their life and not be preoccupied with the S&P going up or down."

"Ultimately," Dana says, "the high-net-worth families we take care of come to us because we're a little bit like a private club. If you need really serious help in something, you want to go to a specialist. For example, if you're sick, you want to figure out how to get to the top-notch hospitals, and even once you get there, you want to find the best practitioners. People with significant wealth have that same question—not just how they find a financial advisor, but how to find the best financial advisor for their particular needs. They ask, 'Who's your best practitioner for people like me?' For high-net-worth families, I try to be one of those best practitioners."

"The bottom line is that clients at all levels of wealth are much more financially sophisticated than they were twenty, fifteen, or even ten years ago. This means that expectations are much higher. Interestingly, this is true for most professions. If I'm a doctor, with all the medical information available on the Internet, I have to stay current. Today we have a more sophisticated and knowledgeable financial consumer than ever before, and this is especially true of families with significant wealth. We have to be better than beyond average, in our knowledge as well as our service."

GIVING BACK AND TAKING CARE

Dana feels very fortunate for his success and for having the opportunity to help others. This is the main reason he spends a good deal of time volunteering in the community, something he has now done for several years. "It's important to me," he stresses. "When you are involved with the community, you give yourself the opportunity to give back to the people who have helped you, and you also meet people who make things happen."

Dana gives his time and money to a number of charities and foundations. He is or has been on the boards of trustees for several organizations, including Detroit Public TV, the Community Foundation for Southeastern Michigan, The Futures Foundation (a developmental service for handicapped individuals), and The Beaumont Foundation (a leading hospital foundation). In addition, Dana is one of the founders of the Planned Giving Council for southeast Michigan and also served as the organization's first president. He has also supported the United Way for many years.

On a more individual note, with respect to taking care of himself personally, Dana says that "basically it's fun for me to work. However, my wife and I travel a fair amount, and I do try to stay fit, because as you get older, if you're not fit, you can't think as well.

There's definitely a correlation between staying physically fit and staying mentally fit, so I try to start my mornings at the health club."

LOOKING FORWARD THROUGH THE EYES OF EXPERIENCE

One might think that Dana, with a career approaching five decades, and who in his sixties looks a decade younger, is probably more interested in planning his retirement than building his business, but that's far from the case. "This is a business," he says, "where the older you get, often the better you get. It's one thing to read about historical ups and downs in a book; it's another thing to have actually lived through them. There's simply nothing like having been there, which in part is why there are many famous investors in their seventies, eighties, and even nineties. Investing is a business where you can remain active for very extended periods of time."

"One of the reasons we're in the mortgage mess we're in today," Dana continues, "is that many of the people running today's banks and brokerage firms, and many of the analysts, had not previously lived through a real problem like this one. People with more experience might have been tipped off earlier as to the use of off-balance-sheet special investment vehicles with no reserve requirements. Essentially, the longer you've been around, the more things you've seen over and over, and today's crisis is really not much different than the crisis of twenty years ago—it's just another bubble bursting. The players are different, but the music's the same."

Dana considers the current mortgage crisis in more detail: "The twenty-something and thirty-something investment bankers, traders, and analysts looked at the data that said housing prices had been going up for fifteen years. They may have assumed the housing market would continue to grow and proceeded to lend to people with, in hindsight, questionable credit, and not have anticipated it would become a problem. 'Even if there are problems with these borrowers, since housing prices are still going up, we'll be OK on the value of their collateral.' Well, if you look at fifteen years of data and your own personal experience, you can conclude that this is indeed how the world works. But if you've been around for a while, you know the world *doesn't* work that way. Housing prices do go down, and they have not always gone up. But a bunch of twenty-something and thirty-something analysts, investment bankers, and traders missed that entirely and collectively marched off the cliff."

Dana and his team do, in fact, take precautions against dramatic market drops. "Great wealth can be made by people who borrow money and then make money on that borrowed money. So leverage gives you a tremendous potential upside, but if we look at the Great Depression, in the aftermath of 1929 it was leverage that put people out of business. Stocks don't go to zero, but if you've borrowed money to own your stocks, your equity goes to zero. So we temper our advice to clients in terms of being debt averse, and we have minor debt in our clients' investment balance sheets. If worse comes to worst, our clients, in general, still own the bluest of the blue chips, and we believe they are unlikely to lose everything because of a margin call."

Dana's focus on broad diversification is another measure against worst-case possibilities. In addition, then, to adding more private equity and natural resources exposure, Dana and his team are aiming their clients at an increased international position. "International is a big part of what we do," Dana says. "We are trying to bring client portfolios up to one-third international, that is, having a third of their equity commitment be international. But this is a learning process, and most people have a home bias, be it for their town or their country. Even though returns may be higher in other places, people tend to be comfortable with what they know."

A FITTING FUTURE

As for continuing to grow his business, Dana is just as interested in securing the next big account as he was when he walked into his office at Merrill Lynch 39 years ago. "When I hear about someone who is selling his company, I'm on the telephone trying to get that appointment, just like I did when I used to sell mutual funds in the early days," he says. "The difference today is that I am more selective about whom I do business with. And, of course, we don't just make random cold calls to someone who's sold a business, because those people get literally fifty or sixty overnight packages and pitches. If there's been a sale of a business, we'll see who we know who can make an introduction to the proper contact."

"Ours is almost entirely a referral-based business," Dana notes, "and until a few years ago, I took every referral regardless of the size of the account. I've now realized, however, that no matter how much I want to help everyone, if I take everyone on, I can no longer do the best job for my existing clients. So now I'm far more focused on deepening each relationship."

"Also, not every potential client is appropriate for us. When I meet with a client for the first time and talk about who they are and who we are, I'm trying to understand what they want to accomplish. Unless they are interested in engaging us as their principal advisor, it's not a good fit for us. If I'm to be just one of several advisors and not the quarterback, well, that's not what we do best, it's not in the best interests of the potential client to work with us, and we can save each other a lot of time by not getting started. Again, we are not interested in being a vendor of specific financial products; we are interested in being the client's principal financial advisor and taking care of all their financial needs. At this stage of the game, I'm just not interested in anything less."

"Similarly," Dana continues, "if someone signs on with us and is really still out there shopping for performance, we're never going to build a deep, long-term relationship, and they'll be harder to work with besides. If they hire us because they've heard we perform well and then performance lags, they'll either want to make the wrong financial move at just the wrong time, or they'll just go on to the next advisor. So, as we go through the interview process with potential new clients, *we're interviewing them just as much as they're interviewing us*. If we find out that they aren't willing to have us be their principal financial advisor, then odds are it won't be a good fit for them or us, and we let them know that up front."

"Ultimately," Dana concludes, "there's just an ocean of money out there looking for investment advice, and a whole herd of competitors looking to provide that advice. I believe that clients want to associate themselves with caring financial advisors who have a long record of providing sound advice and service. In the end, all that a financial advisor can really do is make a serious commitment to building meaningful relationships with clients and providing a comprehensive approach to advice and service, and these are things I work hard at doing every day."

CHAPTER 13: NADIA CAVNER GROUP

BANCORPSOUTH INVESTMENT SERVICES
SPRINGFIELD, MISSOURI

Nadia Cavner

N early every year I attend Nadia Cavner's annual client appreciation event. With 1,000 attendees, this spectacular event is always a truly memorable experience. The first year I attended I sat in an empty chair at a table with five couples. During dinner I asked each couple to describe ways in which Nadia had impacted their lives—for better or worse—whether related to investing, planning, or anything else. Some of the stories I expected, such as Nadia helping one couple plan for their four children's education, or Nadia helping to attain a dream retirement or vacation home. What I didn't expect were the many personal stories, such as when a loved one had passed away and Nadia was there tending to details and lending a shoulder to cry on. On average, I heard six stories from each couple. Then it dawned on me that there were over 500 couples in that room. Using simple math, I determined that Nadia had touched the lives of these people somewhere around 3,000 times. It's this kind of impact on their clients' lives that makes me so passionate about what advisors do for their clients, and I was experiencing it firsthand.

While it's true that Nadia Cavner has always had an affinity for working with money—at age 10 she began picking stocks successfully, and through most of her college days she worked as an amusement park cash control supervisor—even more central to her success has been the strength of her heart and her commitment to serving others in all walks of life. "My philosophy of life," she says, "is to put forth tremendous goodwill and compassion for others. My husband Howard, who is a minister, has a sticker in his study that says 'Practice simple acts of kindness,' and from day one I've built my business on this principle."

Nadia's kindness, and the deeply rooted faith that inspires it, can be seen in everything she does. For her clients, it shows in the way she deals with them both on a day-to-day basis—"we try to have absolutely the best customer service in town and to do our jobs with the most integrity possible"—and in her famous annual Client Appreciation Dinners. But it also shows in Nadia's (and her family's) extraordinary philanthropic endeavors, which range from substantial financial contributions to her service on multiple nonprofit boards to her recent sponsorship of the Dalai Lama in Washington, D.C.

An extraordinary woman with an extraordinary practice, Nadia is widely recognized for her accomplishments. With some 1,500 clients and nearly $400 million under management, she has been consistently ranked among the nation's very best advisors, women advisors, and banking brokers, and has been the subject of numerous national and local magazine and newspaper articles. Recently Nadia received the Missourian of the Year award, and in November of 2007 she was recognized as the Outstanding Philanthropist of the Year.

Combining heart and head, philanthropy and investment prowess, Nadia Cavner is a tremendous resource for her clients, her hometown, and the many others whose lives she touches. And all of this is made more remarkable by the fact that when she moved to the United States at the tender age of 14, she barely spoke English and essentially had to grow up overnight.

A MOVING STORY

Nadia, whose nationality is Assyrian and whose faith is Roman Catholic, was born in Iran. "My dad was in the oil industry. He was always interested in the stock market. When I was about ten, he set up a portfolio for my sister and me (but not my much younger brother) on one of the U.S. stock exchanges. We were each given about $10,000 to work with, a nice sum of money at that time."

"We were in charge of our own portfolios," Nadia recalls, "and my dad would have us research different companies. Once a month after dinner we would sit down, go over our stock picks, and see who had done better in the previous month. I clearly remember how much better I did than my sister, who was a couple of years older. That's something that always stuck with me, and while this was where my interest in the market first developed, I had no inkling at that point that I would want to be in the industry one day."

Things soon changed for Nadia and her family due to ongoing Middle East violence associated with the then Shah of Iran. "I'll never forget what happened when I was about thirteen and a half," she says. "We were sitting in the front of our church and a bomb went off. It was a very frightening noise, and to this day a sudden loud noise can shake me to my bones. Thank God no one was killed, but seeing a place of worship—a place where you go for comfort—blown up like that was very disturbing. As a child you are very impressionable, and so that event has always stayed with me."

"It became very dangerous for us to stay," Nadia continues, "and shortly after the bomb incident our parents decided that we needed to move to what they called a Christian country. My dad had some friends that he had done oil business with in Dallas, and within two or three months the decision was made for us to move—first the children and then later our parents. I was fourteen when I joined my sister, who was already in Dallas, and my younger brother came later."

"I traveled here alone, and I hardly spoke any English when I arrived. I really had to grow up overnight. When I used to tell this story to my daughter, Maral—especially how I hardly spoke the language—she'd say, 'I don't think I'd have gone.' Then I'd tell her that I didn't have a choice. I had to go. About ten years later my parents finally came over. Essentially, then, I was on my own with my sister in Dallas/Fort Worth for ten years, and we really had to take care of each other. We were also blessed with some great friends whose parents took us under their wings and guided us. I remember, for instance, when my friend's dad took me to get my driver's license. Really, we were blessed with some great friendships and the love of the people of Texas."

In Fort Worth, after attending Nolan High School, Nadia started her college career at Texas Wesleyan University, a small liberal arts school, where she received her business management degree. Nadia then enrolled in an MBA program at TCU (Texas Christian University) where she met her future husband, Howard, who was getting his Master's of Divinity at TCU's Brite Divinity School on his way to being a minister. The two were married, and then moved to Springfield, Missouri.

"You can only imagine," Nadia says with a smile, "how little Springfield was over twenty years ago. Now the area has a population of two hundred and fifty thousand or so, but back then Springfield was much smaller, maybe eighty thousand people. So I would come up to visit Howard and say, 'Oh my gosh, there's no way I can live here in this small town.' But I will tell you now that this small town has been great to me."

BECOMING A BROKER

In Springfield, Nadia took a part-time position as a bank teller. "After just a couple of months," she recalls, "a new accounts supervisor position came open, which was sort of like being an operations officer on the retail brokerage side. I worked at that position for about three years. Now, the bank had a brokerage arm as well, and even though I would give the resident broker all the referrals that came through me, he never really seemed to spend any time with these customers. I'll never forget one particular instance—one of those great defining memories in my life—when I referred a lady to him. He came to my desk and met her and said, 'I'm getting ready to go to lunch, so I only have about two or three minutes. I can either tell you about our municipal bonds, or I can tell you about our corporate bonds. You choose which one, because we really need to get going on this.'"

"Well, I thought to myself, 'If someone in his position just showed my referrals a little enthusiasm, if such a person just truly took his time with these clients and explained things to them, took care of them, and nurtured the relationship, that person could really do well.' Not surprisingly, this fellow eventually left. So I called the COO of the brokerage—he probably thought I was out of my mind, especially since there weren't many women in our industry back then—and asked him if he would give me a chance to get my license and start working for the brokerage arm of the bank. I could tell that he was thinking, 'Who is this woman?' But he said, 'I'll tell you what. I'll give you thirty days to get your series 7, your series 63, and your insurance and other licenses.'"

"Can you imagine," Nadia continues, "I was given just thirty days to get all my licenses? He must have thought I had no idea at all what this world was about. Well, I knew enough to know that it wasn't a real possibility, but I thought that if I took my series 7 and scored well, that would show him that I was intelligent and committed enough to what I wanted to do. And that's just what I did. For thirty days I didn't do anything at all but study like mad. Day and night, 24/7, I did nothing but study. I passed my series 7 license test. That got his attention. He knew I was serious."

ROOKIE OF THE YEAR

Nadia, who was in her late twenties when she received her first license, experienced rapid success from that point on. "My first client was a referral from my husband, someone he knew. And my second client was someone whose aunt I had helped when I was on the banking side. She told me she always remembered how kind I was to her aunt, so when she inherited funds from her aunt, she brought those funds to me."

"In my first year," Nadia continues, "I was named 'Rookie of the Year.' In my second year I was the firm's top producer nationwide. Suddenly, the man who had given me thirty days to get all my licenses just couldn't do enough for me, including offering me more assistants, and we became great friends. Since then, I've been the top producer nationwide with every firm I've been with. It's really been a great ride for me."

One aspect of that great ride has been holding on during numerous ownership changes of the brokerage firm that Nadia has worked for. In addition to a single move that Nadia herself made three years ago, she has experienced six bank mergers and seven broker/dealer changes during her career. "It has been a bit of a nightmare," Nadia admits, "since it seemed that about every six months we were either changing our broker/dealer or the bank we worked for." Nadia points out, however, that "people do business with people, not with a sign outside the door. So while our institution's name has changed, we have remained the consistent face behind it all."

BUILDING HER BUSINESS: REFERRALS AND RESPONSIBILITY

Unlike most financial advisors, Nadia states," I have never made a cold call in my life. Can you believe that? My business has always been based on referrals from clients, friends, and family. Referrals have absolutely been one of the centerpieces of our success, our bread and butter, from day one. I truly believe that if you are caring enough, and make plenty of 'warm' calls to your existing clients—showing them respect, giving them great service, and doing your best for them—then you won't have to make cold calls. I'm having one of my best years again, and I can honestly tell you that 99 percent of my new sales are coming from my existing book of business."

As an example of the kind of referrals that Nadia generates, consider the woman who opened an account with Nadia after watching her help out her aunt at the beginning of her career. "She's still a dear client," Nadia says. "She lives in a small town in Missouri, and I bet she has referred half of that town to me." Elderly clients very often refer their kids from the big cities. With respect to such "generational referrals," Nadia notes that the family member making the referral is usually thrilled to do so. "You just wouldn't believe the excitement in their voices."

For Nadia, receiving so many referrals "is a tremendous blessing, and I don't take it lightly, because it comes with a tremendous responsibility." That responsibility, she says, "is to continue to do my absolute best for the people who rely on me. It means giving them the best service, building the best team, and keeping myself abreast of all relevant market changes. It also means taking good care of myself, being a good friend to them, and making sure that we are both on the same page. I truly look at the entire circle of my relationship with each of my clients, and always make sure to pick up the phone and thank them for their generous referral and express what that means to my business. And then I always follow up with a nice thank-you note."

Another dimension of the responsibility that Nadia feels is her refusal to institute any client minimums. "We do not have account minimums," she says. "I just don't believe in that. In life, in whatever you are doing, you owe it to yourself to give back, whether that's to your community or to those who aren't as fortunate as you. I have clients who invest $30,000 a month, but I also have clients who invest $50 a month. I truly believe that it's just as important to help the blue-collar guy who works just as hard as anyone else and perhaps needs more assistance than most. Some people may think I'm crazy for not having minimums, but if I'm successful and someone needs my help, I can't just turn away from them. In my heart, I know that wouldn't be the right thing to do."

On occasion, however, Nadia will turn down business. "I have turned down business when I feel the client and I are not on the same wavelength, if they don't understand what I'm telling them, or if there isn't a good line of communication in place. It doesn't happen too often, but it does happen."

Something else that doesn't happen too often is client attrition. "We have lost very few clients," Nadia notes, "but I have to admit that when we do lose one, it just shatters me. I would have to say that the fact that I take it so very hard is one of my weaknesses."

"In most cases," Nadia continues, "we have a good enough relationship that my clients will tell me their reasons for leaving. Usually it's because they've moved, and they felt it would be easier to work with a local advisor. In some cases it's because they were never really comfortable with having me as their advisor. It's hardly ever about their return rate. When we do lose a client, I always go over it with my team, see who had the last contact, and try to figure out what took place so we can learn from our mistakes."

TEAMING UP TO SERVE A BIG CLIENT BASE

Nadia works with some 650 to 700 households, or a total of about 1,500 clients, and manages nearly $400 million on their behalf. Most of these clients, she says, "are individuals, although we have a few corporations and work with their 401Ks. And most of the individuals we work with are either retired or getting ready to retire."

To work effectively with so many clients and provide the kind of top-notch service that Nadia prides herself on, she and her team of six segment their clients. "We have our client list divided between A,

B, and C clients," Nadia says. "Our largest clients are quite large—I have clients that have $15 million with me—and naturally I deal more with these higher-end clients. But that doesn't mean that any of our clients don't have access to me if they need me or want to talk to me."

"Importantly," Nadia continues, "I have a very seasoned staff. Becky Angus has been with me for over sixteen years, Steven Clark and I have worked together for over twenty years, and Devona Breeden has been with me for eight years. It helps a great deal to have a wonderful, confident, staff. "

"Becky is our main point of customer service," Nadia says. "She takes a lot of the calls on the service side. Devona is our trading guru and does a phenomenal job processing the investment paperwork for clients. Steve focuses mainly on marketing, and backs us up on customer services, trading, and initial asset allocations for clients. Michelle Dugger is our receptionist. She makes all the appointments, takes all the calls, and backs up whoever needs help on service. But really, she's mainly in charge of my schedule. She's a very important person for us. And then there's Megan Keith, who is our newest full-time staff member, and we also have part-time employees."

"My team has evolved as my business has kept growing," Nadia notes. "I try to bring on team members whose personality will fit well, and make them feel like they're part of the family. I think the stability of the team has helped the business a great deal. Also, it's very important for us as a team to get along. I can honestly tell you that I've never had a team member come to me with a complaint about another team member. While we do have pressures, especially when the market is down, we keep things lighthearted and nobody takes anything personally." Devona amplifies this point: "While our ages are different, I think our personalities are all very similar. Everyone is very comfortable here, we laugh a lot, and we never get mad at each other."

"Ultimately," Nadia says, "it's important for us to love and support each other, to know that the customers come first, and to do our best every day. But not only is it important that everyone is a good team player, it's important that it comes from the heart, because other people can sense when someone is sincere or not. So our team laughs a lot, and when someone answers the phone, they often giggle with the clients. Everyone on my team is very conscientious, and they all say something kind and grateful when they finish up conversations with clients."

"I attribute much of our success," Nadia continues, "to the wonderful communication that we have. Our office is set up so that we can all pretty much see and talk to each other at just about any given time during the day, which really makes things so much easier. Everyone has a good idea of what's going on and who's doing what, and if someone needs to step in, they do. We regularly communicate through email and have weekly staff meetings, too, but if an issue that we need to talk about arises in the middle of the day, we huddle up right there and then, work it out, and move on."

What, then, does a typical day for Nadia look like? "We usually come in through the back door," she says, "because the bank doesn't open until nine a.m. I come in and take about twenty minutes for myself to check my email and go through the *Wall Street Journal*, *USA Today*, and our local paper. Those are the three bibles that I go through. I include the local paper because my clients often want to talk about what's going on in Springfield. 'Did you hear about so-and-so?' And then certain clients will have read an article in the *Journal* or *USA Today* and will expect me to know about it. Then I surf the Web to see if there's anything new that's happened since the newspapers were printed. Then I open my office door, check in with my team, and usually start having appointments at about eight-thirty. On average, I have seven or eight appointments a day, so my time is pretty structured."

TIME, NOT TIMING

"I've always believed that success in the market is due to time, not timing," Nadia notes. "That is, you have to have a solidly diversified portfolio and stick with it, and try to not jump in and act and react to day-to-day-news, constantly trying to time the market, buying and selling, buying and selling. I really think you should stick with a good diversified asset allocation long-term. What I tell my clients is this: 'It's like we're on a nice long plane ride. Along the way, I'll tell you to fasten your seatbelts, and sometimes it will be bumpy and you'll have to hang on. And sometimes as your pilot I'll take the seatbelts sign off and tell you its safe to move around the cabin. God willing, everyone will arrive safe and sound. In any case, it's not going to be a short ride or a short-term relationship.'"

As for specific investments, Nadia says, "We do a very good job in terms of diversifying our clients' asset allocations. I don't use money managers, but instead work very closely with a handful of quality fund families, like Franklin Templeton and Putnam Investments. I also use variable annuities and fixed annuities, and I use fixed-income products. And I don't use any hedge funds. Overall, I can say that I truly like the family of funds that I work with."

"Of course," Nadia adds, "I'm not going to tell you that I was looking forward to coming in every day during the bear market of 2000. We all have down times in our lives, but I believe that if, during a down market, you stick with your book and just communicate even more than you normally do with your clients, holding their hands and making sure they don't make the wrong move, you end up becoming much stronger. A lot of my strength, knowledge, and understanding comes from having gone through a couple of pretty major bear markets. But for us, just as for everybody else, 2000 was a tough time."

How does Nadia work with a new client? "First," she says, "I gather all the information I need, starting with the initial meeting. I make sure I'm clear about their entire asset picture, including where they are now financially, their debt ratio, and what their goals are. I truly look at the entire big picture, and do a plan that takes into account their entire world. It's very important that I have the entire picture of their world. I point out that if they had an ongoing headache, they wouldn't go see their physician and say he can only take their blood pressure."

"So I ask about everything from A to Z," Nadia continues, "from their health to their parents' health to what, if anything, they might be inheriting. With respect to their health, I say, 'If you've got something serious and are going to be gone in six months, I need to know that, because it will affect your asset allocation.'"

"If they don't have all the necessary paperwork with them at the initial meeting, then we usually meet a second time to make sure we have everything we need. By the third meeting I'm ready to put forth my proposal and tell them what areas I think they're doing well in and what areas need improvement. Based on the information I have and on their time frame, I may tell them where they need to save more."

EDUCATING HER CLIENTS

"Our clients inherently trust Nadia," notes Becky. "The market is complicated, but the way she explains various products to them, like mutual funds and annuities, gives them a very good concept of what she's offering. When clients have assets in the stock market, their balances will fluctuate, but because they trust Nadia, and because of the way she's educated them—'Just hang in there' and 'Stay the course'—we don't get a lot of phone calls, even during down markets. She really prepares her clients very well."

Sometimes that education concerns critical areas a client might have otherwise missed. For example, Nadia says, "It doesn't matter how young they are, I always look at their life insurance. I have a formula that I use. In one case I had a couple, and although the wife had a nice job, the husband was the real breadwinner. If anything happened to him, she wouldn't have been able to maintain their lifestyle. I insisted that they quickly take care of this, and asked him to almost triple his life insurance, going through his employer where he could get the best premium rates. To his credit, he did so within forty-eight hours."

"He was a big strong, man, a football player, in his early thirties," Nadia continues. "Well, he contracted some kind of virus and—no exaggeration—sixty days later he was dead. To this day, the wife regularly shows me her appreciation. Now, I could have totally missed this: They had nice-sized assets, and I could have gotten totally engrossed in that direction. That's why I always tell my staff that *it's imperative that we do our jobs right*. So when clients ask me if I really think they need that much more insurance, what I tell them is that if anything happens to one of them, the survivor will have enough to deal with emotionally without having a financial shortfall as well."

Another area that Nadia has her clients carefully look at is retirement in a day and age when people are living longer. "I had a couple who were clients. When the husband retired, he decided he was just going to put everything in a money market account in a bank, and that at their age that would be just fine. He was an engineer, and I'll never forget the detailed breakdown he had done. But he assumed that they would live for a maximum of another eight or ten years, and that if they needed a little bit more, they could do a reverse mortgage on the house and would be good to go. Well, I asked him and his wife what would happen if they lived longer, and whether it was important for them to leave some money for their kids."

"They listened to what I was saying," Nadia says, "and I put together a really nice plan for them. Well, they each lived almost ten years longer than he had originally planned for, and they would have totally run out of money if they'd just gone with the money market idea. All three of their kids are good clients of mine now, and I was able to roll over a nice sum to each of them. It worked out great, and along the way, you wouldn't believe how many times this sweet man would say, 'Nadia, what would I have done if I hadn't listened to you?' Those moments are just priceless to me."

One educational domain where Nadia has strong feelings concerns the effect of the financial media on her clients. "Realistically," Nadia says, "you can't expect people to shut off the television entirely. We don't do that ourselves, and we can't really expect our clients to do it. As with anything else, the key is moderation. The TV news that many people have on 24/7, literally all the time, is often overdramatized just to draw attention, since you can't repeat the same thing over and over and expect people to watch. But it's not true that whoever can scream the loudest will make the most money. Instead, once again it's important for clients to realize that success in the market comes with time, not timing, and the key is to have a well diversified portfolio and hold onto it for the long term. I leave it to the professional fund companies to do what they do best in terms of buying and selling securities. I'm very frank with my clients about all this, and often tell them that in my opinion, they would simply be better off if they shut off the television in their homes."

SERVICE AND TRUST

"There's no question whatsoever," Nadia says, "that our business is a relationship business. Everybody here is clear that service makes you or breaks you, which is why we make sure we provide excellent service. Importantly, when clients feel comfortable with you, they can trust you. During our first interview, I often tell my new clients that I want them to go home and think about whether they are truly comfortable with me. It's very important that we are on the same wavelength."

Perhaps because of her natural warmth and depth of caring—and to some degree perhaps because she is a woman ("I truly believe that we have an edge there")—Nadia has experienced many clients' opening up deeply with her. "I am often amazed," she says, "at how our clients open up to us. Sometimes it turns into a full-blown counseling session. Let's say someone has lost a spouse and is crying. I'll just reach over and touch their hand, or go around the desk and sit next to them. I was with a client yesterday who just lost her husband and I hugged her probably four or five times as she told me about their fifty-five years of marriage. It wasn't easy. She said, 'My husband trusted you, and I trust you too. Please tell me what I need to do here.'"

"Sometimes," Nadia goes on, "I worry that there's an image of our industry as cold-hearted money machines. I really, honestly, resent that, because that's not who I am or what I do. I don't know if it's from my heritage—there's a lot of hugging and kissing in Assyrian families—or just a genuine feeling that comes from my heart, but the care and affection I show for my clients is very genuine and has helped my business immensely. I feel my team and I go out of our way to take care of our clients, so when I speak to different industry groups and other advisors, I tell them that it's imperative that we not be seen as cold-hearted brokers who are just here to deal with our clients' money and their money only. We are compassionate, loving people. We are family members. We are heavily involved in charitable pursuits."

Nadia was not always willing to reveal her caring and emotional nature. "My stance developed over time as I evolved as a person. During the first year of my career I would have felt nervous if someone cried at my desk for whatever reason. I would have felt too intimidated to reach over and touch their hand. But now I'm not intimidated at all. My God, during our annual client appreciation dinners, I stand near the door as everyone comes in and give them a firm handshake. Some guys just really go at it and love nothing more than a firm handshake!"

Another aspect of providing service and building trust is the many personal touches that Nadia and her team provide. "We send birthday cards to our clients," she says, "and I write a personal, handwritten note on every card. I've done this for years. Think about it: A lot of our clients are in their eighties. By then, a lot of their friends are gone, or their spouses may be gone. So when they get a card from us, or if I have Becky give them a phone call on their birthday, they are just delighted, and that's an understatement."

Nadia also maintains an active external presence in her clients' lives. "In the last three weeks I've gone to four funerals or wedding showers. That doesn't happen all the time, but we have many clients who are dear to us, and when you share a moment like these with someone, you build trust. The market will inevitably go up and down, but when you have this kind of long-term, in-depth relationship with them, they are a lot less likely to make a bad decision and suddenly yank everything out."

"Ultimately," Nadia adds, "it comes back to the fact that we really do try to practice simple acts of kindness. So, for example, almost 100 percent of the time when a client opens an account with us, we send a very nice basket of goodies to eat. That basket might include some strawberry jam that will stay with the client for a long time. We always try to think of things that will last and give them a good feeling."

Nadia and her team also have a strict rule about always letting the client hang up first on all phone calls. "This is very important," Nadia says, "because hanging up on a client has a very negative effect on them." Devona adds, "I'll just say, 'Did I answer all your questions?' Usually they'll say goodbye, but if they don't, I'll just ask them again, 'Is that all you needed?' Usually it works out."

Becky adds, "Nadia has always taught us to put the customer first. And to treat them with respect and try and always respectfully assess the situation we're in. I've learned a lot from Nadia, especially watching her be with clients and support them during down markets."

Devona makes a similar observation. "When I walked into the office for the very first time, it was really warm. Everyone took their time when answering the phone. And Nadia treats all her customers like her own family. She can tell you all about their families and remembers everyone's name." Becky concurs: "Nadia really does give a personal touch. She'll go to funerals and weddings, and gets invitations for graduations just because the customers feel like she's a part of their families."

THE BIG EVENT

Just to make sure that her clients know how she feels about them, Nadia hosts an annual Client Appreciation Dinner that, with over 1,000 attendees, has become one of Springfield's premier social events. "As the name indicates," Nadia says, "this is really an evening to appreciate our clients' business and their referrals. It's also to let them know that I'm not just a cold-hearted stockbroker. Part of my goal has been for my clients to see me as a good mom and a good wife. My wonderful daughter Maral introduces me—she's been doing this since she was six and needed a stepstool to reach the microphone on the podium—and my husband always opens the dinner with a heart-felt prayer. So my clients have seen my kid grow up in front of their eyes, and they can't wait to see her each year. And during my husband's blessing before dinner, you can hear a pin drop."

"We started these dinners in 1998. We rent the biggest ballroom in town, which is really a convention center. Then we have a fabulous, elaborate dinner that lasts from five-thirty until seven-thirty. We have a piano playing, the tables are beautifully decorated, and the clients leave with a nice little gift and a note from me as a token of our appreciation."

"Before the main dinner," Nadia adds, "we have a smaller VIP reception with about two hundred people. We have some toasts and a speaker, and I go around to all two hundred attendees and shake their hands. Then I open the main event with a nice commentary about how many folks are in attendance, and how many different states are represented. Because I have clients in so many states we have people who come in from all over the country. Then I thank my top referring clients for their loyalty and referrals. Next I introduce the VIPs, who in the past have included the state attorney general, governor, and the heads of various financial institutions. We also have a keynote speaker for the event, who might be the chairman of one of the institutions we work with."

"It's just a wonderful event—it's really like a huge family reunion—and is spoken about throughout the industry. Everyone in town knows about it and talks about it as well, and in some ways it's the 'place to be seen.' People so look forward to it: I've had clients who've changed their surgery dates and vacations to avoid missing it. We tell people to dress Sunday nice—we thought about doing a black tie, but figured that might cause some clients who've been away from the business world for a while to shy away from the event. We want all our guests to be comfortable and enjoy themselves. Ultimately, the dinners are an effective way for us to take care of over a thousand clients in a single shot."

A CHARITABLE CHAMPION

Nadia's deep caring and service-oriented approach extends not just to her clients, but to all areas of her life. In fact, saying that Nadia is deeply involved in charitable causes and philanthropic pursuits would be a definite understatement. It's not surprising, then, that in 2007 Nadia was named the Outstanding Philanthropist of the Year by the Ozark Region Chapter of the Association of Fundraising Professionals, or that she was previously named a Missourian of the Year by the American Red Cross.

Nadia's volunteer efforts span the national, statewide, and local levels. On a national level, she is a member of the Executive Committee of the American Bible Society and serves on its finance committee. On the statewide level, Nadia was appointed by Missouri's governor as a member of the Missouri Health and Educational Facilities Authority. "A lot of great work is done here," Nadia says, "and I get tremendous exposure to some great universities, hospitals, cities, and small communities." Nadia was also appointed by the Missouri Secretary of State to the Advisory Board of the Securities and Exchange Commission.

Locally, Nadia serves on the Advisory Board of the Finance Committee of the Springfield Community Foundation and on the Lost and Found board (for children who have lost their parents). Nadia and her husband Howard have given generously to local area charities, and are creating a family foundation to make their charitable efforts more effective. At Nadia's 2006 Annual Client Appreciation Dinner, the Cavner family gave a $10,000 check to each of six different local charities, including the Parenting Life Skills Center, the Carol Jones Recovery Center for Women, the Kitchen (a homeless services agency), the Council of Churches, United Ministries in Higher Education, and Westminster College. And in 2007, Nadia and her family pledged to donate at least $30,000 to the Kitchen, and possibly as much as $80,000 if another $50,000 in matching funds could be found elsewhere.

The Cavners have also made significant donations to the Breast Cancer Foundation of the Ozarks, the American Bible Society, and the Dalai Lama. They also started a foundation to help support Greenwood Laboratory School's first ever girls' high school soccer team and made several donations to Missouri State University. The Cavners also make numerous donations to other charitable causes. For example, they recently donated to Female Leaders in Philanthropy, which is dedicated to "ease the pain of childhood hunger in our community—one backpack at a time." And all this is in addition to the many hours that Nadia spends each year working to stage and promote events of various types, as well as the time she spends on the boards she serves on.

"I do give a large percentage of my income to charities," Nadia acknowledges. "My charitable commitments kind of have a life of their own." Becky nicely sums up Nadia's charitable efforts: "I see the way that Nadia and her husband, and their daughter, give passionately to charities, and that's taught me a lot about what's important. Nadia has tremendous compassion for people and has taught us all that it's important to take care of them. Just being around her has made me more of a giver."

A HAPPY HEART

"Having been the top producer for so many years," Nadia says, "I don't get up in the morning thinking my mission is to continue to be the top producer for the company. I just don't think in those terms. I come to work with my heart happy and my soul ready to go. I still get excited and just dive right into it. It's just so important to keep that attitude about life in general. For example, I was recently going out to this great dinner, and Becky said, 'You're making it sound like you've never gone out to dinner in your whole life.' But to me, that kind of excitement is what life is all about. A lot of times we become so burdened by our lives, but instead, it's important to be happy and grateful. What it all comes back to is that if you have a happy heart, you care. We all have bad days, but for me it's not often, and I don't have two different personalities, one at work and one at home."

To keep her heart happy, Nadia makes sure to take good care of herself and her family. For fun, she plays golf, and she keeps physically fit. "I have a personal trainer," she says, "whom I've been with now since 2001. I work out faithfully with her three times a week, and then usually at least once or twice during the week I do extra cardio at my home gym. I love my treadmill and Stairmaster, and we live in a nice wooded area so we have a great place to go jogging."

"We love to travel," Nadia adds, "and as a family we usually go to Europe once or twice a year. We also love to ski, and usually go for two or three days a couple of times a year. I just love our family time, and love to take walks with my husband and my daughter. And my daughter is very involved in soccer and tennis. We are a very close-knit family and I genuinely enjoy that."

Perhaps Nadia's one "weakness" along these lines is that after just three or four days of vacation, she typically finds herself eager to come back to work. "I love to go on vacations," she says, "but as Howard can tell you, after three or four days into it, I'm anxious to get back to work. I'm not necessarily proud of this fact, but I find that three days is just about the right amount of time for me to be gone. Even when we go to Europe, if my husband and daughter still want to play more, that's fine by me—they shouldn't have to cut their vacation short just because I'm ready to come back. But if my family wants to stay for a week, usually by the fourth day, I'm back."

Ultimately, for Nadia, it always comes back to a combination of a prodigious heart, a deep sense of service and responsibility, plenty of smarts and investment knowledge, and a solidly rooted faith in herself and her work. A perfect example is the recent $25,000 gold-level sponsorship undertaken by the Cavners of the Dalai Lama's November 2007 visit to Washington, D.C., where he received the Congressional Medal of Honor. "I'm a Roman Catholic," Nadia says, "but I work hard to reach out to other faiths."

It's this multidimensional sense of deeply rooted faith that becomes clear to everyone who experiences Nadia. "My faith does come across to people," Nadia agrees, "and it's true that I'm a very grounded and deeply rooted person. That's an excellent way to describe me." Clearly, Nadia Cavner knows who she is, what she's doing, and why she's doing it, to the great benefit of her clients and so many other individuals and organizations.